Unix User's Handbook

The Lance A. Leventhal Microtrend® Series

Lance A. Leventhal, Ph.D., Series Editor

Unix User's Handbook

Tim Parker

Microtrend® Books

Library of Congress Card Catalog Number: 91-53067

Library of Congress Cataloging-in-Publication Data
Parker, Timothy
Unix user's handbook: the one-stop reference for Unix information / Timothy Parker.
p. cm. — (Lance A. Leventhal Microtrend series)
Includes bibliographical references
ISBN: 0-915391-47-3 (pbk.)
1. Operating systems (Computers) 2. Unix (Computer operating system)
I. Title. II. Series
QA76.76.063P366 1993
005.4'3—dc20 91-53067 CIP

Microtrend® Books
Slawson Communications, Inc.
165 Vallecitos de Oro
San Marcos, CA 92069

Edited by Lance A. Leventhal, Ph.D., San Diego, CA
Production by Joanne Roth, Slawson Communications, Inc.
Front cover design by John Odam Design Associates

Printed in the United States
10 9 8 7 6 5 4 3 2 1

Table of Contents

Preface

Background

Ken Thompson and Dennis Ritchie of Bell Laboratories created Unix in the 1960s as a multitasking operating system for small computers. During the 1970s, informal distribution channels led to its adoption by many schools, nonprofit organizations, and companies, who tailored it to their own needs. The result was a proliferation of versions, with common basic principles and outlooks but minor differences in commands, approaches, and implementations.

With the emergence of Unix as a commercial product, the number of versions grew, with most leading companies having their own incompatible brands. The need for standards was obvious. Users demanded more consistency, and companies wanted to promote their products. Clearly only a few could receive the support and maintenance required for widespread adoption.

Currently, several "standard" Unixes exist with support from particular factions or uses in special application areas or on specific platforms. AT&T's System V Release 4 (SVR4) has become the most common, and many companies are now revising their versions to comply with it.

Purpose of This Book

This book covers the leading current versions of Unix and the standard definitions that most vendors now adopt. It provides a reference to the commands available to most users. Each entry has a standard form, including a brief description, compatibility section, syntax, version information, defaults, return values, associated files, cross-references, discussion, notes, and examples. The idea is to provide quick access to well-organized information without excessive detail. The book includes only typical user commands, not those intended primarily for administrators, programmers, and other specialized groups.

The book is more than just another list of commands. It is intended to be clear, readable, and even (heaven forbid!) interesting. It explains the commands' practical purposes and significance, and shows examples that are both realistic and relevant. Most standard Unix reference manuals fail miserably in all these areas!

The compatibility sections cover the major versions, namely:

Open Software Foundation's OSF/1

The Santa Cruz Operation's Unix (SCO Unix)

The Santa Cruz Operation's Xenix (SCO Xenix)

AT&T System V Release 3.2 (SVR3.2)

AT&T System V Release 4 (SVR4)

X/Open Portability Guide (X/Open)

The book is intended primarily as a quick reference. You can use it to find consistent descriptions of all user commands. You can also use it to expand your knowledge of Unix commands, see how particular versions work, and find practical examples.

How the Book Is Organized

The primary part of the book consists of command entries in alphabetical order. Each entry is self-contained, and starts at the top of a page for easy reference.

The appendixes include an acronym list, a glossary, and a list of resources you can consult for more information.

Intended Audience

This book is suitable for any Unix user, from the beginner who wants to see how to perform basic tasks to the advanced user who wants to understand unfamiliar options. It is especially well-suited to those who lack the background or patience to search through the traditional bulky documentation.

The book should be of special interest to those who use or must understand, support, or be familiar with several versions of Unix. Such people include consultants, software developers, product evaluators, database administrators, customer engineers, technical writers, telephone support personnel, maintenance programmers, system analysts, computer and network administrators, microcomputer managers, teachers, trainers, and students. They now have a single compact source that applies to all major versions.

How the Reader Will Benefit

This book gives you one place to look up any Unix user command. No more struggling with huge sets of manuals that you find later are outdated or for the wrong version. Furthermore, the information is in a standardized, comprehensible format and includes realistic examples. You can also use the book to investigate or evaluate versions of Unix, understand articles, reports, and technical notes, answer questions (and achieve exalted status as a famous Unix guru), and write or read proposals, documentation, advertisements, and sales literature. What else would you like for the mere price of a book? Enjoy!

Acknowledgments

The book you now have (thank you!) differs greatly from the one I envisioned four years ago. I originally planned to summarize the differences among the many Unix versions then in use. As time passed, major companies announced plans to revise their versions to comply with a single standard (SVR4), and the distinctions among them diminished. Therefore, this book now covers only the primary versions in today's—and the near future's—Unix.

The sheer numbers of Unix commands forced another compromise. I intended to include all of them, but as I found over 1000 in my first drafts, I decided to limit my coverage to commands a typical user will encounter. I have thus excluded supervisory and administrative commands. They must wait unhappily in a queue somewhere for a future volume. (Here users defer to administrators, unlike the situation on most systems). Similarly, I have excluded commands specifically for programmers (such as make, RCS, and SCCS) to be covered elsewhere. By the end of this project, I will be personally responsible for destroying an entire forest!

A book is seldom the work of one person, although I fully expect to take all the blame. In this case, most of the layout and style is the result of suggestions by Dr. Lance Leventhal of Slawson Communications. He and his associates waited (sometimes patiently) while I went through draft after draft, adding commands and removing references, until we arrived at the current contents. Dr. Leventhal's editing is responsible for ensuring consistency and practicality in the discussion and examples throughout the book, and is much appreciated. Joanne Roth of Slawson did the production. Thanks also to Slawson's Ron Tucker, who harassed me continually to finish the manuscript. Your turn will come, Ron, as soon as I finish my fine voodoo doll. I only hope I have enough pins!

Several companies supplied information about their Unix versions, and I thank them for their cooperation. I particularly thank The Santa Cruz Operation (SCO) for keeping me updated on their Unix and Xenix products.

On a more personal note, my friends provided the moral and mental support needed to endure a seemingly endless project. Many times I felt like quitting, but a few kind words and veiled threats (plus demands by my creditors) would get me going again. Thanks to Ingrid Farag, Alan Hobson, Linda Humeniuk, Roy MacLean, Carole Ohan, Patricia Philips, Bill Smallwood, and Ed Treijs. My parents always provide love and support (sometimes even allowing me to pay for them by credit card), and I appreciate them greatly.

Tim Parker
Toronto, 1992

Dedication

This one is for my nieces and nephews
Tammy Lynn, Tammy, Tanya, John, and Ryan

with love

About the Author

Tim Parker is a consultant, writer, and programmer based in Toronto, Ontario, Canada. He is the Editor of *UNIQUE: The Unix Systems Information Source*, and Contributing Editor to *Unix Review*, *Canadian Datasystems*, and *Canadian Computer Reseller*. He also contributes regularly to several other computer magazines.

His Unix experience extends over fifteen years, a period he spent both writing about Unix and programming for it. He was a founding writer of *Computer Language* magazine, and has published three other books, including one on Unix. He has also published over 400 articles and reviews.

Born in England, he moved to Canada in 1965. He was educated at the University of Toronto, University of Ottawa, and the Ottawa-Carleton Institute for Graduate Work and Research. Since leaving graduate school, he has pursued a career as a writer and consultant.

When not working with computers (or every other month, whichever is more often), he spends as much time as possible outdoors. He is a private pilot, scuba diver, marathoner, skier, and white water kayaker, and readily admits to trying anything for an adrenaline rush (except writing another Unix reference book or coping with any more of Lance Leventhal's red pencil).

About the Series Editor

Lance Leventhal is the author of 25 books, including *Turbo C Quickstart*, *80386 Programming Guide*, *68000 Assembly Language Programming*, and *Microcomputer Experimentation with the IBM PC*. His books have sold over 1,000,000 copies and have been translated into many foreign languages. He has also helped develop many microprocessor-based systems and has been a consultant for Disney, Intel, NASA, NCR, and Rockwell.

Dr. Leventhal served as Series Editor on Personal Computing for Prentice-Hall and as Technical Editor for the Society for Computer Simulation. He has lectured on microprocessors, operating systems, and C programming throughout the United States for IEEE, IEEE Computer Society, and other groups.

Dr. Leventhal's background includes affiliations with Linkabit Corporation, Intelcom Rad Tech, Naval Electronics Laboratory Center, and Harry Diamond Laboratories. He received a B.A. degree from Washington University (St. Louis, Missouri) and M.S. and Ph.D. degrees from the University of California, San Diego. He is a member of AAAI, ACM, ASEE, IEEE, and IEEE Computer Society.

Introduction

Each command entry starts with a single-line description of its function. Then come sections that explain the command and its options. The order is:

- Description
- Compatiblity
- Alternative
- Syntax
- Diagnostics
- Versions
- Arguments
- Options
- Error Handling
- Defaults
- Returns (return values)
- Warnings
- Limitations and Restrictions
- Files
- See Also (cross-references)
- Discussion
- Notes
- Examples

Not all sections appear for every command. Only the major ones are explained below.

Compatibility

This section lists the six versions the book covers, and indicates whether each includes the command. The references used to determine compatibility are:

> OSF/1: *OSF/1 Operating System Command Reference*, Open Software Foundation, Prentice-Hall, Englewood Cliffs, NJ, 1991.
>
> SCO Unix: *SCO Unix System V/386 Operating System User's Reference*, The Santa Cruz Operation, Santa Cruz, CA, 1989.
>
> SCO Xenix: *SCO Xenix System V Operating System User's Reference*, The Santa Cruz Operation, Santa Cruz, CA, 1988.
>
> SVR3.2: *Unix Programmer's Manual, Volume 1: Commands and Utilities*, AT&T, Unix System Library, Holt, Rinehart and Winston, New York, 1986.
>
> SVR4: *Unix System V Release 4 User's Reference Manual*, AT&T, Unix Press/Prentice-Hall, Englewood Cliffs, NJ, 1990.
>
> X/Open: *X/Open Portability Guide Issue 3 XSI Commands and Utilities*, X/Open Group, Prentice-Hall, Englewood Cliffs, NJ, 1989.

In cases where versions lack a significant command, I have indicated alternatives. You can also consult the See Also section for related commands.

Syntax

This section shows the command's syntax. The conventions are:

- square brackets enclose options
  - [-a] indicates that the argument "-a" is an option
- multiple arguments may appear as a list
  - "aeiou" indicates that any or all of the arguments may appear at the same time
- a vertical bar means that only one option can appear in a single command
  - [a|e|i] indicates that "a", "e", or "i" can appear, but only one at a time.

ellipses indicate one or more occurrences, usually of a filename

file . . . indicates that one or more filenames may be supplied, separated by spaces

an argument to an option is identified in the description

[-cchar] shows that -c is the option, and it takes an argument "char" immediately after it. Remember that options are always single characters, usually prefixed with a hyphen.

boldface indicates commands, and italics occasionally distinguish computer names that one could easily confuse with everyday words. Where meanings are clear without special markings, I have avoided them in the interests of simplicity and consistency.

Versions

When versions have different options or arguments, this section summarizes them. The usual variations are added options. Each version has its own heading, with the additions described briefly. Versions appear in alphabetical order.

You should read this section to ensure that your version has the options you want to use. The list of options also identifies ones that apply only to specific versions.

Arguments and Options

These sections contain lists of the command's arguments and options, along with brief descriptions. When necessary, I indicate the versions involved. I have also noted cases in which options are mutually exclusive. The arguments are in the order in which they appear in the syntax; the options are in alphabetical order with symbols and numbers first and lowercase letters before capitals (for example, 'N' appears just after 'n').

Frequently, an option itself has an argument, which I identify on the syntax line and explain in the options section.

Files

This section lists files the command uses or creates, with a brief description of their purpose. In many cases, users cannot access the files directly, but it is helpful to know that they exist. A common problem is for such ancillary files to be discarded, deleted, or corrupted accidentally, leading to strange results from commands without apparent errors. Some Unix versions may change the names of the paths.

See Also

This section lists related commands that may perform a similar or opposite function. Sometimes they provide an alternate way to do a task. The cross-references may also help when you cannot remember the exact command you want, but know a related one.

Discussion

This section covers the command, its purpose, and its practical significance. It may also include version-specific information. In most cases, it explains the common options. The emphasis here is on how and when users commonly employ the command.

Notes

This section may include related information about versions, the ownership of files, and other secondary subjects.

Examples

This section provides examples of the command's typical use, with sample output in some cases. It usually illustrates major options. I have drawn most examples from actual applications, articles, or conversations with users. Only occasionally, out of sheer desperation and over the belligerent and sarcastic objections of my editor, have I resorted to the trivial or silly examples typical of most books.

Other Sections

Other sections that may appear include Diagnostics, Error Handling, Defaults, Returns (return values), Warnings, and Limitations and Restrictions. Their purposes are generally self-explanatory.

Final Note

In the tradition of Kernighan, Ritchie, Pike, Feuer, and others (from Bell Laboratories and elsewhere), I have not hesitated to include a little humor from time to time. Unix is a serious subject, but it has its comical aspects and weird terminology as well. One cannot be serious always and survive! As Shakespeare wrote, "With the help of a surgeon, he might yet recover, and prove an ass."

Notes to SunOS, Solaris, and Berkeley (BSD) Users

SunOS/Solaris

Sun Microsystems originally used a version of Berkeley Unix for its SunOS. BSD4.3 formed the basis for the latest revisions. Solaris 1.0 moved Sun (through its SunSoft subsidiary) from BSD toward the AT&T (SVR) variants to be more compatible with the industry.

Solaris 2.0, which will be Sun's basic operating system product, is SVR4 compliant. So users can simply refer to the SVR4 information in this book.

Berkeley (BSD) Unix

The BSD (Berkeley Software Distribution) variant of Unix was popular in the 1980s, but with the move toward a standard Unix, it became less common. Most BSD-based commercial products have migrated to SVR4. In the process, SVR4 has incorporated some key features of BSD Unix. Clearly, the emergence and leadership position of Sun Microsystems, with many people drawn from the Computer Systems Research Group at University of California, Berkeley, has had a major impact.

This book does not include BSD compatibility information, as its user community has diminished dramatically. As a rough guide, BSD users can use SVR3.2 information, coupled with OSF/1.

Excluded Commands

This book emphasizes commands of interest to typical users. In the interests of conserving space and my own sanity, I have excluded the following:

- Commands of interest only to administrators
- Text processing commands (such as **nroff**, **tbl**, and **troff**) because of their complexity and specialized use
- Commands of interest only to programmers, such as RCS (revision control system) and SCCS (source code control system)
- The shells themselves (**csh**, **ksh**, and **sh**) because of their complexity. They deserve (and have) books of their own.
- Communications-related commands not available in many systems (such as **ftp**).

If I receive enough encouragement or complaints, I will cover these in later editions or other books.

accept

Description:

Allows print requests to be sent to a specific printer or class of printers

Compatibility:

OSF/1	No
SCO Unix	No
SCO Xenix	Yes
System V Release 3.2	No
System V Release 4	No
X/Open	No

Syntax:

/usr/lib/accept dest

Arguments:

dest   printer name or a class of printers

Files:

/usr/spool/lp/*   printer spool directories

See Also:

disable; enable; lp; lpstat; reject

Discussion

accept allows a particular printer, or class of printers, to accept print requests. A system administrator generally uses it when adding a new printer to the system, or after disabling one for maintenance. Only enabled printers can be used for printing.

Notes

accept is separate only for SCO Xenix. It is part of the **lpstat** command in other versions.

accept is usually accessible only to the system administrator.

Examples

To allow a printer called *hplaser* to accept print requests, enter

```
accept hplaser
```

To allow an entire class of printers to accept commands, use its name. All printers belonging to it can then accept print requests.

apply

Description:
Runs a command repeatedly with different arguments

Compatibility:

OSF/1	Yes
SCO Unix	No
SCO Xenix	No
System V Release 3.2	No
System V Release 4	No
X/Open	No

Syntax:
apply [-achar] [-number] cmd arg [...]

Options:
- \- provides the number of arguments to pass to cmd
- -a uses char instead of "%" to designate argument substitution strings

Discussion
apply runs cmd on all specified arguments in turn. Usually they are applied individually (see Examples), but you can specify the number with the "-" option. -0 means to run cmd without arguments.

You can specify character sequences on the command line using the percentage sign to indicate substitution. You can change indicators with the -a option. **apply** reads the arguments in order, substituting as specified.

You should enclose complex commands in single quotation marks to prevent the shell from converting metacharacters.

Examples

The command

```
apply -2 diff file1 file2 file3 file4
```

runs **diff** twice, first comparing file1 and file2, and then comparing file3 and file4.

apply is useful when you want to perform a command repeatedly with different arguments. The command

```
apply 'chown bill %1' /usr/tim /usr/alex /usr/carol
```

runs **chown** on the three /usr directories in turn, changing the ownerships to “bill”. Bill is quickly on his way to dominating the entire world!

apropos

Description:
Displays manual references by keywords

Compatibility:

OSF/1	Yes
SCO Unix	No
SCO Xenix	No
System V Release 3.2	No
System V Release 4	No
X/Open	No

Syntax:
apropos keyword [...]

Argument:
keyword   words to be searched for

See Also:
man; whatis

Discussion
apropos searches for occurrences of keywords, and displays the reference manual page number for each one. It searches for substrings, so searching for "pass" matches "passwd" and "password", as well as all other words with "pass" in them. For example, "compassion" would match, but no one in the computer business has it anyway.

Examples

The command

```
apropos pass
```

searches for all words containing the string “pass”.

apropos displays the page references, which you can then use with **man** directly.

ar

Description:

Creates and maintains file archives

Compatibility:

OSF/1	Yes
SCO Unix	Yes
SCO Xenix	Yes
System V Release 3.2	Yes
System V Release 4	Yes
X/Open	Yes

Syntax:

ar [-c|-d|-h|-m|-r|-p|-q|-t|-w|-x] [closuv] [-V] [position] archivename [name ...]

Versions:

OSF/1: adds the -c, -h, -w, o, and u options. The hyphen preceding options is itself (recursively!) optional.

SVR4: adds the -V option.

Options:

-c suppresses messages normally produced when creating an archive (OSF/1 only)

-d deletes named files from the archive

-h sets modification times to the current date and time. If no filenames are specified, all files are affected. (OSF/1 only)

-m appends named files to the end of the archive unless a positional modifier appears (see the list below)

-p prints named files from the archive

-q quick append of named files to the archive (does not check whether they already exist)

-r replaces named files in the archive

-t prints the archive's table of contents

-V prints the version number (SVR4 only)

-w displays the archive file's symbol table (OSF/1 only)

-x extracts named files from the archive

position indicates where to place the file. Valid values are "b" or "i" for "before", and "a" for "after" the specified filename.

Valid modifiers are:

c suppresses messages

l places temporary files in the current working directory instead of the system default temporary directory (see Notes)

o sets the modification time of the copied file to the time of the archived member when used with the -x option (OSF/1 only)

s forces regeneration of the archive table (see Notes)

u copies only files changed since they last entered the archive (see -r) (OSF/1 only)

v verbose output, provides file by file reporting

See Also:

tar

Discussion

ar maintains files in an archive. You can use archives to group files for storage as a single entity or for transfer to another machine. **ar** creates portable archive files with header information. By convention, they have a ".a" suffix.

You can add, extract, and update files in the archive with the -m (or faster -q), -x, and -r options, respectively. Modifiers can suppress or expand diagnostic output. OSF/1 does not require the hyphen before options.

When adding files to an archive, **ar** will add one twice if it appears twice on the command line. It creates an archive file if one with the specified name does not already exist. You cannot display archive files using a file display utility (such as **more**), as the stored format differs from the original. Instead, you must extract the file first.

Notes

The -l modifier is obsolete for most Unix versions as **ar** does not create temporary files. It is still supported to prevent errors in existing scripts. Future revisions will drop it.

The -s modifier forces regeneration of the library symbol table.

Examples

To create an archive arc_files.a and add all .c files to it, issue

```
ar -qv arc_files.a *.c
```

The v modifier displays **ar**'s actions as it archives files. If the archive already exists, the files are appended. This command does not verify whether the files already exist in the archive, as -q suppresses the check. The -m option performs the check and replaces existing files.

To list the contents of the archive file, issue

```
ar -tv arc_files.a
```

You can obtain a summary list of the filenames by omitting the v option.

To update an archived file, issue

```
ar -rv arc_files.a file.c
```

This replaces the existing file.c with the new version.

You can add a file to the archive with the command

```
ar -mv arc_files.a newfile.c
```

The -m option verifies that the file is not already in the archive. If you know it isn't, you can use the -q option to speed the process.

You can specify the file's location. The command

```
arc -arv arc_files.a newfile.c file.c
```

places newfile.c after file.c (because of the *a* positional modifier). To delete a file from the archive, issue

```
ar -dv arc_file.a file.c
```

Finally, to extract one, issue

```
ar -xv arc_file.a newfile.c
```

assign

Description:

Assigns and deassigns devices

Compatibility:

OSF/1	No
SCO Unix	Yes
SCO Xenix	Yes
System V Release 3.2	No
System V Release 4	No
X/Open	No

Syntax:

assign [-d] [-u] [-v] [device] ...

Options:

-d	deassigns the device (same as the **deassign** command)
-u	performs error checking only to ensure that device is assignable
-v	descriptive output
device	any assignable device not currently assigned

Returns:

0 if successful

1 if unsuccessful

2 if the device cannot be assigned (usually because of another assignment)

Files:

/dev/asglock	file to prevent concurrent access
/etc/atab	table of assignable devices

See Also:

deassign

Discussion

You can use **assign** to try to assign a specific device (such as a tape unit or floppy drive) to you. This would give you exclusive access, preventing others from using it. The device cannot be assigned already, nor can you assign it for another user.

In most installations, **assign** is unnecessary, as devices allow general read and write access. Its common use is to prevent others from conflicting with your commands, such as backups, when the device is far from your terminal. For example, **assign** can ensure that no one overwrites your floppies.

assign without arguments displays a list of devices and their current assignments.

Notes

To use **assign**, the directory /dev must be owned by "bin" and have read and write access. Assignable devices in the directory must be owned by "asg". The administrator must establish these settings.

Examples

To assign yourself exclusive access to the tape drive /dev/rmt0, enter

```
assign /dev/rmt0
```

Ah, the thrill of ownership! Now is a great time to go on that two-week backpacking trip in the mountains, far from the angry outcries of would-be tape users.

at

Description:

Executes a command at a specified time

Compatibility:

OSF/1	Yes
SCO Unix	Yes
SCO Xenix	Yes
System V Release 3.2	Yes
System V Release 4	Yes
X/Open	Yes

Syntax:

at [ckms] time [date] [increment]

at -l [jobID ...] [user] [-o]

at [-i|f] -r jobID ... [-u user]

at -qletter time [date] [increment] (SCO Unix and Xenix only)

at [-f file] [-m] time [date] [increment] (SVR4 only)

at -n [user] (OSF/1 only)

Versions:

OSF/1: adds the -c, -f, -i, -k, -m, -n, -o, -s, and -u options. -l and -r allow a user name as an argument.

SCO Unix and Xenix: support the -q option for queue status reports. Other versions use the **atq** command.

SVR4: allows the -f and -m options.

Arguments:

-l lists scheduled jobs. OSF/1 allows a user name to be specified; others use a job ID to identify the user.

-q puts the job in the queue for one of the following commands (SCO Unix and Xenix only):

```
a   at
b   batch
c   cron
```

-r removes previously scheduled commands

time may be 1 or 2 digits taken as hours, or 4 digits taken as hours and minutes, or hh:mm, The suffix "am" or "pm" may appear. The suffix "zulu" (a convenient mnemonic) indicates use of Greenwich Mean Time (GMT). The words "noon", "midnight", and "now" are recognized.

date may be specified by month name, day, and year (optional), or day of the week (full spelling or three-letter abbreviation). The words "today" or "tomorrow" may appear.

increment is a number followed by "minutes", "hours", "days", "weeks", "months", or "years" in either plural or singular form.

Options:

-c uses the C shell (**csh**) for the request (OSF/1 only)

-f reads commands from "file" (SVR4 and OSF/1 only)

-i activates interactive deletion (OSF/1 only)

-k uses the Korn shell (**ksh**) for the request (OSF/1 only)

-m sends mail to the user after the command finishes (SVR4 and OSF/1 only)

-n displays the number of queued files for user

-o lists jobs in queued order (OSF/1 only)

-s uses the Bourne shell (**sh**) for the request (OSF/1 only)

-u deletes all jobs for the specified user (OSF/1 only)

Error Handling:

Displays invalid syntax, time, and date commands on standard output when actually submitted

Defaults:

Reads from standard input unless redirected.

Assumes a 24 hour (international) clock unless specified otherwise.

Assumes the next occurrence of the specified time if no day is specified.
Assumes the next year if the month specified is before the current one.
Routes all output to your mailbox unless you specify otherwise.

Files:

/usr/lib/cron	main cron directory
/usr/lib/cron/at.allow	allowed users
/usr/lib/cron/at.deny	denied users
/usr/lib/cron/queuedefs	queue information
/usr/spool/cron/atjobs	spool area

OSF/1 uses /var/adm instead of /usr/lib, and /var/spool instead of /usr/spool.

See Also:

atq; atrm; batch; cron; crontab; kill; nice; ps

Discussion

at mails standard output and standard error to the user unless they are redirected. It retains all environment variables, the current directory, and the umask settings in effect when given, even if the user logs off before the specified execution time.

Unix uses the files /usr/lib/cron/at.allow and /usr/lib/cron/at.deny to control access to **at**. Both have one user name per line. If neither exists, only the superuser can use **at**. To allow global usage, create an empty at.deny file.

A file queued using **at** is copied into the /usr/spool/cron/atjobs directory and assigned the job ID as its name. It will have the environment variables defined first, followed by the submitted commands. Queue information is in the file usr/lib/cron/queuedefs.

Notes

You can list or remove only your own jobs unless you are the superuser.

You can have **at** reschedule itself by invoking it recursively. The best approach is to use a file redirected into it. For example, suppose the file *onsystem* contains the following:

```
who
echo "sh onsystem" | at 1900 tue next week
```

When submitted once, it will reschedule itself each time to run the following Tuesday at 7:00 PM. Such automatic repetitions are useful with backup and cleanup routines.

The command **at now** produces an error message, as it is always too late to execute now. There must be some deep philosophical significance to this, but I have no idea what it is.

SVR4 adds the commands **atq** and **atrm** for displaying scheduled jobs and removing them, respectively.

OSF/1 uses /var/adm and /var/spool instead of /usr/lib and /usr/spool respectively.

Examples

After you specify a valid time and date, **at** waits for you to enter the commands to execute, terminated with Ctrl-D.

```
at 2100 Aug 21
who <Ctrl-D>
```

The best approach is to put the commands in a shell script, then redirect the input. OSF/1 and SVR4 use the -f option to read the file directly.

For example, to execute **who** using **at**, create a file containing it. If the file is test.at, you can submit it for execution at 7:00 PM today with any of the following commands:

```
at 700pm < test.at
at 1900 < test.at
at 19:00 today < test.at
```

Note the variations in time and date format. For example, the following commands are legal:

```
at 0900pm Jul03 < test.at
at 2100 Jul 03 < test.at
```

You can use increments to modify any argument. The word "next" is equivalent to "+1":

```
at 0900pm +2 weeks < test.at
at 9 pm Monday next week < test.at
at 2100 next month < test.at
```

The system responds to a job submitted to **at** with a message such as:

```
job 651286801.a at Tue Aug 21 21:00:00 EDT 1990
```

The 651286801.a is the job ID. The last letter indicates the type:

a	**at** job
batch	**batch** job
e	**ksh** job (OSF/1 only)
f	**csh** job (OSF/1 only)

To list the jobs you have queued, use **at -l**. Most versions include the user name:

```
user = tim 651286800.a Tue Aug 21 21:00:00 EDT 1990
user = tim 651286801.a Tue Aug 21 21:00:01 EDT 1990
```

OSF/1 and SVR4 users can list the queue with the **atq** command.

The command to remove the first job in the list is

```
at -r 651286800.a
```

Unix does not report anything, but a check of the queue with **at -l** will show that the job has vanished. OSF/1 and SVR4 users can issue **atrm** to remove jobs.

atq

Description:
Displays jobs queued to run at specified times

Compatibility:

OSF/1	Yes
SCO Unix	No
SCO Xenix	No
System V Release 3.2	No
System V Release 4	Yes
X/Open	No

Alternative:
at -l

Syntax:
atq [-c|-n] [user ...]

Options:
-c displays jobs in the order submitted

-n displays only the total number of jobs in the queue

Files:
/usr/spool/cron spool area

/var/spool/cron spool area for OSF/1

See Also:
at; atrm; batch; cron; kill; nice; ps

Discussion

atq displays a list of jobs submitted through **at** to run later. It shows only ones you have submitted, unless you are the superuser. The superuser can list all jobs, or a specific user's.

Notes

Only OSF/1 and SVR4 have **atq**. With other versions, use **at -l** instead.

atrm

Description:

Removes jobs queued by **at** or **batch**

Compatibility:

OSF/1	Yes
SCO Unix	No
SCO Xenix	No
System V Release 3.2	No
System V Release 4	Yes
X/Open	No

Syntax:

atrm [-|-a|-f|-i] [jobID ...]

Versions:

OSF/1: uses the - option to remove all jobs.

SVR4: uses the -a option to remove all jobs.

Options:

-	removes all jobs in the queue (OSF/1 only)
-a	removes all jobs in the queue (SVR4 only)
-f	suppresses all information about the removal
-i	asks the user to confirm each removal
jobID	job ID or user name

Files:

/usr/spool/cron	spool area
/var/spool/cron	spool area for OSF/1

See Also:

at; atq; batch; cron; kill; nice; ps

Discussion

atrm removes jobs submitted through **at** or **batch** to run later. You can obtain job IDs with the **atq** command. If a job ID appears, only it is deleted. If the superuser includes a user name (such as "tim"), **atrm** deletes all jobs that user has submitted. So much for poor "tim"! He has become the tragic "man without a valid user account," left to wander from computer to computer, searching desperately in trash icons for partially consumed CPU cycles.

The -a (SVR4) or - (OSF/1) option removes all jobs you have submitted. If you are a superuser, it flushes the entire queue.

The -i option asks for confirmation on each job. If you answer "y", it removes the job.

awk

Description:

Pattern scanning and processing language

Compatibility:

OSF/1	Yes
SCO Unix	Yes
SCO Xenix	Yes
System V Release 3.2	Yes
System V Release 4	Yes
X/Open	Yes

Syntax:

awk [-F sep] [parms] ['match'] [-f 'matchfiles'] [file ...]

Options:

-f file of options to be performed for each matched pattern

-F defines the input field separator to be "sep"

match a string enclosed in single quotation marks containing patterns to be matched

parms parameters passed to **awk** in the form x=..., where x is an **awk** variable. Valid ones are:

ARGC	command line argument count
ARGV	command line argument array
FILENAME	current input file
FNR	current record number in the current file
FS	input field separator
NF	number of fields in a record
NR	current record number
OFMT	output format for numbers

OFS	output field separator
ORS	output record separator
RS	input record separator

Defaults:

With no files specified, **awk** assumes standard input. The filename "-" indicates it specifically.

awk variables have the following default values:

FS	blank
OFMT	%.6g
OFS	blank
ORS	newline
RS	newline

Limitations and Restrictions:

You must enclose the "match" string in single quotation marks to prevent interpretation by the shell.

Whitespace in the input file is not preserved in the output if fields are used.

See Also:

grep; sed

Discussion

awk scans each input file for matches to a set of patterns given in "match". You can specify the action to be taken for each pattern either in the command or in a file following the -f option. We call the specifications *pattern-action statements.*

awk compares each line to the patterns and takes the corresponding action. If no action appears, it prints the matching line. If no pattern appears, it performs the action on every line.

An action can be a single statement or a collection. **awk** recognizes the following statements:

{ [statement] ... }

break
continue
delete array[subscript]
do statement while (conditional)
exit [expression]
for (expression ; conditional ; expression) statement
for (var in array) statement
if (conditional) statement [else statement]
next
print [expression] [>expression]
printf format [, expression] [>expression]
return [expression]
while (conditional) statement

The "next" statement skips the remaining patterns on the current input line. The "exit" and "return" statements can have an exit status given by "expression". The option ">expression" means redirection to a filename given by "expression".

Patterns are Boolean combinations of expressions. Valid ones take the form:

expression regularoperation expression
expression ~ expression
expression ! expression
variable in array

Regular operations are any of the six C relational operators. A matching operator is either ~ (contains) or ! (does not contain). An expression is any valid regular expression of the type used by **egrep**. When used in patterns, it must be surrounded by slashes.

Columns in the input file are indicated by $1 for the first, $2 for the second, and so on. $0 refers to the entire line. The words BEGIN and END indicate the start and end of a section.

awk supports the following arithmetic functions:

atan2
cos

exp
int (truncates to an integer)
log
rand (random number between 0 and 1)
sin
sqrt
srand (sets seed value for rand specifically, or uses time of day if no argument appears).

awk also supports the following functions:

close(name)	closes the file or pipe “name”
cmd|output	pipes the output of “cmd” into “output”
getline	moves to the next input record and assigns it as $0
getline <file	sets the next input record ($0) from “file”
getline var	sets variable “var”
getline var <file	sets variable “var” from the next record of “file”
gsub(for,repl,in)	replaces successive occurrences of the expression (same as sub)
index(str,b)	gives the position of string “b” in string “str”, or 0 if it does not occur
length(str)	gives the length of the argument, or the whole line if no argument
match(str,exp)	gives the position of expression “exp” in string “str”, or 0 if it does not occur. Sets RSTART to the starting position and RLENGTH to the length of the matched string.
split(str,arr,sep)	splits string “str” into array elements arr[1], arr[2], ... arr[n]. It returns the value of “n”. If the field separator “sep” does not appear, the default (a space) is used.
sprintf(fmt,exp,...)	formats all expressions according to the printf “fmt” format
sub(for,str,in)	substitutes string “str” for the first instance

	of the expression "for" in each occurrence of string "in". It returns the number of substitutions. If "in" is omitted, it uses the current record.
substr(str,start,len)	returns a substring of length "len" in string "str", starting at position "start"
system(cmd)	executes command "cmd" and returns its exit state

awk allows user defined functions, which may be recursive. The format is

```
function name(arguments) { statements }
```

Notes

awk is a very powerful processing language. For more information about it, the definitive source is the book by its authors: Aho, A., et al. *The awk Programming Language*, Reading, MA: Addison-Wesley, 1988. There are even **awk** compilers available.

Examples

awk can do complex operations. It is ideally suited to examining files and changing their formats. Simple examples of its use are:

- display lines longer than 60 characters

  length > 60
- display the total number of lines

  END { print NR }
- print the fifth, third, and fourth columns

  { print $5, $3, $4 }
- print all lines containing "tim"

  /tim/
- sum the fourth column and display the result

  ```
      { sum += $4 }
  END { print "The sum is ", sum, " with an average of ", sum/NR}
  ```

backup

Description:

Performs incremental backups

Compatibility:

OSF/1	No
SCO Unix	No
SCO Xenix	Yes
System V Release 3.2	No
System V Release 4	No
X/Open	No

Syntax:

backup [key [arguments] filesystem]

Options:

The key consists of characters from the set:

0-9 number of the backup level (0 is a complete backup, the highest level). Backs up files modified since the date in /etc/ddate for lower levels. The 0 option backs up the entire filesystem. If no date is defined, **backup** saves all files below the specified level.

d tape density. The density in bpi is the next argument. The default is 1600 bpi. Densities are expressed in inches only. Metric units are not supported.

f backs up to the next argument instead of the default device

k size of the backup volume. The next argument gives its size in kB. Overrides d and s options.

s tape size. The next argument is the size in feet. The default is 2300. Metric units are not supported.

u writes the date to /etc/ddate/ if the backup succeeds

Defaults:

The key defaults to "9u", an incremental backup (only files changed since the last higher level backup).

Backs up the default filesystem to the default device unless an override appears.

Warnings:

When backing up to floppies, be sure to have enough formatted disks available. When inserting a new volume, close the drive door properly or the entire backup will fail and must be restarted. If you have completed 15 disks of a 20-disk backup, you will be quite unhappy.

Files:

/etc/ddate	contains an entry for each file system and backup level, with the date of the last successful backup
/etc/default/backup	default backup information

See Also:

dump; dumpdir

Discussion

backup copies all files changed after a specified date to a backup medium. Backups can be to disk or tape.

backup allows ten "backup levels", numbered from 0 (complete backup) to 9 (incremental—files changed since last higher level backup). In practice, the intermediate levels are seldom used.

That is, a common approach is to do a level 0 backup, then perform level 9 backups. Each contains all files changed since the level 0 backup (not just since the last level 9)

If one volume is insufficient, you will be asked to change volumes, then press Return.

backup is the same as the Xenix **dump** command.

Examples

The common way to use **backup** is to create a full backup first with the command

```
backup 0u
```

followed by incremental backups using

```
backup 9u
```

When the incremental backups become too large, or at selected intervals, you should make a new level 0 backup.

Intermediate levels exist in theory, but levels 0 (full backup) and 9 (incremental backup) are much easier to track in practice.

banner

Description:
Prints headings in large letters

Compatibility:

OSF/1	Yes
SCO Unix	Yes
SCO Xenix	Yes
System V Release 3.2	Yes
System V Release 4	Yes
X/Open	Yes

Syntax:
banner string ...

Arguments:
string is a set of characters to be printed in large format on standard output.

See Also:
echo

Discussion
banner forms letters from seven rows and up to seven columns, with spaces in-between. You can embed spaces in a string by surrounding them with single or double quotation marks.

If more than one argument is specified, each appears on a separate line.

The maximum number of characters per line is version dependent, but is usually ten. Excess characters are ignored.

Examples

banner is useful for identifying printouts or program names in a highly visible way. A common use is to separate output on shared or networked printers.

```
banner tim

#####       #       #      #

  #         #       ##    ##

  #         #       #  ##  #

  #         #       #      #

  #         #       #      #

  #         #       #      #

  #         #       #      #
```

You should embed spaces and special characters in quotation marks:

```
banner "tim *"

#####       #       #      #            #    #

  #         #       ##    ##              ##

  #         #       #  ##  #            #######

  #         #       #      #              ##

  #         #       #      #            #     #

  #         #       #      #

  #         #       #      #
```

You can redirect **banner** or embed it in a shell script.

You can split the output over several lines by enclosing each part in quotation marks. The command

```
banner "Backup""in Progress"
```

displays “Backup” on one line, and “in Progress” below it.

basename

Description:

Removes directory names from pathnames

Compatibility:

OSF/1	Yes
SCO Unix	Yes
SCO Xenix	Yes
System V Release 3.2	Yes
System V Release 4	Yes
X/Open	Yes

Syntax:

basename string [suffix]

Arguments:

string is the string from which the directory names are to be stripped.

Options:

suffix will also be removed. You can thus remove an extension at the same time, leaving the base filename for use in accessing related files or creating new ones.

See Also:

dirname

Discussion

basename deletes any prefix ending with / and can remove a suffix as well. The common use is in shell programming.

Examples

basename can strip off directory and suffix information from a filename. The command

```
basename /usr/tim/c/testprog.c .c
```

displays the output *testprog* on the console. If we had not specified the suffix ".c", **basename** would not have removed it.

Shell scripts commonly use **basename** to specify names. The following example compiles a file and moves the output into the current directory:

```
cc $1
mv a.out 'basename $1 .c'
```

If the script was named *compileit,* you would invoke it with

```
compileit /usr/tim/c/testprog.c
```

The command compiles testprog.c in the /usr/tim/c directory, then moves its output (called a.out by default) to the current directory as testprog. Here **basename** strips the current directories' names and the .c suffix from the argument. The result is then the destination for **mv**.

You can also use **basename** to set variables. The command

```
NEWFILE='basename /usr/tim/c/testprog'
```

sets the variable NEWFILE to testprog.

batch

Description:

Executes commands at a specified time

Compatibility:

OSF/1	Yes
SCO Unix	Yes
SCO Xenix	Yes
System V Release 3.2	Yes
System V Release 4	Yes
X/Open	Yes

Syntax:

batch

Files:

/usr/lib/cron	main cron directory
/usr/lib/cron/at.allow	allowed users
/usr/lib/cron/at.deny	denied users
/usr/lib/cron/queuedefs	queue information
/usr/spool/cron/atjobs	spool area

See Also:

at; cron; crontab

Defaults:

Reads from standard input unless redirected.

Mails standard output and standard error output to the user unless redirected.

Retains all environment variables, the current directory, and umask settings.

Discussion

batch accepts commands to be executed when system load permits. It resembles **at**, but does not allow time and date specifications. All commands submitted reside in a queue.

When submitted, **batch** displays a job ID number. You can remove it if it has not yet executed with the **at -r jobID** command (see **at**).

Unix uses the files /usr/lib/cron/at.allow and /usr/lib/cron/at.deny to control access to **batch**. Both have one user name per line. If neither exists, only the superuser can use **batch**. To allow global usage, create an empty at.deny file.

Examples

batch allows immediate background processing. It is easiest to use with redirected shell scripts. For example, to execute **who** using **batch**, create a file containing it. If the file is test.batch, you can submit it for execution with

```
batch < test.batch
```

batch need not have its input redirected. After you issue it, the shell will let you enter commands line by line, terminated with Ctrl-D.

You should use **batch** for long programs that require no user interaction, such as database sorts and document formatting. It minimizes their impact on system performance, and lets you continue working at your terminal. For example, to use the text formatter **nroff** to format a large text chapter2, you could issue the commands:

```
batch
nroff chapter2 > chapter2.nroff
<Ctrl-D>
```

to submit the **nroff** command to the **batch** queue. When a job is submitted, the system responds with a message such as:

```
job 651286801.b at Tue Aug 21 21:00:00 EDT 1990
```

651286801.b is the job ID.

batch routes all output to your mailbox unless you specify otherwise. An example of rerouting errors is

```
nroff chapter2 2>&1> chapter2.nroff | mail tim
```

It formats chapter2 and puts the output in chapter2.nroff, mailing all errors to "tim". I suppose this is better than the electronic junk mail I usually get ("You may have already won 1,000,000 hours of free computer time!").

bc

Description:

Unlimited precision calculator

Compatibility:

OSF/1	Yes
SCO Unix	Yes
SCO Xenix	Yes
System V Release 3.2	Yes
System V Release 4	Yes
X/Open	No

Syntax:

bc [-c] [-l] [file...]

Options:

-c	compiles only (run with **dc** later)
-l	makes mathematical library available (includes exponentials)
file	provides input for **bc**

Defaults:

Uses standard input unless an input file is specified.

The default library is /usr/lib/lib.bc.

Files:

/usr/bin/dc	desk calculator program
/usr/lib/lib.bc	mathematical library

See Also:

dc

Discussion

bc uses a C-like language as a preprocessor for the **dc** calculator. It invokes **dc** automatically unless you use the -c option to send the **dc** input to standard output. Pressing Ctrl-D terminates **bc.**

bc allows comments enclosed in /* and */. It provides single letter variable names and array elements defined as a variable name followed by an expression in square brackets. All variables are global. You can use a letter as a variable, a function, and an array simultaneously.

bc assumes that its input consists of statements and routes them to standard output unless the main operator is an assignment. Semicolons and newline characters may separate statements.

bc supports the following operators:

+	addition
-	subtraction
*	multiplication
/	division
%	remainder
^	exponentiation
++	unary plus
--	unary minus
==	exactly equal to (exact string matches and numerical equality)
<=	less than or equal to
>=	greater than or equal to
!=	not equal to
<	less than
>	greater than

Compound assignments use the following operators:

=+, =-, =*, =/, =%, =^

bc supports the following statements:

break

for (expression; expression; expression) statement

if (logical expression) statement

null statement

quit

while (logical expression) statement

The “quit” statement is interpreted when read. The “for” statement requires three arguments.

Functions can be defined with:

```
define <name> (name, ..., name) {
        auto name, ..., name
        statement; ... statement
        return (expression)
}
```

The /usr/lib/lib.bc library includes the following mathematical functions:

a(x)	arctangent
c(x)	cosine
e(x)	exponential
j(n,x)	Bessel function
l(x)	log
s(x)	sine

All trigonometric functions require arguments in radians.

Assignments to *scale* set the precision in digits. Assignments to *ibase* or *obase* set the input and output number radix, respectively.

Examples

You can use the calculator interactively by entering commands after issuing **bc** by itself. For example, enter:

```
$bc
scale = 2 /* sets 2 decimal places */
1/5
```

and the system responds with

```
0.20
```

bc displays the result of each calculation when you press Enter, except for assignments. You can embed comments when using **bc** interactively, as in the above example.

The following creates a function *e* that approximates an exponential:

```
scale = 20
define e(x) {
    auto a, b, c, i, s
    a = 1
    b = 1
    s = 1
    for(i=1; 1==1; i++){
        a=a*x
        b=b*i
        c=a/b
        if(c==0) return(s)
        s=s+c
    }
    }
```

scale, *a*, *b*, *c*, *i*, and *s* are variables.

You can display *e*'s values for the first 25 integers with

```
for(i=1; i<=25; i++) e(i)
```

The values are imprecise due to the crude algorithm.

bdiff

Description:
Compares files too large for **diff** (more than about 3,500 lines)

Compatibility:

OSF/1	Yes
SCO Unix	Yes
SCO Xenix	Yes
System V Release 3.2	Yes
System V Release 4	Yes
X/Open	No

Syntax:
bdiff file1 file2 [n] [-s]

Options:
n number of lines to put in each temporary file

-s suppresses diagnostics from **bdiff** (but not **diff**)

Defaults:
The default length of each split file is 3,500 lines.

See Also:
diff

Discussion
bdiff extends **diff** to large files. It divides a file into smaller temporary ones, then runs **diff** on each of them. The output is identical to **diff**'s.

If either filename is a dash, **bdiff** uses standard input.

Examples

The command

```
bdiff file.1 file.2 5000
```

divides both file.1 and file.2 into temporary files 5,000 lines long, and compares them.

bfs

Description:
Scans large files

Compatibility:

OSF/1	Yes
SCO Unix	Yes
SCO Xenix	Yes
System V Release 3.2	Yes
System V Release 4	Yes
X/Open	No

Syntax:
bfs [-] name

Options:
- suppresses printing of sizes

Limitations and Restrictions:
Files can be up to 1024kB and 32,000 lines. Allows up to 255 characters on a line.

See Also:
ed

Discussion
bfs handles large files and allows **ed** commands to navigate through the text. It is read only (i.e., it does not allow editing).

bfs prompts for input with an asterisk. Prompts are toggled on or off with the P key and Return. **bfs** displays the size of the file unless suppressed.

bfs displays error messages if prompting is on. If it is off, you can display them with the ? command.

bfs supports all **ed** addressing commands and adds the following:

>	forward search without wraparound
<	backward search without wraparound
:label	places a label in a command file
xb/a/label	jumps to "label" if the expression "a" is valid
xbn label	jumps to "label" if the last return code is nonzero
xbz label	jumps to "label" based on the last return code from a "!command" command
xc [switch]	if "switch" is 1, output from the "p" and null commands is "crunched" (tabs and spaces are reduced to one space, and blank lines are deleted); if "switch" is 0, output is not crunched.
xf file	takes further commands from "file"
xt n	truncates output from the "p" and null commands to "n" characters. Default is 255.
xo file	diverts output from the "p" and null commands to "file", or to standard output if no "file" is specified.
xv[var][ ][val]	assigns the value "val" to variable "var". Spaces are optional, so both xv625 and xv6 25 assign "25" to the variable "6".

bfs extends several **ed** commands. The differences are:

+	means one or more times. [0-9]+ is equivalent to **ed**'s [0-9][0-9]*

\{m,n\} — the "m" integer value inside "\{" and "\}" indicates the number of times to repeat the preceding expression. If "n" is specified, it is the maximum number of repetitions. The limit is 255. A comma following "m" with no "n" value means to repeat without limit.

$n — following an expression, this stores its return value in the "n+1"th argument. A maximum of 10 expressions is allowed.

Notes

As **bfs** does not use a buffer, it is faster than **ed**. The common use is to determine where you can split a file with **csplit**. The smaller pieces are then easier to edit. In case you are wondering, there is no "big file delete" command.

biff

Description:

Notifies you when mail arrives

Compatibility:

OSF/1	Yes
SCO Unix	No
SCO Xenix	No
System V Release 3.2	No
System V Release 4	No
X/Open	No

Syntax:

biff [y | n]

See Also:

mail; mailq

Discussion

biff informs you when mail arrives during your current session. When active, it sends a message showing the header information and first seven lines of the text. That should be enough to tell whether you have something significant or merely a reminder of the weekly love offering for the system administrator.

Most users put **biff y** in their .login or .profile files to execute when logging on. **biff** settings are lost when you log out.

Examples

To turn on mail notification, enter

```
biff y
```

You can display the current setting by typing **biff** with no arguments.

cal

Description:
Prints a calendar

Compatibility:

OSF/1	Yes
SCO Unix	Yes
SCO Xenix	Yes
System V Release 3.2	Yes
System V Release 4	Yes
X/Open	Yes

Syntax:
cal [[month] year]

Options:
month must be a number between 1 and 12 inclusive, or letters that identify a unique month.

year is between 1 and 9999 inclusive.

Defaults:
When used without arguments, **cal** prints the calendars for this month, and the previous and next ones. When a month or month and year is given, **cal** prints just its calendar. If only a year is given, **cal** prints all its calendars.

Notes
You must specify years as four digits; 92 refers to 92 AD (probably not what you want!), not 1992. This approach is a convenience for Roman historians, Biblical scholars, and archaeologists.

cal uses the English calendar. It switched from Julian to Gregorian in September 1752, so **cal** cannot establish accurate days of the week before then, just in case you were wondering.

Examples

cal can display any month's calendar, such as:

```
cal Jul 1993
cal 7 1993
```

You need enter only enough letters to specify the month's name uniquely. Thus "mar" will do for March, and "s" for September. If the letters are ambiguous (such as "ma"), **cal** reports "non-unique month name".

calendar

Description:
Reminder service

Compatibility:

OSF/1	Yes
SCO Unix	Yes
SCO Xenix	Yes
System V Release 3.2	Yes
System V Release 4	Yes
X/Open	Yes

Syntax:
calendar [-]

Options:
- examines all users' calendar files

Files:
/usr/lib/calprog determines today's and tomorrow's dates

Cautions:
The calendar file must have read permission for the service to work.

See Also:
cron

Discussion

calendar checks a file in your current directory to determine if any lines in it have today's or tomorrow's date. If so, it mails them to you. On weekends, the "tomorrow" check extends to the next Monday.

You can create a file containing a single line with the month and day and a note. You can abbreviate the month or spell it out, and the day can simply follow it or be separated by a slash. When a match occurs, **calendar** sends the note to your mailbox.

When **calendar** has an argument (a hyphen is sufficient), it scans all users for a "calendar" file in their home directory and sends the results. Superusers can **cron** the process for automatic execution just after midnight each day. The user's "calendar" files must have read permission for it to work.

Examples

In your home directory, you can create the file "calendar" with a single line for each event you want to receive mail on. You can specify months and days in many formats, such as:

Jan 5	Appointment with palm reader
2/14	Benedict Arnold's birthday
March 12	Send flowers to secretary (he's allergic to them!)
Apr 15	Income tax due
May 1	Book summer vacation in Tibetan monastery
6/21	Company picnic (good time for trip to Mars)

When the user runs **calendar**, it scans the file "calendar" in the current directory and mails any items that have today's or tomorrow's date. Friday's matches extend over the weekend to Monday, but **calendar** does not track holidays.

The system administrator usually runs **calendar** in a **cron** file each day just after midnight, so it checks all users' files for matches and mails them automatically. The joys of computerized nagging, just in case you don't get enough at home!

cancel

Description:

Cancels a request to the line printer

Compatibility:

OSF/1	Yes
SCO Unix	Yes
SCO Xenix	Yes
System V Release 3.2	Yes
System V Release 4	Yes
X/Open	Yes

Syntax:

cancel [id ...] [printer ...]

cancel -u userid [printer]

Versions:

SVR4: adds the -u argument.

Options:

-u	login of the user who made the print request (SVR4 only)
id	print request ID
printer	printer name

See Also:

lp; lprm; lpstat

Discussion

Cancels a print request submitted with a command such as **lp**. It requires either a printer name or a print request ID.

If an ID is given, it is cancelled. If a name is given, the request currently printing on it is cancelled.

Examples

To cancel the print request "laser-1234", enter

```
cancel laser-1234
```

You can determine print request IDs with **lpstat**. To cancel the request currently printing on printer "laser", use

```
cancel laser
```

It cancels the current request and queues the next one.

"Who could have cancelled your print request just before the big meeting? I'm so sorry you were unprepared and didn't get the promotion you were expecting. It's all that terrible computer's fault!" (*How to Succeed in Business Without Really Trying*, computer version).

cat

Description:

Concatenates and displays files

Compatibility:

OSF/1	Yes
SCO Unix	Yes
SCO Xenix	Yes
System V Release 3.2	Yes
System V Release 4	Yes
X/Open	Yes

Syntax:

cat [-b] [-e] [-n] [-r] [-s] [-t] [-u] [-v] file ...

Versions:

OSF/1: adds the -b, -n, and -r options.

X/Open: supports only the -s option.

Options:

-b omits line numbers on blank lines (used with -n) (OSF/1 only)

-e prints a $ at the end of each line when used with -v. Ignored otherwise.

-n displays line numbers (OSF/1 only)

-r reduces consecutive blank lines to a single one (OSF/1 only)

-s suppresses warnings about nonexistent files

-t shows tabs as '^I' and form feeds as '^L' when used with -v. Ignored otherwise.

-u produces unbuffered output

-v shows nonprinting characters. For example, it displays Ctrl-C as '^C' and DEL as '?'. It does not show tabs and form feeds (use -t to do that).

See Also:

more; pr

Discussion

You use **cat** to display files or move them to either standard output or another file. It can also combine files or display them on a terminal.

Examples

The command

```
cat testfile
```

displays testfile on standard output. **cat** can display several files, one after another.

You can concatenate files and rename the combination with the command

```
cat file_1 file_2 > file.new
```

It creates a new file file.new, containing file_1 followed by file_2. If file.new already existed, its contents would be deleted without warning. A version that appends to a file is

```
cat file_1 file_2 >> file.new
```

It appends file_1 and file_2 to file.new.

If you are **cat**ting large files to the screen, you may want to use a filter such as **more**. Otherwise, the text may scroll by too quickly to see.

catman

Description:
Creates formatted reference pages

Compatibility:

OSF/1	Yes
SCO Unix	No
SCO Xenix	No
System V Release 3.2	No
System V Release 4	No
X/Open	No

Syntax:
catman [-M path] [-n|-p|-w] [section ...]

Options:
-M updates reference pages in path. Multiple entries are separated by a colon (see Examples).

-n prevents creation of the **whatis** database

-p displays actions that would have occurred, but does not actually do any formatting

-w creates **whatis** database without doing any formatting

Defaults:
/usr/share/man is the default path.

See Also:
man; whatis

Discussion

catman formats all unformatted manual reference pages. It examines each page and replaces obsolete ones.

If it makes any changes to the manual, it also updates the **whatis** database.

If **catman** is invoked with arguments not preceded by a hyphen, it assumes they are reference sections to be examined.

catman is not a copycat crimefighter who drives around in a Catmobile, works in a Cat Cave, and makes his sidekick Robin very nervous.

Examples

To update manual section 4, enter

```
catman 4
```

To see if any pages in the entire manual need updating without actually changing anything, use the -p option:

```
catman -p
```

cd

Description:

Changes working directory

Compatibility:

OSF/1	Yes
SCO Unix	Yes
SCO Xenix	Yes
System V Release 3.2	Yes
System V Release 4	Yes
X/Open	Yes

Syntax:

cd [directory]

Options:

directory	valid directory name

Error Handling:

If the argument does not exist, **cd** searches for a similar name and asks whether you want to make it the working directory.

Defaults:

cd by itself returns to the user's home directory.

See Also:

pwd

Examples

If you are in the directory /usr/tim and want to switch to /etc, the command is

```
cd /etc
```

You must have access permission to the /etc directory to enter it.

To return to your home directory, just enter **cd** by itself as in:

```
$ pwd
/usr/spool/cron
$ cd
$ pwd
/usr/tim
$
```

To go up one level in the directory structure, use the special filename ".." The command

```
cd ..
```

always refers to the directory immediately above the current one.

If you specify a nonexistent directory, **cd** looks for a similar name. For example, suppose you try to change to the nonexistent directory /usr/tom:

```
$ cd /usr/tom
cd /usr/tim? y
ok
$ pwd
/usr/tim
```

When **cd** asks for approval to change to a directory, "n" means no, and anything else is "yes". Unix wants a firm, unequivocal "No" here!

checkmail

Description:

Checks for undelivered mail

Compatibility:

OSF/1	No
SCO Unix	Yes
SCO Xenix	No
System V Release 3.2	No
System V Release 4	No
X/Open	No

Syntax:

checkmail [-a] [-f] [-m]

Options:

-a shows both delivered and undelivered addresses

-f suppresses printing of the subject line

-m checks undelivered messages from all users

Discussion

checkmail lists the addressees and subjects of all undelivered mail from you on your local machine. You can use it to determine if mail has been sent to its recipient. Unfortunately, it does not help with the postal service.

Mail is usually undelivered due to a network problem (such as failure to connect through the modems). **checkmail** lists mail that has not been sent through the network.

chgrp

Description:

Changes the group ID

Compatibility:

OSF/1	Yes
SCO Unix	Yes
SCO Xenix	Yes
System V Release 3.2	Yes
System V Release 4	Yes
X/Open	Yes

Syntax:

chgrp [-f] [-h] [-R] group file

Versions:

OSF/1: adds the -f and -R options.

SVR4: adds the -h and -R options.

Arguments:

group is either the group name or ID number.

file is the file to be changed.

Options:

-f suppresses error reports (OSF/1 only)

-h changes the group of symbolic links (otherwise, **chgrp** changes the file, not the link) (SVR4 only)

-R descends through directories recursively (OSF/1 and SVR4 only)

Error Handling:

chgrp examines the /etc/group file to confirm that the group name or number exists before changing ownerships.

Limitations and Restrictions:

Only the file's owner and the superuser can change the group ID.

Files:

/etc/group	valid group ID names and numbers
/etc/passwd	user information

See Also:

chmod; chown; groups; grpcheck

Discussion

Files have permissions that apply to members of the owner's group. **chgrp** lets you change the group ID. It supports wildcards.

Group IDs are in the file /etc/group. **chgrp** accepts either the group name or its ID number.

Examples

The group ID is assigned when a file is created. It defaults to the creator's group. In a directory listing, the group name is in the fourth column, as in

```
-rw-r----- 1 tim prog    24 Aug 01 16:08 test
```

In this entry, the file's owner is "tim", who belongs to the group "prog". The file permissions (see **chmod**) indicate that group members have read permission, but all others have no rights.

To change the group ID of file "test" to "research", enter

```
chgrp research test
```

If group "research" is number 52 in the /etc/group file, an obscure alternative is

```
chgrp 52 test
```

An excellent choice if your aim is to preserve your job and show your scorn for lowly maintenance programmers!

To change the group ID of all files in the current directory to "research", enter

```
chgrp research *
```

The /etc/group file lists all valid groups and their users. A typical sequence is:

```
prog::51:tim,bill,mary
research::52:tim,david,jane,sam
accting::53:jim,art,kathy
sales::54:mike,laurie,jack
```

The first part of each line is the group name. After two colons comes the group ID number, followed by all members. A user can belong to several groups. Users can be assigned to groups by changing the /etc/group file. However, corrupting it may have serious effects (including preventing logins), so be careful. **grpcheck** checks whether the /etc/group file has been corrupted.

chmod

Description:

Changes access permissions

Compatibility:

OSF/1	Yes
SCO Unix	Yes
SCO Xenix	Yes
System V Release 3.2	Yes
System V Release 4	Yes
X/Open	Yes

Syntax:

chmod [-f] [-R] [who][+|-|=] [permission] file ...

chmod [-f] [-R] mode file

Versions:

OSF/1: adds the -f and -R options.

SVR4: adds the -R option.

Arguments:

file is the filename to be changed. Wildcards are permitted.

mode is the logical OR (equivalent to a sum) of the following octal values:

4000	set user ID on execution
20X0	set group ID on execution if X is odd (1-7)
	set mandatory locking if X is even (0-6)
1000	set the sticky bit
0400	read by owner
0200	write by owner

0100	execute by owner (search in directories)
0040	read by group
0020	write by group
0010	execute by group (search in directories)
0004	read by others
0002	write by others
0001	execute by others (search in directories)
0000	no permissions

Options:

-f does not report errors (OSF/1 only)

-R moves through directories, changing files recursively (OSF/1 and SVR4 only)

who may be a (all), g (group), o (other), or u (user).

+-= indicates whether to add (+), subtract (-), or set (=) permissions.

permission consists of the letters:

l	mandatory locking
r	read
s	set
t	sticky bit
w	write
x	execute

Defaults:

Affects all users unless otherwise specified

See Also:

chgrp; chown; umask

Discussion

File and directory permissions determine who can read, write, and execute a file or access a directory. The permissions are set when a file is created, according to the user's default permissions. **chmod** can change them. To see a file's permissions, use **l** (or **ls -l**). A typical result is

```
-rw-r--r-- 1 tim  prog   134  Aug 02 13:15 test
```

The first column indicates the file's type and permissions. The first character indicates whether it is a directory ("d") or an ordinary file ("-").

The next three characters ("rw-" in the example) are the user permissions. Then come the group permissions ("r--"), and finally the other users' (world) permissions ("r--"). Permissions are of three types:

- r read, allows the file to be examined
- w write, allows the file to be modified and overwritten
- x execute, allows the file to be treated as a program

The three types appear in the order above. In the example, the user (the file's owner) has read and write permission, whereas the group and all others have only read permission. A hyphen indicates no permission.

In the following example, the user has read, write, and execute permission, the group has read and execute permission, and all others have no permission:

```
-rwxr-x--- 1 tim  prog   134  Aug 02 13:15 test
```

chmod changes who has access to a file or directory, and what kind of access they have. It has two modes, symbolic and absolute.

Symbolic mode uses letters to indicate the activity. You must specify three things: who is affected, what kind of changes to make, and the new permissions.

To indicate whom **chmod** affects, use the following letters:

- a all users (the default)
- g owner's group ID
- o others (all users)
- u user, or owner of the file or directory

Those affected then have the changes in permission indicated.

They can be:

- \+ add permissions

- \-   remove permissions
- =   assign to the permissions

The permissions themselves use the following letters:

- l   mandatory locking
- r   read
- s   sets the owner bit
- t   sets the sticky bit
- w   write
- x   execute (or search for directories)

The owner bit sets the user ID for a file to that of the person executing **chmod**. If the group ID bit is set, the file assumes the ID of the executing user ID's group. When set on a directory, the owner bit determines user and group ownership of all files in it.

The sticky bit applies to directories. When it is set, no one except the owner or superuser can delete a file. Both owners and superusers can set sticky bits.

Mandatory locking refers to the file locking read or write permissions while a program is accessing it. A file cannot have group execution permission and be locked.

Absolute mode uses an octal number as an argument to chmod. The number is the logical OR (equivalent to a sum) of the octal values in the table above. Symbolic mode is easier to remember and use, but shell scripts often use absolute mode. A calculator or a utility program is the best way to handle octal numbers; taping down two fingers or amputating them with your Swiss Army knife is not recommended.

Examples

The symbolic mode is the easiest way to use **chmod**. The command must specify the three elements "who", "change", and "permissions". For example, to allow the owner to execute a file "test" enter

```
chmod u+x test
```

To allow all users to execute "test", enter

```
chmod a+x test
```

or more simply

```
chmod +x test
```

(the default is all users).

To allows all users to read, write, and execute the file, enter

```
chmod +rwx test
```

The command

```
chmod g-rwx test
```

removes read, write, and execute permissions for the group, but does not change the "user" and "other" permissions. The equal sign sets the permissions to the specified levels.

For example, the following directory:

```
-rw-r-----  1  tim  prog  134  Aug 02  13:15  test1
-rwxr-xr--  1  tim  prog  128  Aug 02  13:41  test2
-rw-r--r--  1  tim  prog  156  Aug 02  14:02  test3
```

could have several **chmod** commands executed:

```
chmod +rwx test1
chmod g-rx test2
chmod u=rwx test3
```

The result is the directory listing:

```
-rwxrwxrwx  1  tim  prog  134  Aug 02  13:15  test1
-rwx---r--  1  tim  prog  128  Aug 02  13:41  test2
-rwxr--r--  1  tim  prog  156  Aug 02  14:02  test3
```

chmod does not affect the file date and time.

You can change several sets of permissions with a single command by separating the parts with commas. The command

```
chmod g+r,o+rw test
```

changes the file's group permission to include read, and its other permissions to include read and write.

chmod supports wildcards, so to give all .out files execute permission, enter

```
chmod +x *.out
```

Absolute mode is more difficult to use. To give a file "test" read, write, and execute permission for all users, enter

```
chmod 0777 test
```

The 0777 is the result of logically ORing the read, write, and execute permission octal numbers for owner, group, and others. To give the file read and write permission for the owner only, enter

```
chmod 0600 test
```

The command

```
chmod -rwx test
```

provides the ultimate in file security. No one can read, write, or execute "test"! It is like the famous movie that was so violent, repulsive, and obscene that it got an "XX" rating (no one admitted!).

chown

Description:
Changes owner ID

Compatibility:

OSF/1	Yes
SCO Unix	Yes
SCO Xenix	Yes
System V Release 3.2	Yes
System V Release 4	Yes
X/Open	Yes

Syntax:
chown [-f] [-h] [-R] owner file

Versions:
OSF/1: adds the -f and -R options.

SVR4: adds the -h and -R options.

Arguments:
owner is a valid user ID

file is the filename. Wildcards are supported.

Options:
-f does not report errors (OSF/1 only)

-h changes the owner of symbolic links (otherwise, **chown** changes the file, not the link) (SVR4 only)

-R descends through directories recursively (OSF/1 and SVR4 only)

Files:
/etc/passwd user ID file

See Also:

chgrp; chmod

Discussion

chown validates all user IDs before changing them by comparing them to the /etc/passwd file. The user ID can be either the user's login name or ID number.

The system controls access to **chown**. It seldom allows users to change file ownership.

Examples

To change the owner of file "test" to "tom", enter

```
chown tom test
```

chown supports wildcards, so you can change all files in the current directory to have owner "tom" with

```
chown tom *
```

The /etc/passwd file contains a list of all valid users and their passwords. A typical extract from it is:

```
tim:HaYTwg9a:201:51:Tim Parker:/usr/tim:/bin/sh
bill:aSDqETAd:202:51:Bill Smith:/usr/bill:/bin/sh
david:GHAsysRT:203:52:David Wilson:/usr/david:/bin/csh
```

The file consists of several lines, with items separated by colons. The items are the user ID, password (encrypted), ID number, group ID number, a comment, home directory, and the file to execute when the user logs on (usually a shell).

Passwords in /etc/passwd are encrypted, and are very difficult to decipher. Changing it can affect the user's password, preventing login. So modify it cautiously, as though you were working on high-voltage equipment.

chroot

Description:
Changes the root directory for a command

Compatibility:

OSF/1	No
SCO Unix	No
SCO Xenix	No
System V Release 3.2	No
System V Release 4	No
X/Open	Yes

Syntax:
chroot directory command

See Also:
cd

Discussion

chroot runs a command supplied as an argument using a different root directory from the default. It changes the initial working directory to the new root directory for the command.

Access to **chroot** is usually restricted.

Examples

The command

```
chroot /usr/tim cat > temp
```

will **cat** whatever is typed into file "temp" relative to directory /usr/tim instead of the default root directory. All references to files will be made relative to the new root directory.

clear

Description:
Clears the terminal screen

Compatibility:

OSF/1	Yes
SCO Unix	Yes
SCO Xenix	Yes
System V Release 3.2	Yes
System V Release 4	Yes
X/Open	Yes

Syntax:
clear [term]

Options:
term is the terminal identification, if not already set.

Error Handling:
Issues an error message if standard output is not a terminal

Files:

/etc/termcap	terminal definitions
/usr/lib/terminfo	terminal information database

Discussion
If the terminal lacks a clear capability, **clear** uses newline characters to scroll the screen. For a printing terminal, it issues a form feed.

If the terminal type is not set by the environment TERM variable, it may be specified as an argument. All terminal types must be in the /etc/termcap file.

Examples

To clear a terminal, issue **clear**. It blanks the screen and moves the cursor to the top left corner (the home position).

cmchk

Description:

Reports the block size of hard disks

Compatibility:

OSF/1	No
SCO Unix	Yes
SCO Xenix	Yes
System V Release 3.2	No
System V Release 4	No
X/Open	No

Syntax:

cmchk

Discussion

cmchk displays the hard disk block size in 512-byte blocks. Only system administrators typically use it.

Notes

cmchk is an SCO extension to Unix and Xenix.

cmp

Description:
Compares two files

Compatibility:

OSF/1	Yes
SCO Unix	Yes
SCO Xenix	Yes
System V Release 3.2	Yes
System V Release 4	Yes
X/Open	Yes

Syntax:
cmp [-l | -s] file1 file2

Options:
-l prints the byte number and values for each difference

-s returns an exit code only

Returns:
0 files are identical

1 files differ

2 file is inaccessible or missing

See Also:
diff; diff3

Discussion

cmp displays the byte and line numbers of differences in two files. It is useful to determine whether two versions or copies of a file are identical. It uses standard input if either file is specified by a hyphen.

You should use **cmp** to compare binary files. To compare text files, use **diff** or **diff3**.

Examples

Use **cmp** to compare program (binary) files that do not contain just printable characters. To compare the binary files test1 and test2, enter

```
cmp test1 test2
```

It displays differences by line number, indicating the bytes that differ.

With the -l option, **cmp** prints the byte number in decimal and the differing bytes in octal.

The -s option, used mainly in programs, returns only a result code indicating whether the files differ.

For files differing in length (e.g., STRU and STRUCTURE), **cmp** reports that it reached the end of the shorter one if it finds no differences.

col

Description:

Filters reverse line feeds

Compatibility:

OSF/1	Yes
SCO Unix	Yes
SCO Xenix	Yes
System V Release 3.2	Yes
System V Release 4	Yes
X/Open	Yes

Syntax:

col [-b] [-f] [-l lines] [-p] [-x]

Versions:

OSF/1: adds the -l option.

Options:

-b assumes the output device cannot backspace. If multiple characters are to appear in the same position, only the last one is printed.

-f allows forward half line feeds

-l buffers the specified number of lines in memory (OSF/1 only)

-p ignores unknown escape sequences, passing them as regular characters

-x prevents conversion of whitespace to tabs during output.

Defaults:

col converts whitespace to tabs unless the -x option appears.

The default buffer size (unless overridden by -l) is 128 lines (OSF/1 only).

Limitations and Restrictions:

col cannot handle more than 800 characters on a line.

It cannot back up more than 128 lines.

It ignores vertical motions above the first line.

Discussion

You can use **col** to prepare output from programs such as text formatters for printers or other devices that do not allow reverse or half-line movement.

col does not support superscripts on the first text line, as it does not allow upward motion there.

col recognizes only the following control characters:

- alternate character off (SO)
- alternate character on (SI)
- backspace
- forward half linefeed (ESC 9)
- newline
- return
- reverse linefeed (ESC 7)
- reverse half linefeed (ESC 8)
- space
- tab
- vertical tab (VT)

SI and SO are used for alternate character sets.

Examples

Use **col** when a printer lacks backspacing and half line spacing. Typical examples are old printers and some daisywheel devices.

A common use of **col** is to format text, such as tables that require special printer maneuvering, for the **nroff** text formatter. For example, you could use **col** to pipe output from the table program **tbl** with

```
tbl filename | nroff | col | lp
```

"What pipes and timbrels? What wild ecstasy?" (Keats)

colcrt

Description:
Filters text processing files for screen viewing

Compatibility:

OSF/1	Yes
SCO Unix	No
SCO Xenix	No
System V Release 3.2	No
System V Release 4	No
X/Open	No

Syntax:
colcrt [-|-2] [file ...]

Options:
- \- suppresses underlining
- -2 displays all half-lines to be printed (effectively double spacing the output)

See Also:
col; more; pg

Discussion
colcrt filters output from a text processor (such as **nroff**) for display on a terminal.

colcrt changes underlined text to dashes and places them on a new line underneath the normal output lines. Subscripts and superscripts should be displayed with the -2 option to allow half-line spacing.

Notes

colcrt trims all lines to 132 bytes. Overstriking is lost.

colcrt cannot back up more than 102 lines.

Examples

To display a file with underlining suppressed, enter

```
colcrt - filename
```

colrm

Description:

Extracts columns from a file

Compatibility:

OSF/1	Yes
SCO Unix	No
SCO Xenix	No
System V Release 3.2	No
System V Release 4	No
X/Open	No

Syntax:

colrm start [end]

Arguments:

start	start column
end	end column

See Also:

cut; paste

Discussion

colrm removes columns from a file. It takes input from standard input, so redirection is necessary. With only a start column specified, it removes everything from that position on. With both start and end columns specified, it removes them and everything in between.

Examples

To remove columns two through four inclusively from the file test_file and redirect the output to a file, enter

```
cat test_file | colrm 2 4 > filename
```

comm

Description:

Finds common lines in sorted files. Has nothing to do with communications despite the name.

Compatibility:

OSF/1	Yes
SCO Unix	Yes
SCO Xenix	Yes
System V Release 3.2	Yes
System V Release 4	Yes
X/Open	Yes

Syntax:

comm [-123] file1 file2

Options:

[123] suppresses printing of the corresponding columns

See Also:

cmp; diff; sort; uniq

Warning:

If the files are not in sorted ASCII order, **comm**'s results are unreliable.

Discussion

comm reads file1 and file2, which should both be sorted in ASCII sequence, and produces three columns of output. The first contains lines only in file1, the second ones only in file2, and the third ones common to both.

A numerical flag suppresses the printing of the corresponding column.

Examples

comm requires two sorted files. To print just entries unique to the first file, suppress the second and third columns with

```
comm -23 file1 file2
```

If the two files contain the following entries (sorted in the default collating sequence):

file1	*file2*
Aardvark	Antelope
Buffalo	Cat
Cat	Dinosaur
Dinosaur	Eagle
Elephant	Fox
Fox	Godzilla
Gopher	

the output from **comm** is:

Aardvark		
	Antelope	
Buffalo		
		Cat
		Dinosaur
Elephant		
	Eagle	
		Fox
Gopher		
	Godzilla	

The first column contains entries unique to file1, the second ones unique to file2, and the third ones common to both. You can suppress any columns using command line options. You can even suppress them all with -123 if you feel your system simply needs some exercise.

compress

Description:
Compresses files

Compatibility:

OSF/1	Yes
SCO Unix	Yes
SCO Xenix	Yes
System V Release 3.2	No
System V Release 4	Yes
X/Open	No

Syntax:
compress [-cCdfFnqv] [-V version] [-b bits] [file]

Versions:
OSF/1: adds the -C, -n, -v, and -V options.

SVR4: does not support -d and -q. The -f option forces compression.

Options:
-b specifies the maximum number of bits to use in encoding (between 9 and 16)

-c writes to standard output and does not delete the original file

-C makes the output compatible with version 2.0 of **compress** (OSF/1 only)

-d expands a compressed file

-f overwrites the previous output file (SVR4: forces output)

-F forces writes to the output file even if no space is saved

-n suppresses addition of a header (OSF/1 only)

-q generates error messages only (no output)

-v displays the percentage reduction for each file (OSF/1 only)

-V uses the specified version number (OSF/1 only)

Returns:

0 normal termination

1 command failed

2 no compression: file size did not decrease

Defaults:

Uses 16 bits for compression

See Also:

ar; pack; uncompress; zcat

Discussion

compress compresses a file. It then deletes the original (unless you use the -c option). The compressed file has the original one's name with ".Z" appended. Its permissions and ownerships are the original's.

If no filename is supplied, **compress** uses standard input and directs the result to standard output.

If **compress** cannot save space, it does nothing unless forced by the -F flag.

You can read compressed files with **zcat** and expand them with the -d option or **uncompress**.

compress differs from **pack** in its compression algorithm (it uses Lempel-Ziv rather than Huffman coding). **pack** is more efficient.

Notes

For information about compression methods, see M. Nelson, *The Data Compression Book* (San Mateo, CA: M & T Books, 1991).

Examples

Compression is useful for seldom accessed files. To compress a large text file called "war_and_peace", enter

```
compress war_and_peace
```

This creates a new file called war_and_peace.Z and deletes the original. To preserve the original, use

```
compress -c war_and_peace
```

The -F option allows a set of files to be compressed or expanded automatically (by a script, for example). This is useful for distribution or for creating archive floppies.

copy

Description:

Copies a group of files

Compatibility:

OSF/1	No
SCO Unix	Yes
SCO Xenix	Yes
System V Release 3.2	No
System V Release 4	No
X/Open	No

Syntax:

copy [-adlmnorv] source destination

Arguments:

"source" may be a file, special file, or directory. If it is not a directory, **copy** is the same as **cp**.

"destination" must be a file or directory name that differs from "source".

Options:

-a	asks the user before copying
-ad	asks the user whether the -r option applies to directories
-l	uses a link if possible (except with special files and directories) by adding one instead of copying the file
-m	sets modification time and date to source
-n	requires destination to be new (no overwriting of files)
-o	files assume owner and group of source; otherwise, owner is user
-r	examines (and copies) directories recursively
-v	verbose display of filenames copied

Defaults:

Sets the copied file's modification time and date to those of the system unless you use the -m option. -m retains the original file's time and date.

Copying files changes ownership to the user who issues the **copy** command. You can override this with the -o option, which retains the original file's owner and group (essential to preserve security and access rights).

See Also:

cp

Discussion

copy can copy entire directories. If its source and destination are files, it behaves exactly like **cp.**

The -a option makes **copy** ask the user for permission to continue. If the response does not begin with y, the copy is not performed. The -ad option is similar, but it asks the user only about directories. The -a and -ad options imply the -v (verbose) option.

When logged in as superuser, use the -o (and sometimes -m) option to avoid setting the ownership of copied files to root, preventing users from accessing them. Users may not appreciate your housekeeping efforts if they are shut out of their own files.

You cannot copy a directory to a file.

Examples

To copy directory /usr/tim to /usr/bill and display the names of the files as they are copied, enter

```
copy -v /usr/tim /usr/bill
```

copy supports wildcards and specific filenames (it then acts like **cp**). The commmand

```
copy -orv /usr/tim/*.doc /usr/bill
```

copies all .doc files in /usr/tim or its subdirectories to the /usr/bill directory, retaining their groups and owners.

cp

Description:
Copies files

Compatibility:

OSF/1	Yes
SCO Unix	Yes
SCO Xenix	Yes
System V Release 3.2	Yes
System V Release 4	Yes
X/Open	Yes

Syntax:
cp [-f] [-h] [-i] [-p] [-r] file1 [file2 ...]

cp file [file2...] directory

Versions:
OSF/1: supports the -f, -h, -i, -p, -r, and -R options.

SVR4: supports the -i, -p, and -r options.

Options:
-f suppresses overwriting prompt (OSF/1 only)

-h follows symbolic links (OSF/1 only)

-i prompts for confirmation before overwriting file2 (OSF/1 and SVR4 only)

-p preserves modification time and permissions (OSF/1 and SVR4 only)

-r copies directories recursively, including special files as regular ones (OSF/1 and SVR4 only)

-R copies directories recursively, but recreates special files instead of copying them (OSF/1 only)

See Also:

copy; cpio; ln; mv

Discussion

To copy a file, you must specify the source and destination. The two must differ. If you supply a target directory name, it must exist or the command will fail. You cannot copy a directory to a file.

With the OSF/1 and SVR4 -r option, **cp** copies all subdirectories if the source is a directory. The -R and -r options (OSF/1 only) treat special files (symbolic links and device files) differently. The -R option is preferable to avoid damaging special files.

Examples

The command

```
cp /usr/tim/bills /usr/tmp/bankrupt
```

copies a single file. To copy several, use wildcards. The command

```
cp -p /usr/tim/*.doc /usr/mike
```

copies all .doc files in /usr/tim into the directory /usr/mike. If /usr/mike does not exist, the copy fails. The -p option (OSF/1 and SVR4 only) preserves modification times.

cpio

Description:

Copies archive files

Compatibility:

OSF/1	Yes
SCO Unix	Yes
SCO Xenix	Yes
System V Release 3.2	Yes
System V Release 4	Yes
X/Open	Yes

Syntax:

cpio -i [bBcdfkmrsStuvV6] [-C buffersize] [-E file] [-H format] [-I file] [-M message] [-R ID] [pattern]

cpio -o [aABcLvV] [-C buffersize] [-H format] [-O file] [-M message]

cpio -p [adlLmuvV] [-R ID] directory

Versions:

OSF/1:

supports all options with the following exceptions:

cpio -i: does not support the -E, -H, -k, -R, and -V options.

cpio -o: does not support the -A, -H, -L, and -V options.

cpio -p: does not support the -L, -R, and -V options.

SVR4:

cpio -i: adds -E, -H and -R options.

cpio -o: adds -A, -H, and -L options.

cpio -p: adds -L and -R options.

Options:

-6 processes a Unix Sixth Edition file

-a resets access times of input files after copying

-A appends files to the archive (requires -O option) (SVR4 only)

-b reverses order of bytes in each word (use with -i)

-B blocks I/O to 5,120 bytes per record. Default is 512.

-c writes header information in ASCII character form for portability

-C blocks I/O to the specified value

-d creates directories if they do not exist

-E reads a list of filenames to be extracted (one name per line in "file") (SVR4 only)

-f copies all files except those in [pattern]

-H reads or writes header information in one of the following formats (SVR4 only):

crc/CRC	ASCII with per-file checksums (expanded device numbers)
odc	ASCII header with small device numbers
tar/TAR	tar
ustar/USTAR	IEEE Data Interchange Standard

-I reads an input file

-k tries to skip corrupt headers and I/O errors

-l links files instead of copying when possible

-L follows symbolic links (SVR4 only)

-m retains previous file modification time and date

-M defines a message to display when a user must switch media

-O directs output to a file

-r renames files interactively

-R reassigns file ownership to a valid login in /etc/passwd. Available only to superuser. (SVR4 only)

-s swaps bytes within each halfword

-S swaps halfwords within each word

-t prints a table of contents of the input

-u copies unconditionally

-v displays a list of filenames as copied

-V prints a dot for each file seen

Defaults:

cpio assumes four-byte words throughout and 512-byte records, unless changed with the -B or -C option.

cpio will not replace a newer file with an older one. The -u option forces a replacement, regardless of modification dates.

Limitations and Restrictions:

Only the superuser can copy or link special files using **cpio**. It limits pathnames to 128 or 256 characters, depending on the implementation.

See Also:

ar; tar

Discussion

cpio has three formats. **cpio -o**, the copy out format, reads a list of pathnames. It copies the files in the paths, along with pathnames and status information.

cpio -i extracts files from an archive (assumed to be the product of a previous **cpio -o** command). You can supply a list of patterns of files to be extracted, enclosed in double quotation marks to prevent confusion with filenames. It accepts multiple patterns. With no pattern specified, it extracts all files.

cpio -p (pass) reads an archive to create a list of files that are created conditionally and copied into the destination directory.

The patterns that can be used with **cpio** are all regular expressions similar to those used in **sh**. They allow metacharacters, including "?", "*", and "[...]" (for ranges). The backslash serves as an escape character. The "!" metacharacter means "not", so "!doc*" excludes files beginning with "doc".

An extracted file retains the archive version's permissions. The owner and group are the current user's, unless he or she is the superuser in which case the originals apply.

The -I option allows removable media (such as floppy disks). When one is full, **cpio** waits for the user to replace it and type a carriage return. This option applies only to the **cpio -i** format. The -M option can define a message for display when a change of media is necessary. A "%d" in the text prints the sequence number of the next media needed.

The -r option lets you rename files as they are copied. It prompts the user for a new name for each file. If nothing is entered, the file is skipped. A period means to use the original name.

The -v option displays a list of filenames as **cpio** processes them. When used with the -t option, it generates a table of contents that resembles the output from the **ls -l** or **l** command. The special -V option prints a dot for each file **cpio** processes. It provides a visual progress indicator.

Notes

cpio archives are portable between implementations of System V. Use the -c option to ensure portability if the source and destination machines differ.

Examples

You can use **cpio** to write and read an archive file, usually onto a removable medium. The output format often pipes the standard output of another command. For example,

```
ls | cpio -oc > filename
```

directs files from **ls** through **cpio** to a new file called "filename". The -o option specifies the output format. The -c option ensures portability; use it with all **cpio** commands unless you are sure they apply only to a single machine.

You can redirect **cpio**'s output to a floppy or other device instead of a file. For example, to archive the **ls** command's output to a floppy, enter

```
ls | cpio -oc > /dev/rdsk/f0q15dt
```

substituting the correct device name. **cpio** prompts for floppy changes if the files do not fit on one diskette.

To extract the files created and saved in "filename", enter

```
cat filename | cpio -ic
```

It directs the output from **cpio -i** through a pipe to **cat**. You can extract specific files from the archive or match a pattern. To extract all files ending in ".doc", but exclude ones starting with "letter", enter

```
cat filename | cpio -ic "*.doc" "!letter*"
```

To extract directories matching the patterns, include the -d option.

cpio -p copies or links filenames piped to it to another directory. The command

```
find / -name *.c | cpio -pdlv c_progs
```

copies or links all .c files that the **find** command locates, and places them in directories under a directory c_progs. The -d option allows **cpio** to create directories as needed. Omitting the -l option eliminates linking and copies all files. The -v option reports the command's actions as it performs them.

With replaceable media, **cpio** prompts you when the one in use is full. The default message is:

```
If you want to go on, type device/file name when ready.
```

When it appears, you must enter the device's name. If you are using a system with two floppies, you can alternate between them. You can change the prompt with the -M option.

cron

Description:

Executes commands at a specified time

Compatibility:

OSF/1	Yes
SCO Unix	Yes
SCO Xenix	Yes
System V Release 3.2	Yes
System V Release 4	Yes
X/Open	Yes

Syntax:

cron

Files:

/etc/default/cron	**cron** default information
/usr/lib/cron	**cron** directory
/usr/lib/cron/atjobs	**at** directory
/usr/lib/cron/log	**cron** accounting information
/usr/lib/cron/queuedefs	**cron** data file
/usr/lib/cron/.proto	**cron** environment information
/usr/spool/cron/crontabs	**crontab** directory

See Also:

at; crontab

Discussion

cron is a Unix daemon that executes commands at specified times and dates. You submit processes to it using **at, batch,** or **crontab**.

All **cron** actions are recorded in the file /usr/lib/cron/log if logging has been activated by setting the variable CRONLOG to YES in /etc/default/cron.

Notes

cron is usually started in the /etc/rc2 scripts invoked when the system is brought up in multiuser mode. It does not terminate until the system shuts down.

If logging is on (it is off by default), the **cron** log file can rapidly become very large. The administrator should clean it to release disk space.

crontab

Description:

Schedules commands to be executed at intervals

Compatibility:

OSF/1	Yes
SCO Unix	Yes
SCO Xenix	Yes
System V Release 3.2	Yes
System V Release 4	Yes
X/Open	Yes

Syntax:

crontab [file]

crontab -e|-l|-r|-v

Versions:

OSF/1: adds the -v argument.

SVR4: adds the -e argument.

Arguments:

-e edits a current **crontab** file, or creates one if none exists. Uses the default editor defined in system variable EDITOR (default is **vi**). (SVR4 only)

-l lists the user's **crontab** file

-r removes the user's **crontab** file from the **crontab** directory

-v displays the name of your **crontab** file and the time and date of submission (OSF/1 only)

Files:

/usr/lib/cron	main **cron** directory
/usr/lib/cron/cron.allow	list of allowed users
/usr/lib/cron/cron.deny	list of denied users
/usr/lib/cron/.proto	**cron** environment information
/usr/lib/cron/queuedefs	**cron** data file
/usr/spool/cron/crontabs	**crontab** directory

OSF/1: uses /var/adm instead of /usr/lib.

See Also:

at; cron

Discussion

crontab schedules commands for execution at regular intervals. It submits files to **cron**. Each user's commands are in the file /usr/spool/cron/crontabs/username where username is the user's login name.

When called with no options and a file name as an argument, **crontab** copies the specified file to the **crontab** directory, replacing any previous entry for the user.

The -r option deletes the user's **cron** file, and the -l option lists it.

Output from commands submitted to **cron** is mailed to the user. It may include error messages as well as normal program output.

A **crontab** file consists of lines of six fields, separated by spaces, tabs, or other whitespace. The fields and their ranges are:

minute	0-59
hour	0-23
day of month	1-31
month	1-12
day of week	0-6 (0 = Sunday)
command	

The first five fields are integers. Numbers separated by a minus indicates an inclusive range. Ones separated by commas indicate the numbers specified (not inclusive). An asterisk means all values.

The day of the month and week may appear. This allows specific dates and weekly execution of commands.

The command in the sixth field position is a string executed by the shell. % symbols in it are translated into newline characters. The shell executes only to the end of the first line or the newline character. The rest of the string represents standard input for the command.

A user may not use **crontab** if the file /usr/lib/cron/cron.allow exists and his or her name is not in it. A similar restriction applies if the file /usr/lib/cron/cron.deny exists and the user's name is in it. An empty cron.deny file allows anyone to use **crontab**. When neither cron.allow nor cron.deny exists, only the superuser can use **crontab**. Both files have one user name per line.

Warning:

Under SVR4, if you enter the **crontab** command with no argument, do not use Ctrl-D to exit or you will save a blank file. Use Del instead.

Examples

A typical **crontab** file is:

```
0      4 * * * calendar -
15     1 1 * 0 /usr/lib/uucp/uucpclean
10,40  * * * * /usr/bin/setperms
```

The first line executes **calendar** with the argument "-" every night at 4:00 AM. The second line executes **uucpclean** (to remove **uucp** spool directories) at 1:15 AM every Sunday (0 in the fifth column) and on the first of every month (1 in the third column). The third line executes the program "setperms" at ten and forty minutes past each hour every day.

cron reads **crontab** files only on startup and when a new file is submitted using **crontab**. Changes to the **crontab** file that are not submitted using the "crontab filename" format are not recognized.

To suppress output from commands submitted to **cron**, redirect them. For example,

```
0   *   *   *   *   date > /tmp/testfile 2> /dev/null
```

sends the output of the **date** command to /tmp/testfile, and sends errors to /dev/null (discarding them). If the output is not redirected, the user's mail may become unwieldy.

crypt

Description:

Encrypts or decrypts files

Compatibility:

OSF/1	No
SCO Unix	Yes
SCO Xenix	Yes
System V Release 3.2	Yes
System V Release 4	Yes
X/Open	No

Syntax:

crypt [-k]

crypt [password]

Options:

-k uses the key in the CRYPTKEY environment variable

Warnings:

If you encrypt two files with the same key and then combine them (using **cat** or **copy**, for example), decryption will decode only the first one. Use the **csplit** command to separate them afterward. You can then decrypt the second part.

You may encrypt encrypted files again using any key. When decrypting, however, be sure to apply the keys in the reverse order.

Discussion

crypt encrypts or decrypts files based on a password. It reads from standard input and writes to standard output unless redirected. Encryption and decryption must use the same key.

crypt requests a password if none appears on the command line. With the -k option, it uses the key in the CRYPTKEY environment variable.

The security level of the encryption depends on how long the key is. A three-letter key is easier to break than an eight-letter one. At the very least, decoding a **crypt**-produced file requires substantial computational power. The key used on a command line does not appear when someone else does a **ps** (or similar) command; **crypt** destroys the records of the key as soon as you enter it.

Notes

The U.S. Government limits the distribution of the **crypt** library and utility. They may not be exported freely. Most Unix implementations omit **crypt** from the standard distribution set, but you can request it.

Examples

To encrypt a file "secrets" with the password (key) "alpha", enter

```
crypt alpha < secrets > newfile
```

It encrypts "secrets" and stores the encrypted text as "newfile". If the key "alpha" were not supplied, **crypt** would ask for the password, turning the console off while the user types it.

To decrypt the encrypted file, enter

```
crypt alpha < newfile > newerfile
```

It decrypts "newfile" and saves the contents in "newerfile". In this example, "newerfile" and "secrets" should be identical.

csplit

Description:
Splits files according to context

Compatibility:

OSF/1	Yes
SCO Unix	Yes
SCO Xenix	Yes
System V Release 3.2	Yes
System V Release 4	Yes
X/Open	Yes

Syntax:
csplit [-f title] [-k] [-s] file arguments

Arguments:
Can have the following formats:

/expr/	the line containing the regular expression "expr"
%expr%	same as above, but no file created for this section
lineno	down to the line number specified
{number}	repeat argument, used with any of the above

Options:

-f	creates files with the names title00, title01, etc.
-k	does not remove previously created files in case of error
-s	suppresses printing of all character counts

Error Handling:
If an error occurs, **csplit** removes all created files unless you use the -k option.

Discussion

csplit divides a file into sections, as defined by the arguments. By default, it names them xx00 through xxn (n is determined by the number of arguments). The number of sections cannot exceed 99.

csplit reads from the start of the file up to (but not including) the first specified line. The second section contains that line and everything up to (but not including) the second specified one, or the end of the file. The process continues until it uses all arguments.

You should enclose regular expressions in double quotation marks if they contain blanks or special characters.

csplit does not delete the original file.

Examples

To split the large file king_lear into sections of 1000 lines each (to make editing easier), enter

```
csplit -k king_lear 1000 {99}
```

We set the number of repetitions to the most sections **csplit** can produce (99). The -k option prevents it from erasing created files if it ends up with a first section of less than 1000 lines (and hence cannot complete the process). It still generates an error message. The sections are named rather obscurely as xx00 through xxn, where n is the total number minus 1.

To change the names to the more meaningful section00 through section99, use the -f option:

```
csplit -f section king_lear 100 {99}
```

To break a file at specific strings, give them as arguments. For example,

```
csplit four_seasons '/summer/' '/autumn/' '/winter/'
```

causes the first section to extend from the start of the file to the line above the first one containing "summer", the second section from the line containing "summer" to the one above "autumn", and so on. You may add an offset to (or subtract one from) the regular expression, so the argument

```
'/snow/'+3
```

breaks at the third line after the text "snow".

You can use **cat** to recombine a file divided with **csplit**. For example, you could recombine the files in the first example above to form a duplicate of king_lear. If there are eight sections, the command is

```
cat xx0[0-7] > new_king_lear
```

ct

Description:

Starts a connection to a remote terminal

Compatibility:

OSF/1	Yes
SCO Unix	Yes
SCO Xenix	Yes
System V Release 3.2	Yes
System V Release 4	Yes
X/Open	No

Syntax:

ct [-h] [-v] [-sspeed] [-wmins] [-xnum] number ...

Arguments:

number telephone number with at most 58 characters. Valid characters are the numbers 0 through 9, "-" (delay), "=" (wait for secondary dial tone), "*", and "#".

Options:

- -h does not hang up current line
- -s sets speed in baud
- -v verbose output to standard error
- -w number of minutes to wait for a line
- -x sets debugging level to "num"

Defaults:

1200 baud line speed

Files:

/usr/adm/ctlog	log file
/usr/lib/uucp/Devices	list of automated calling units
/usr/lib/uucp/LCK...	temporary files

See Also:

cu; getty; nohup; uucp

Discussion

ct uses an attached modem and dials a telephone number. It tries each automated calling unit (ACU) given in the file /usr/lib/uucp/Devices until it finds an available one that matches the speed given on the command line or the default value. If none exists, it asks how long it should wait for one. The wait time can also appear on the command line with the -w option.

When it establishes a connection, **ct** spawns a **getty** process, allowing users to log in remotely. It is then on-line to the remote number. If several telephone numbers appear on the command line, **ct** tries each one in sequence until it gets a connection.

ct hangs up the line when finished (the remote terminal receives a Ctrl-D) unless you use the -h option. When the remote terminal logs off, **ct** prompts with the message "Reconnect?". Any answer starting with "y" causes **getty** to start again and allow logins; otherwise, it drops the line. When -h is not specified and **ct** finds a usable line, it sends the message "Proceed to hang-up?". If you answer with "y", it connects. Any other response causes it to terminate.

The -x option activates a debugger that relays output to standard error. The level of detail is set by the argument, a number between 0 and 9 inclusive. Level 9 is the most detailed. With the -v option, **ct** sends a running narrative to standard error.

Examples

ct allows a remote terminal with a modem to connect to your system. It calls the modem's telephone number and allows a user to log on.

The command

```
ct -s2400 9-1234567
```

causes **ct** to look for an available line that supports 2400 baud. Once it finds one, it dials 9, pauses, and then dials the rest of the number (this is usually the sequence to call out through a company exchange).

To prevent the remote terminal from hanging up, or your being prompted for a hangup, use the **nohup** command with the -h option:

```
nohup ct -h -s2400 9-1234567
```

cu

Description:
Calls another Unix system

Compatibility:

OSF/1	Yes
SCO Unix	Yes
SCO Xenix	Yes
System V Release 3.2	Yes
System V Release 4	Yes
X/Open	Yes

Syntax:
cu [-d] [-e|-o|-oe] [-h] [-lline] [-n] [-sspeed] [-t] [-xnum] number

cu [-d] [-e|-o|-oe] [-h] [-sspeed] [-xnum] -lline [dir]

cu [-d] [-e|-o|-oe] [-h] [-xnum] system

Versions:
SCO Unix and Xenix: do not support the -d option.

Arguments:
number telephone number with at most 58 characters. Valid characters are the numbers 0 through 9, "-" (delay), and "=" (wait for secondary dial tone).

system a UUCP system name in /usr/lib/uucp/Systems (ignores -l and -s)

Options:
-d prints diagnostic traces

-e uses 7-bit even parity

-h emulates local echo for half-duplex terminals

-l	specifies the device name
-n	prompts for the telephone number
-o	uses 7-bit odd parity
-oe	uses 7-bit data with either parity
-s	sets speed in baud. Can include a range as in -s300-4800.
-t	for auto-answer ASCII terminals
-v	verbose output to standard error
-w	number of minutes to wait for a line
-x	sets debugging level
dir	keyword indicating direct connection

Defaults:

8-bit characters with no parity unless you include -e, -o, or -oe

Files:

/usr/lib/uucp/Devices	list of automated calling units
/usr/lib/uucp/LCK...	temporary files
/usr/lib/uucp/Systems	list of systems

See Also:

cat; ct; echo; stty; uname; uucp

Discussion

cu calls another Unix or Xenix system, a remote terminal, or another computer, and handles the interaction. It supports automated ASCII file transfers. It scans the /usr/lib/uucp/Devices file for the first available line.

The speed of the connection is determined by the -s option, or by the available line in the /usr/lib/uucp/Devices file. You can specify the device to use with -l on the command line. This option is for direct connections that do not require a telephone number.

cu interprets the following user commands:

~.	terminates
~!	escapes to the local system shell
~!cmd ...	executes "cmd" on the local system
~$cmd ...	executes "cmd" on the local system and sends the output to the remote system
~%cd	changes directory on the local system
~%put file [to]	copies "file" from the local system to the file "to" (if specified) on the remote system
~%take file [to]	copies "file" from the remote system to the file "to" (if specified) on the local system
~~line	sends "~line" to the remote system
~%b	sends a Break to the remote system
~%break	sends a Break to the remote system
~%d	toggles the -x option debugging level
~%debug	toggles the -x option debugging level
~t	prints the values of the termio variables for the user's terminal
~l	prints the values of the termio variables for the remote line
~%nostop	toggles between no input control and DC3/DC1 (Ctrl-S and Ctrl-Q) input control

Both the "take" and "put" commands allow **cu** to transfer files. It can transfer only ASCII files. When transferring, it indicates each block with a digit on the terminal. To use "put" and "take", both systems must have **cat**, **echo**, and **stty**.

The **uname** command displays the UUCP name of the system referred to by a command. One system can connect to another, which then connects to another, and so on. In this case, you must stack tildes appropriately. For example, "~~!uname" returns the name of the second system, and "~~~!uname" the name of the third.

Notes

Only users with write access to the /usr/lib/uucp/Devices file can use the *dir* option.

Examples

The command

```
cu -s1200 1234567
```

dials the number on the first available line that supports 1200 baud.

The command

```
cu timsystem
```

examines /usr/lib/uucp/Systems for a line that refers to timsystem and uses the number and speed there to call it.

cut

Description:
Deletes fields from a file

Compatibility:

OSF/1	Yes
SCO Unix	Yes
SCO Xenix	Yes
System V Release 3.2	Yes
System V Release 4	Yes
X/Open	Yes

Syntax:
cut -clist [file...]

cut -flist [-d char] [-s] [file...]

Options:

-clist	list of integers specifying character positions
-d char	indicates field delimiters (default is tab)
-flist	list of fields separated by a delimiter
-s	suppresses lines with no delimiter (used with -f)

Limitations and Warnings:
cut cannot handle lines exceeding 511 characters. If no arguments appear after the -c or -f option, or if there is a space afterward, it returns the error message "no fields".

See Also:
grep; paste

Discussion

cut deletes columns from a file or table. It is useful for removing columns of data or unwanted material from each line (filtering). To restore the file, use **paste**. You can combine **cut** and **paste** to reorder columns. To cut lines horizontally, use **grep**.

cut requires either the -c or -f option. -c specifies characters to cut, whereas -f indicates fields (which may not always occur at the same character positions). The list of characters or fields must follow the option immediately (no spaces allowed).

The list **cut** requires as an argument is a sequence of numbers separated by commas. It can include ranges (see Examples). A character must separate fields. The default is "tab", but you can change it with the -d option. The -s option suppresses lines lacking delimiters.

Examples

If you have a four-column telephone directory (name, address, telephone number, and extension), and want to move everything except the addresses to the file "numbers", enter

```
cut -f1,3-4 telfile > numbers
```

To remove specific characters, use the -c option. Suppose you have a file from another operating system that puts a line feed in the 79th position of each line. You can remove it with the command

```
cut -c79 filename
```

cut does not check the character. You can use it to remove line numbers from program code or private information from a file.

You can change the delimiter with the -d option. For example, the /etc/passwd file contains columns separated by a colon. To extract user IDs and names (if added by the system administrator), enter

```
cut -d: -f1,5 /etc/passwd
```

The user ID is the first column, and the name is the fifth.

date

Description:

Sets and prints the date and time

Compatibility:

OSF/1	Yes
SCO Unix	Yes
SCO Xenix	Yes
System V Release 3.2	Yes
System V Release 4	Yes
X/Open	Yes

Syntax:

date [-n|-u] [mmddhhmm[yy]][+format]

Versions:

OSF/1: adds the -n and -u options.

Options:

+ specifies format using field descriptions
-n does not set the time globally on all machines (OSF/1 only)
-u displays and sets time in Coordinated Universal Time (CUT) (OSF/1 only)

Coordinated Universal Time is just Greenwich Mean Time without changes for Daylight Savings.

Defaults:

OSF/1: By default, systems use Coordinated Universal Time. If this has been changed, the -u option forces the display and setting of time in CUT.

Discussion

With no arguments, **date** displays the current system date and time. To set them, follow the syntax precisely. Valid arguments are:

mm	month (1-12)
dd	day of month (1-31)
hh	hour in 24-hour format (0-23)
mm	minutes (0-59)
yy	last two digits of year (00-99)
a	abbreviated weekday (Sun-Sat)
h	abbreviated month (Jan-Dec)
j	day of the year (Julian date, 001-366)
r	time in AM/PM (12 hour) notation
T	time in HH:MM:SS format
w	day of the week (0-6, 0=Sunday)

date converts the date and time to the local display format, depending on the language setting. For example, it converts 00:01 on a 24-hour clock to 12:01AM if the local language is English. Unix systems maintain date and time as GMT (Greenwich Mean Time), with **date** converting them to and from the local time zone.

The + sign argument allows the user to customize the output format. The specification resembles C's printf(). A percentage sign precedes each field descriptor, and all fields are treated as fixed size with zero padding. The descriptors are the same as the **date** arguments (for example, %r for time in 12 hour notation). A newline is represented by %n. Any other text is echoed to output intact.

For a description of the C printf() function, see S.P. Harbison and G.L. Steele, Jr., *C:A Reference Manual*, 3rd ed. (Englewood Cliffs, NJ: Prentice-Hall, 1991).

Notes

Only the superuser can set the date and time. If no year is specified, the current (default) one is assumed.

Examples

To set the current date to Nov 10 and the time to 1:30AM, enter

```
date 11100130
```

To change the output format using the + option, use C printf() options. Thus

```
date +'+%m/%d/%y/%n%H:%M:%S'
```

prints the date and time set above as:

```
11/10/90
01:30:00
```

Similarly,

```
date +' %r %d %m (%a)"
```

displays the date output as

```
04:22:54 PM 27 Mar (Fri)"
```

dc

Description:

Calculator

Compatibility:

OSF/1	Yes
SCO Unix	Yes
SCO Xenix	Yes
System V Release 3.2	Yes
System V Release 4	Yes
X/Open	No

Syntax:

dc [file]

Diagnostics:

nesting depth	too many levels of nested execution
out of headers	too many items kept
out of pushdown	too many values on the stack
out of space	too many digits used
stack empty	the stack lacks enough elements to complete the command
x is unimplemented	the octal number x corresponds to an unimplemented character

See Also:

bc

Discussion

dc is an arbitrary precision arithmetic calculator that uses Reverse Polish

Notation (RPN). It usually operates on decimal integers, but can handle several other formats. If a file name appears on the command line, **dc** reads from it, then from standard input.

Reverse Polish Notation uses a "stack", a set of numbers placed one on top of another. When the top is removed, the number just beneath it becomes the new top. **dc** uses a main stack, and can have auxiliary stacks in registers (memory variables).

dc recognizes the following constructs:

number	a number to be placed on the stack. A preceding underscore indicates a negative value.
+, -, *, /, ^	performs the specified operation on the top two stack values, removes them, and places the result on the top. Exponentiation (^) ignores fractional exponents.
%	divides the top two stack values, removes them, and places the remainder on the top.
[...]	puts the bracketed string on the top of the stack (ASCII values only)
<a	removes the top two stack values, and compares them. Evaluates register "a" if the first is smaller.
>a	removes the top two stack values, and compares them. Evaluates register "a" if the first is larger.
=a	removes the top two stack values, and compares them. Evaluates register "a" if the two are equal.
!	interprets the rest of the line as a Unix command
?	takes a line of input from the source and executes it
;:	used by **bc** for array operations
c	clears the entire stack
d	duplicates the top stack value
f	prints the stack
i	removes the top stack value and uses it as the number radix for further input
I	puts the input base on the top of the stack

k	removes the top stack value and uses it as a non-negative scale factor. All subsequent output uses that many places.
la	copies the value in register a to the top of the stack. The register does not change.
La	moves the top value of stack a to the top of the main stack
o	removes the top stack value and uses it as the number radix for further output
O	puts the output base on the top of the stack
p	prints the top stack value without removing it
q	exits **dc**. If executing a string, it increases the recursion level by two.
Q	exits **dc**. If executing a string, it removes the top stack value and increases the string execution level by it.
sa	removes the top stack value and stores it in register a
Sa	removes the top stack value and moves it to stack a
v	replaces the top stack value with its square root
x	executes the top stack element as a string of **dc** commands
X	replaces the top stack value with its scale factor
z	puts the number of stack elements on the top of the stack
Z	replaces the number on the top of the stack with the number of stack elements.

Notes

bc is a preprocessor for **dc**, and is easier to use interactively. It also provides a more C-like syntax.

dd

Description:

Converts file formats

Compatibility:

OSF/1	Yes
SCO Unix	Yes
SCO Xenix	Yes
System V Release 3.2	Yes
System V Release 4	Yes
X/Open	Yes

Syntax:

dd [option=value...]

Options:

if=file	input filename (standard input is the default)
of=file	output filename (standard output is the default)
ibs=x	input block size (default is system value)
obs=x	output block size (default is system value)
bs=x	input and output block size
cbs=x	conversion buffer size
skip=x	skips x records of input before starting copy
seek=x	seeks x records from start of output file before copying
count=x	copies only x input records
conv=ascii	converts EBCDIC to ASCII
conv=ebcdic	converts ASCII to EBCDIC
conv=ibm	converts ASCII to EBCDIC (slightly different map than conv=ebcdic)

conv=lcase	converts letters to lowercase
conv=swab	swaps each pair of bytes
conv=sync	pads each input record to input block size
conv=ucase	converts letters to uppercase
conv="..,.."	comma separated conversions (defined by user)

See Also:

copy; cp; tar

Discussion

dd copies a file to an output. It can do conversions during the process. Both input and output block sizes can be specified, allowing raw physical I/O to be used. **dd** reports the number of whole and partial input and output blocks.

All sizes are in bytes. Numbers may end with "k", "b", or "w" to indicate multiplication by 1024, 512, or 2, respectively. They may be separated by "x" to indicate multiplication.

Use the "cbs" option only when converting from ASCII to EBCDIC or vice versa. **dd** adds or removes trailing spaces as needed.

Examples

To convert a file from uppercase to lowercase starting with the fifth record, enter

```
dd if=infile of=outfile conv=lcase skip=4
```

The names of the input and output files appear after "if" and "of", respectively.

To read an EBCDIC tape blocked into ten 100-byte images per record (mounted on /dev/rmt0), and convert it to ASCII in the file "convertfile", enter

```
dd if=/dev/rmt0 of=convertfile ibs=1000 cbs=100 conv=ascii
```

deassign

Description:
Deassigns a device

Compatibility:

OSF/1	No
SCO Unix	Yes
SCO Xenix	Yes
System V Release 3.2	No
System V Release 4	No
X/Open	No

Syntax:
deassign [-u] [-v] [device] ...

Options:

-u	performs error checking only
-v	verbose output
device	any assignable device not currently assigned

Returns:

0	if successful
1	if problems encountered

Files:

/dev/asglock	file to prevent concurrent access
/etc/atab	table of assignable devices

See Also:
assign

Discussion

deassign removes a device from exclusive access specified by **assign**.

Examples

To remove exclusive access to the tape drive /dev/rmt0, enter

```
deassign /dev/rmt0
```

Be careful! If you do too many good deeds like this, you could ruin your reputation. People may begin to expect you to clean up coffee spills and broken glass, share your blank disks and office supplies, and do other nice things that produce no immediate reward.

df

Description:

Reports the number of free disk blocks

Compatibility:

OSF/1	Yes
SCO Unix	Yes
SCO Xenix	Yes
System V Release 3.2	No
System V Release 4	Yes
X/Open	Yes

Syntax:

df [-f] [-t] [-v] [filesystem]

OSF/1 only:

df [-i] [-k] [-n] [-t type] [filesystem]

SVR4 only:

df [-begklntV] [-F type] [-o options] [directory]

Versions:

OSF/1: adds several options (see Syntax above).

SVR4: adds many options (see Syntax above).

X/Open: supports only the -t option.

Options:

-b prints only the number of free kilobytes (SVR4 only)

-e prints only the number of free files (SVR4 only)

-f reports only the actual count of blocks in the free list

-F specifies the filesystem on which to operate (SVR4 only)

-g prints the entire filesystem structure (SVR4 only)

-i displays statistics on the number of free inodes (OSF/1 only)

-k prints the filesystem allocation in kilobytes. Do not use it with other options due to the different output format. (OSF/1 and SVR4 only)

-l reports only the local filesystem (cannot be used with -o) (SVR4 only)

-n displays previously obtained statistics from all mounted filesystems. Does not request new statistics. (OSF/1 only)

-n displays only the filesystem name (cannot be used with -o) (SVR4 only)

-o specifies FSTtype-specific options. Used by administrators only. (SVR4 only)

-t reports total allocated blocks as well as free ones (SVR4: overrides -b, -e, and -n)

-t displays statistics for the specified filesystem types only (OSF/1 only). Valid types include:

5sfs	System V file system
mfs	Memory file system
nfs	Network File System
pc	Xenix
ufs	Berkeley Fast File System (default value)

-v reports the percentage of used blocks, as well as counts of used and free ones

-V echoes the command line but does not execute it. Displays it with expanded information from the /etc/mnttab or /etc/vfstab files. (SVR4 only)

See Also:

du; fsck

Discussion

df prints the number of free blocks and free inodes available for the specified filesystem, or all filesystems if none is specified. The -f option displays only the number of free blocks and inodes, -t reports free and used blocks and inodes, and -v reports percentages used as well. The options cannot be combined.

Blocks are reported in 512-byte units.

Notes

Secure systems may restrict access to **df**.

diff

Description:

Compares two text files

Compatibility:

OSF/1	Yes
SCO Unix	Yes
SCO Xenix	Yes
System V Release 3.2	Yes
System V Release 4	Yes
X/Open	Yes

Syntax:

diff [-befh] file1 file2

OSF/1 and SVR4:

diff [-b] [-c|-C number|-D string|-e|-f|-h|-n] [-i] [-t] [-w] file1 file2

diff [-b] [-c|-e|-f|-h|-n] [-i] [-l] [-r] [-s] [-S name] [-t] [w] directory1 directory2

Versions:

OSF/1 and SVR4: The latest release of **diff** greatly expands its abilities, adding many options (see Syntax) and the ability to examine directories.

Options:

All versions:

-b ignores trailing blanks

-e produces a script of **ed** commands to recreate file2 from file1

-f produces a script of commands to convert file1 to file2 (cannot be used with **ed**)

-h fast pass - may miss some differences

filex file name or "-" for standard input

OSF/1 and SVR4 only:

- -c lists differences in three lines of context. Includes filenames and creation dates, then changes separated by a line with twelve asterisks. Lines removed from file2 are marked with "-", ones added to file2 with "+", and ones that change in both files with "!".
- -C same as -c, but adds "number" lines of context.
- -D merges file1 and file2 with C preprocessor controls included. Including "string" produces file2, whereas omitting it produces file1.
- -n produces a script in the order opposite to the -e option. Displays a count of changed lines.
- -l produces output in long format (pipes each text file through **pr**)
- -r applies **diff** to all subdirectories recursively
- -s reports identical files (normally not reported)
- -S starts at file "name" in the directory

Returns:

0 no differences

1 some differences

2 errors encountered

Warnings:

ed scripts produced with the -e or -f options may not work correctly on lines consisting of a single period.

See Also:

bdiff; cmp; comm; diff3

Discussion

diff indicates differences between two files, and describes line changes required to the first one to make them identical. It requires two file names, or a hyphen indicating standard input. If a directory is specified, **diff** assumes the same filename in both it and the current directory (see Examples).

diff produces a set of lines similar to **ed** commands to convert the first file into the second. By replacing "adds" with "deletes", and reversing the order of the changes, you can also convert the second one into the first. To generate lines that **ed** can use directly, specify the -e option. The -f option also generates conversion commands, but **ed** cannot use them directly.

The -h option does a less exacting, faster pass on the files. It is ideal for use when the differences are distinct, not bunched together. You cannot combine it with the -e or -f option.

The -b option ignores trailing blanks (spaces and tabs). All strings of blanks compare equal.

diff's output indicates the type of change required. An *a* means to add text after the indicated line, *d* to delete text, and *c* to change it.

OSF/1 and SVR4: **diff** can cperate on entire directories, examining each file in two of them for differences.

Examples

The simplest use of **diff** is to compare two versions of a file using the format

```
diff file1 file2
```

It generates output like:

```
1,3d0
<
< while true
< do
42c38
< done
—
```

The < at the start of a line indicates that the first file is affected, whereas > indicates the second file. Remember that **diff**'s output shows how to change the first file into the second. The first line means that you must delete lines 1 through 3, which appear below the command. The second tells you to change line 42 of the first file to resemble line 38 of the second. The contents of the line appear below the command. With the -e option, the output allows **ed** to make the changes automatically.

You need not specify the filenames if they are the same, but in different directories. If the file "letter" is in both /usr/tim and the current directory /usr/tmp, the **diff** command to compare them is

```
diff /usr/tim letter
```

diff is useful for comparing source program files. It can tell you what someone has changed in a file, and which copy is the latest version. It is useful for determining whether a file has been changed inadvertently (through an accidental save or incorrect name) or deliberately (by a virus or malicious action). **diff** can also compare or check data files.

diffmk

Description:

Marks differences between files

Compatibility:

OSF/1	Yes
SCO Unix	No
SCO Xenix	No
System V Release 3.2	No
System V Release 4	No
X/Open	No

Syntax:

diffmk [-b] [-ab'mark'] [-ae'mark'] [-cb'mark] [-ce'mark'] [db'mark'] [-de'mark'] file1 file2

Options:

-ab uses *mark* to indicate where added lines begin

-ae uses *mark* to indicate where added lines end

-b ignores tabs and whitespace differences on a line

-cb uses *mark* to indicate where changed lines begin

-ce uses *mark* to indicate where changed lines end

-db uses *mark* to indicate where deleted lines begin

-de uses *mark* to indicate where deleted lines end

See Also:

diff; diff3

Discussion

diffmk compares two versions of a file and creates a new one that indicates differences between them. By default, it uses **nroff** formatting marks, unless you specify otherwise on the command line.

Examples

To compare /usr/tim.1 and /usr/tim.2, enter

```
diffmk tim.1 tim.2
```

The output will contain **nroff** formatting marks. The command

```
diffmk -ab'>Ins' -ae '<Ins' -cb'>Chg' -ce'<Chg' -db'>Del'
   de'>Del' tim.1 tim.2 >diff.tim
```

will create the new file diff.tim that has inserts from tim.1 marked with “>Ins”, inserts from tim.2 with “<Ins”, changes from tim.1 with “>Chg”, and so on.

diff3

Description:

Compares three files

Compatibility:

OSF/1	Yes
SCO Unix	Yes
SCO Xenix	Yes
System V Release 3.2	Yes
System V Release 4	Yes
X/Open	No

Syntax:

diff3 [-e|x|E|X|3] file1 file2 file3

Versions:

OSF/1 and SVR4: add the -E and -X options.

Options:

-e produces an **ed** script that incorporates differences between file2 and file3 into file1

-E same as -e but marks changes where all three files differ, bracketed with “<<<<<<“ and “>>>>>>” (OSF/1 and SVR4 only)

-x produces a script for **ed** incorporating into file1 differences in the three files

-X same as -x but marks changes where all three files differ, bracketed with “<<<<<<“ and “>>>>>>” (OSF/1 and SVR4 only)

-3 produces an **ed** script that incorporates differences between file1 and file3 into file1

Warnings:

Script files produced with the -e option do not work correctly for lines consisting of a single period.

Input file size is limited to 64kB.

See Also:

bdiff; cmp; diff; diffmk

Discussion

diff3 compares three files and indicates differences among them. It can generate an **ed** script to correct the first file for differences in the others.

diff3 displays differences among the three files prefaced with one of the following codes:

====	all three files differ
====1	file1 differs
====2	file2 differs
====3	file3 differs

After the file indicator, **diff3** indicates the type of change in one of two ways:

file x: line m a

file x: line m, line n

The first means to append the following text after line m in file x, the second to change the following text in lines m through n. If a single line is involved, only one number appears.

The -e option generates an **ed** script with the changes needed to convert file1 to reflect differences between file2 and file3. (In other words, those prefaced by '====' and '====3'.) The -x option updates file1 to reflect differences in the three files (those prefaced by '===='). Finally, the -3 option generates a script to update file1 to reflect differences between it and file3, ignoring file2 (those prefaced by '====3' only).

Examples

If you have the following three files:

file_1:	file_2:	file_3:
Gold	Gold	Silver
Platinum	Amber	Amber
Jade	Uranium	Uranium

the output from one format of **diff3** is:

```
$diff3 -e file_1 file_2 file_3
1,3c
Silver
Amber
Uranium
```

indicating that the three lines indicated must be added to file_1.

dircmp

Description:
Compares directories

Compatibility:

OSF/1	Yes
SCO Unix	Yes
SCO Xenix	Yes
System V Release 3.2	Yes
System V Release 4	Yes
X/Open	Yes

Syntax:
dircmp [-d] [-s] [-w number] dir1 dir2

Versions:
OSF/1 and X/Open: do not support the -w option.

Options:
-d performs **diff** on each pair of like-named files

-s suppresses output of identical filenames

-w changes the output width to a specified number of characters (default is 72)

Warnings:
The display of even empty directories includes headers and footers, and scrolls down the screen rapidly. You should route it to either the printer or **more** via a pipe.

See Also:
cmp; diff

Discussion

dircmp examines two directories and produces lists of unique and common files.

The -d option uses **diff** to examine files with the same name to determine if they are identical. The -s option prints only a list of files unique to the two directories.

Examples:

To compare /usr/tim and /usr/bill, enter

```
dircmp /usr/tim /usr/bill | more
```

Pathnames are relative, so if you are in the /usr directory already, you can enter simply

```
dircmp tim bill | more
```

It routes the output to **more** via a pipe so you can read it on the terminal.

dircmp produces a header with the time, date, and names of the two directories. The first part of the output lists files unique to each directory, and the second part shows common ones.

A sample output is:

```
Jan 24 13:40 1991 tim only and bill only Page 1

        ./letter.804             ./file1.c

        ./letter.new             ./test

        ./book.review            ./display.c

                                 ./display2.c

                                 ./display.mak
Jan 24 13:40 1991 Comparison of tim and bill Page 1

        directory                .

        same                     ./.profile

                                 ./mainmenu

                                 ./uw_article
```

All filenames shown are relative to the specified directory. In the first section, the first column shows files unique to /usr/tim, the second ones unique to /usr/bill.

dirname

Description:
Displays the directory part of a pathname

Compatibility:

OSF/1	Yes
SCO Unix	Yes
SCO Xenix	Yes
System V Release 3.2	Yes
System V Release 4	Yes
X/Open	Yes

Syntax:
dirname filename

Arguments:
filename is a string specifying a filename with directory names included.

See Also:
basename

Discussion
dirname is useful primarily in shell programming to extract the directory part of a filename. The command effectively parses the last backslash and any following characters from a string.

If only a single file name is provided, **dirname** responds with a dot to indicate the current directory.

dirname is often used with **basename** to parse strings for shell processing.

Examples

dirname extracts the directory specifications from a filename that includes them by removing the last backslash (directory indicator) and any following characters. For example,

```
dirname /usr/tim/book/chapter.1
```

produces the output /usr/tim/book.

Shell programs commonly have the filename inside substitution marks. Variables may be used to substitute the string to be parsed. A typical way to assign a directory name to a variable is

```
DIRNAME='dirname /usr/tim/book/chapter.1'
```

which assigns /usr/tim/book to the variable DIRNAME. The filename could have been provided by substitution.

disable

Description:

Turns printers or terminals off

Compatibility:

OSF/1	Yes
SCO Unix	Yes
SCO Xenix	Yes
System V Release 3.2	Yes
System V Release 4	Yes
X/Open	No

Versions:

SVR3.2 and SVR4: applies only to printers.

Syntax:

disable [-c] [-r[reason]] printer ...

disable tty...

Arguments:

printer	enabled printer name
tty	enabled tty device name

Options:

-c	cancels currently printing requests
-r	displays the "reason" why the printer is disabled. Uses a default string (version dependent) if no "reason" appears.

Files:

/etc/ttys (SCO Xenix)	devices
/usr/spool/lp/*	temporary files

See Also:

enable; lp; lpstat

Discussion

disable presents logins on a particular terminal, or print requests for a particular printer. To allow them, use **enable**.

System security may restrict the use of **disable**.

Examples

The command

```
disable -r"toner cartridge change" laser
```

prevents print requests for the printer “laser”, and displays the message after the -r option as a reason.

The command

```
disable tty8a
```

prevents logins from the terminal (or modem) attached to port tty8a.

diskcmp

Description:

Compares floppy disks

Compatibility:

OSF/1	No
SCO Unix	Yes
SCO Xenix	Yes
System V Release 3.2	No
System V Release 4	No
X/Open	No

Syntax:

diskcmp [-d] [-s] [-format]

Options:

-d implies the system has two floppies and the comparison is between them

-s uses **sum** to compare contents and produces an error message if the two differ

format disk format. Must be one of the following:

-48ds9	low density 48 tpi (5.25 inch)
-96ds9	high density 96 tpi (5.25 inch)
-96ds15	quad density 96 tpi (5.25 inch)
-135ds9	high density 135 tpi (3.5 inch)
-135ds18	quad density 135 tpi (3.5 inch)

See Also:

cmp; dd; diskcp; format

Discussion

Use **diskcmp** to determine whether two floppies are identical. You can use it after **diskcp**, for example, or simply to compare floppy disks.

It uses the **cmp** command.

If two floppy drives are available, the -d flag compares them. Otherwise, **diskcmp** prompts you to change disks.

Notes

diskcmp cannot compare floppies with different formats.

diskcmp is an extension supplied by the Santa Cruz Operation.

Examples

You can use **diskcmp** by itself or with an option. The command

```
diskcmp
```

compares the floppy disk in the default drive with another disk. The system prompts you to change floppies.

You can specify the type of floppy in cases where system defaults do not apply. For example, to compare two quad density 5 1/4" diskettes in the main system drive, enter

```
diskcmp -96ds15
```

diskcp

Description:

Copies floppy disks

Compatibility:

OSF/1	No
SCO Unix	Yes
SCO Xenix	Yes
System V Release 3.2	No
System V Release 4	No
X/Open	No

Syntax:

diskcp [-d] [-f] [-s] [-format]

Options:

-d	implies the system has two floppies, and the copy is between them
-f	formats the target floppy before copying
-s	uses **sum** to compare the contents and produces an error message if the two are not identical
format	disk format. Must be one of the following:

-48ds9	low density 48 tpi (5.25 inch)
-96ds9	high density 96 tpi (5.25 inch)
-96ds15	quad density 96 tpi (5.25 inch)
-135ds9	high density 135 tpi (3.5 inch)
-135ds18	quad density 135 tpi (3.5 inch)

See Also:

cmp; cp; dd; diskcmp; format

Warnings:

diskcp displays the message "System error" if it cannot complete the copy. If there is a problem with the target floppy (usually a write error), it first tries to reformat the floppy and complete the copy.

Discussion

diskcp makes an exact copy of one floppy onto another. If your computer has two drives that support the same format, the -d option lets you copy directly. Otherwise, **diskcp** prompts you to change the floppy. On one floppy systems, it copies the image to the hard disk temporarily, then to the target.

After making a copy, **diskcp** asks if you want to copy another disk. Any response starting with "y" restarts the process.

Notes

diskcp is an extension supplied by the Santa Cruz Operation.

Examples

To copy a floppy disk, enter

```
diskcp
```

with no options. It uses the source disk's format for the target disk.

doscat

Description:

Copies DOS files to standard output

Compatibility:

OSF/1	No
SCO Unix	Yes
SCO Xenix	Yes
System V Release 3.2	No
System V Release 4	No
X/Open	No

Syntax:

doscat [-m|-r] file ...

Options:

-m copies with newline conversion

-r copies without newline conversion

See Also:

cat; doscp; dosdir; dosformat; dosls; dosmkdir; dosrm; dosrmdir; dtox; xtod

Discussion

doscat copies DOS files from a diskette or partition to standard output. It allows redirection. It behaves like Unix **cat** or DOS TYPE. It does not refer to a small domestic animal who has just happened to learn a few operating system commands.

DOS uses a carriage return and line feed pair to indicate a newline. Unix uses a newline character only. **doscat** strips off the carriage return character automatically unless you use the -r option.

Notes

The **dos** commands allow access to DOS disks and partitions. To use hard disk files or directories, the partition must be bootable. It need not be active.

Sometimes the automatic carriage return strip does not occur. The -m option ensures it.

The DOS-style drive designators appear in the file /etc/default/msdos. To use them, the file must contain the correct Unix device name for each one.

The **dtox** and **xtod** commands can convert end of line sequences between DOS and Unix forms.

doscat does not support extended DOS partitions.

doscat creates temporary files in /tmp.

doscat is an extension supplied by the Santa Cruz Operation.

Examples

The command

```
doscat /dev/rfd096ds15:/doc/letter.4
```

copies the file letter.4 from the DOC directory on a DOS floppy. You can usually refer to the drive name in DOS terminology, so an equivalent command is

```
doscat a:/doc/letter.4
```

in most cases. You must use the Unix-style slash character instead of the DOS backslash when specifying directory paths.

doscp

Description:

Copies files between a DOS disk and a Unix filesystem

Compatibility:

OSF/1	No
SCO Unix	Yes
SCO Xenix	Yes
System V Release 3.2	No
System V Release 4	No
X/Open	No

Syntax:

doscp [-m|-r] file1 file2

doscp [-m|-r] file ... directory

Options:

-m copies with newline conversion

-r copies without newline conversion

See Also:

cp; doscat; dosdir; dosformat; dosls; dosmkdir; dosrm; dosrmdir; dtox; xtod

Discussion

doscp copies files to or from a DOS diskette or partition. It behaves like the Unix **cp** command.

If two filenames appear, the first is the source. If a directory is specified, the files are copied to it.

DOS uses a carriage return and line feed pair to indicate a newline. Unix uses a newline character only. **doscp** strips the carriage return character automatically, unless you use the -r option.

Filenames longer than eight characters and extensions longer than three characters are truncated when copying to DOS. **doscp** displays a message indicating the name change. DOS files are stored in uppercase only. Filename characters that are illegal under DOS are removed when copying to a DOS file.

Notes

The **dos** commands allow access to DOS disks and partitions. To use hard disk files or directories, the partition must be bootable. It need not be active.

Sometimes the automatic carriage return strip does not occur. The -m option forces it.

The DOS-style drive designators appear in the file /etc/default/msdos. To use them, the file must contain the correct Unix device name for each one.

The **dtox** and **xtod** commands can convert end of line sequences between DOS and Unix forms.

doscp does not support extended DOS partitions.

doscp creates temporary files in /tmp.

doscp is an extension supplied by the Santa Cruz Operation.

Examples

The command

```
doscp /usr/tim/letter.4 /dev/rfd096ds15:/doc/letter.4
```

copies the file letter.4 from Unix to the DOC directory on a DOS floppy. You can usually refer to the drive name in DOS terminology, so an equivalent command is

```
doscp /usr/tim/letter.4 a:/doc/letter.4
```

in most cases. You must use the Unix-style slash character instead of the DOS backslash when specifying directory paths.

The command

```
doscp /dev/rfd048ds9:letter.1 /usr/tim/docs/new.letter
```

or

```
doscp a:letter.1 /usr/tim/docs/new.letter
```

copies the DOS file letter.1 from the floppy to the file new.letter in Unix.

The command

```
doscp /usr/tim/new.letter.April a:new.let
```

truncates the filename under DOS to conform to its naming rules.

dosdir

Description:

Lists files on a DOS disk or partition

Compatibility:

OSF/1	No
SCO Unix	Yes
SCO Xenix	Yes
System V Release 3.2	No
System V Release 4	No
X/Open	No

Syntax:

dosdir directory

See Also:

doscat; doscp; dosformat; dosls; dosmkdir; dosrm; dosrmdir; ls

Discussion

dosdir produces a DOS-style directory listing. It uses the format of the DOS DIR command.

Notes

The **dos** commands allow access to DOS disks and partitions. To use hard disk files or directories, the partition must be bootable. It need not be active.

The DOS-style drive designators appear in the file /etc/default/msdos. To use them, the file must contain the correct Unix device name for each one.

dosdir does not support extended DOS partitions.

dosdir creates temporary files in /tmp.

dosdir is an extension supplied by the Santa Cruz Operation.

Examples

The command

```
dosdir /dev/rfd096ds15:
```

or

```
dosdir a:
```

displays the directory of the DOS formatted disk in the floppy drive. The second alternative works on most systems.

You must use the Unix-style slash character instead of the DOS backslash when specifying directory paths.

dosformat

Description:
Formats a floppy diskette to DOS 2.0 specifications

Compatibility:

OSF/1	No
SCO Unix	Yes
SCO Xenix	Yes
System V Release 3.2	No
System V Release 4	No
X/Open	No

Syntax:
dosformat [-fqv] drive

Options:
-f suppresses interactive prompts

-q suppresses messages

-v asks for volume label after formatting

Files:
/etc/default/msdos default DOS drive

See Also:
doscat; doscp; dosdir; dosls; dosmkdir; dosrm; dosrmdir; format

Discussion
dosformat formats diskettes for DOS. It cannot format a DOS hard disk or partition. If no drive is specified, it uses the default in /etc/default/msdos.

Volume names cannot exceed eleven characters.

Notes

You cannot use the designator "A:" with **dosformat** as it is aliased to /dev/install.

The DOS-style drive designators appear in the file /etc/default/msdos. To use them, the file must contain the correct Unix device names.

dosformat does not support extended DOS partitions.

dosformat is an extension supplied by the Santa Cruz Operation.

Examples

The command

```
dosformat /dev/rfd096ds15
```

formats a high density floppy in the drive to DOS format.

dosls

Description:

Lists files on a DOS disk or partition in a Unix format

Compatibility:

OSF/1	No
SCO Unix	Yes
SCO Xenix	Yes
System V Release 3.2	No
System V Release 4	No
X/Open	No

Syntax:

dosls directory

See Also:

doscat; doscp; dosdir; dosformat; dosmkdir; dosrm; dosrmdir; ls

Discussion

dosls produces an **ls**-style directory listing.

Notes

The **dos** commands allow access to DOS disks and partitions. To use hard disk files or directories, the partition must be bootable. It need not be active.

The DOS-style drive designators appear in the file /etc/default/msdos. To use them, the file must contain the correct Unix device names.

dosls does not support extended DOS partitions.

dosls is an extension supplied by the Santa Cruz Operation.

Examples

The command

```
dosls /dev/rfd096ds15:
```

or

```
dosls a:
```

displays the directory of the DOS formatted disk in the same style as the **ls** command. The second form works on most systems.

You must use the Unix-style slash character instead of the DOS backslash when specifying directory paths.

dosmkdir

Description:
Creates a directory on a DOS disk or partition

Compatibility:

OSF/1	No
SCO Unix	Yes
SCO Xenix	Yes
System V Release 3.2	No
System V Release 4	No
X/Open	No

Syntax:
dosmkdir directory list

See Also:
doscat; doscp; dosdir; dosformat; dosls; dosrm; dosrmdir; mkdir

Discussion
dosmkdir creates a directory on a DOS disk or partition. It uses the same format as the DOS MKDIR or MD command.

Notes
The **dos** commands allow access to DOS disks and partitions. To use hard disk files or directories, the partition must be bootable. It need not be active.

The DOS-style drive designators appear in the file /etc/default/msdos. To use them, the file must contain the correct Unix device names.

dosmkdir does not support extended DOS partitions.

dosmkdir is an extension supplied by the Santa Cruz Operation.

Examples

The command

```
dosmkdir /dev/rfd096ds15:/temp
```

or

```
dosmkdir a:/temp
```

creates a directory "temp" on the DOS formatted floppy. The second form works on most systems.

You must use the Unix-style slash character instead of the DOS backslash when specifying directory paths.

dosrm

Description:

Deletes files from a DOS disk or partition

Compatibility:

OSF/1	No
SCO Unix	Yes
SCO Xenix	Yes
System V Release 3.2	No
System V Release 4	No
X/Open	No

Syntax:

dosrm file list

See Also:

doscat; doscp; dosdir; dosformat; dosls; dosmkdir; dosrmdir; rm

Discussion

dosrm deletes files from a DOS diskette or partition. It behaves like the DOS DEL or ERASE command.

Notes

The **dos** commands allow access to DOS disks and partitions. To use hard disk files or directories, the partition must be bootable. It need not be active.

The DOS-style drive designators appear in the file /etc/default/msdos. To use them, the file must contain the correct Unix device names.

dosrm does not support extended DOS partitions.

dosrm is an extension supplied by the Santa Cruz Operation.

Examples

The command

```
dosrm /dev/rfd096ds15:/doc/letter.4
```

deletes the file letter.4 from the DOC directory on a DOS floppy.

dosrmdir

Description:

Deletes a directory from a DOS disk or partition

Compatibility:

OSF/1	No
SCO Unix	Yes
SCO Xenix	Yes
System V Release 3.2	No
System V Release 4	No
X/Open	No

Syntax:

dosrmdir directory list

See Also:

doscat; doscp; dosdir; dosformat; dosls; dosmkdir; dosrm; rmdir

Discussion

dosrmdir deletes a directory from a DOS disk or partition. It uses the same format as the DOS RMDIR or RD command.

Notes

The **dos** commands allow access to DOS disks and partitions. To use hard disk files or directories, the partition must be bootable. It need not be active.

The DOS-style drive designators appear in the file /etc/default/msdos. To use them, the file must contain the correct Unix device names.

dosrmdir does not support extended DOS partitions.

dosrmdir is an extension supplied by the Santa Cruz Operation.

Examples

The command

```
dosrmdir /dev/rfd096ds15:/temp
```

or

```
dosrmdir a:/temp
```

removes directory *temp* from the DOS formatted floppy. The second form works on most systems.

You must use the Unix-style slash character instead of the DOS backslash when specifying directory paths.

dtox

Description:
Changes file formats from DOS to Unix

Compatibility:

OSF/1	No
SCO Unix	Yes
SCO Xenix	No
System V Release 3.2	No
System V Release 4	No
X/Open	No

Syntax:
dtox file1 > file2

Arguments:

file1	DOS source file
file2	Unix destination file

Error Handling:
Reports a syntax error if redirection symbol is omitted

See Also:
xtod

Discussion
dtox converts a file from DOS to Unix format by changing carriage return/line feed pairs to line feeds only. It also removes the terminating Ctrl-Z.

If a filename is omitted, **dtox** uses standard input or output.

Notes

dtox is an extension supplied by the Santa Cruz Operation. Despite the name, it does not remove dreadful chemicals from files.

Examples

The command

```
dtox letter.4 > letter.new
```

reads the file letter.4, removes carriage returns and Ctrl-Zs, and writes the result as letter.new.

dtype

Description:
Determines disk type

Compatibility:

OSF/1	No
SCO Unix	Yes
SCO Xenix	Yes
System V Release 3.2	No
System V Release 4	No
X/Open	No

Syntax:
dtype [-s] device ...

Options:
-s suppresses messages

Returns:

60	error
61	empty or unrecognizable
70	**backup** format
71	**tar** format
72	**cpio** format
73	**cpio** character format
80	DOS 1.x, 8 sectors/track, single sided
81	DOS 1.x, 8 sectors/track, double sided
90	DOS 2.x, 8 sectors/track, single sided
91	DOS 2.x, 8 sectors/track, double sided
92	DOS 2.x, 9 sectors/track, single sided

93	DOS 2.x, 9 sectors/track, double sided
94	DOS 2.x, hard disk
110	DOS 3.x, 9 sectors/track, double sided
120	Xenix 2.x filesystem (needs cleaning)
130	Xenix 3.x or later filesystem (needs cleaning)
140	Unix 1kB filesystem (needs cleaning)

Discussion

dtype determines and prints (unless you use -s) information about the disk type in the device. It also returns an exit code.

Notes

When several devices appear in the argument list, the return code is for the last one.

dtype works reliably only for floppy disks. It may not correctly report disks from operating systems other than Unix, Xenix, and DOS.

dtype is an extension supplied by the Santa Cruz Operation.

du

Description:

Summarizes disk space usage

Compatibility:

OSF/1	Yes
SCO Unix	Yes
SCO Xenix	Yes
System V Release 3.2	Yes
System V Release 4	Yes
X/Open	Yes

Syntax:

du [-a|-f|-l|-r|-s|-u] [dirname]

Versions:

OSF/1: adds the -l option.

SCO Unix and Xenix: add the -f and -u options.

Options:

-a	generates an entry for each file
-f	displays for files in the current system only (SCO Unix and Xenix only)
-l	allocates blocks equally among links (OSF/1 only)
-r	reports unopenable files and directories
-s	displays totals only for each specified [dirname]
-u	ignores files with multiple links (SCO Unix and Xenix only)
dirname	directory or file names

Defaults:

Assumes current directory if "dirname" is omitted

Discussion

The **du** command summarizes disk usage. Its normal output displays the number of blocks in all files and directories specified by dirname.

The normal output is long, and lists directories vertically in two columns. The left one is the number of blocks, and the right the full file or directory names. Individual files do not appear unless you specify the -a option.

To condense the output, use the -s option to display just the total number of blocks. When there are mounted filesystems, the -f option instructs **du** to ignore them, and to report only on the current one.

du counts files with multiple links just once when summing blocks. The -u option ignores files with multiple links.

du does not report on directories it cannot read, or files it cannot open. The -r option causes it to generate an error message if it finds any.

du counts blocks in 512-byte units. If your file system uses 1024-byte blocks, a file that occupies one block will report as two.

Examples

The simplest use of **du** gives a count of a specific directory.

For example,

```
du /usr/tim
```

produces the output

```
1186  /usr/tim/c
42    /usr/tim/scripts
534   /usr/tim/book
124   /usr/tim/docs
2142  /usr/tim
```

indicating 2142 blocks in /usr/tim, divided into four subdirectories. The size of each subdirectory appears. For large directories (such as /usr), the output will be several screens long and should be piped to **more**.

You could report the total blocks used by /usr/tim with the command

```
du -s /usr/tim
```

which produces the output

```
2142  /usr/tim
```

The total includes subdirectories, even though they do not appear.

The numbers produced by **du** are in 512-byte blocks, so you can compute disk usage in kilobytes by dividing by two. In the above example, /usr/tim occupies 1,071 kB.

dump

Description:

Performs incremental backups

Compatibility:

OSF/1	No
SCO Unix	No
SCO Xenix	Yes
System V Release 3.2	Yes
System V Release 4	No
X/Open	No

See Also:

backup; dumpdir

Discussion

dump is identical to the Xenix **backup** command. Refer to **backup** for information.

dumpdir

Description:
Prints the names of files on a backup volume

Compatibility:

OSF/1	No
SCO Unix	No
SCO Xenix	Yes
System V Release 3.2	No
System V Release 4	No
X/Open	No

Syntax:
dumpdir [f filename]

Options:
f uses "filename" as the backup device

Defaults:
Uses the backup device unless you specify the f option. The system administrator defines the device (usually in /etc/default).

See Also:
backup; dump

Discussion
dumpdir lists the names and inode numbers of all files and directories on an archive volume written with **backup**.

It is useful for finding files on multiple backup volumes.

Notes

dumpdir may create temporary files.

echo

Description:
Displays an argument

Compatibility:

OSF/1	Yes
SCO Unix	Yes
SCO Xenix	Yes
System V Release 3.2	Yes
System V Release 4	Yes
X/Open	Yes

Syntax:
echo [string ...]

OSF/1 and SVR4:

echo [-n] [string ...]

Versions:
OSF/1 and SVR4: Include the -n option is included for compatibility with BSD applications. Future releases will probably drop it.

Options:

-n	does not add a newline to the output (OSF/1 and SVR4 only)
string	character string that may include escape sequences inside quotation marks. Valid sequences are:

\b	backspace
\c	print without newline character
\f	form feed
\n	newline
\r	carriage return

\t	tab
\v	vertical tab
\\	backslash
\x	8-bit character given by x (see Examples)

Warnings:

The C shell has a built-in **echo** command. If you want the Unix **echo**, the command must include the directory

```
/bin/echo
```

or the shell will use its intrinsic command. Its version has different syntax from standard Unix (see Anderson, G. and Anderson, P., *The Unix C Shell Field Guide*, Englewood Cliffs, NJ: Prentice-Hall, 1986).

Discussion

echo is primarily useful in shell scripts for writing the argument to the terminal, displaying diagnostic messages, or sending data to a pipe.

Examples

Use **echo** by specifying the display. The command

```
echo This is a test
```

produces the output

```
This is a test
```

on the terminal. You should enclose the argument in quotation marks to prevent substitution by the shell.

You can embed escape sequences using backslashes. The command

```
echo "This is a test \n\n\n"
```

produces the same output as the above example, but adds three line feeds at the end.

You can specify an ASCII character as a backslash followed by its numerical value. The command

```
echo "Test \07"
```

prints “Test” followed by 07, which is ASCII Control-G (or Bell). The terminal will beep after displaying the word “Test”. You can use any ASCII value in this way.

The most common use of **echo** is creating messages inside shell scripts. For example, when a file open error occurs, the following line displays a message and beeps:

```
echo "The file could not be opened! \n\07"
```

ed

Description:
Line editor

Compatibility:

OSF/1	Yes
SCO Unix	Yes
SCO Xenix	Yes
System V Release 3.2	Yes
System V Release 4	Yes
X/Open	Yes

Syntax:
ed [-] [-p string] [file]

Options:
- \- suppresses character counts
- -p sets the prompt string to "string"

See Also:
edit; vi

Discussion
ed is a line editor that works on one file at a time by copying it to a temporary buffer. All changes are made to the buffer, and must be written back to the file to take effect. **ed** has two modes: command and text. In command mode, it recognizes and executes commands. In text mode, it ignores them. You can put it in command mode by entering a period as the first character of a new line.

ed uses a current line pointer to identify positions in the text. All commands assume the current line unless specified otherwise. **ed** allows only one command per line. (Exceptions are l and p, which can be followed by any other command except e, E, f, r, and w, which require a filename as an argument.)

ed supports the following commands:

[#]a	append - enters text mode from command mode. Appends lines to the last addressed one if no number is specified. If a line is specified, text is appended after it.
[#,#]c	change - removes the addressed lines and replaces them with new input
[#,#]d	delete - removes the addressed lines. The line after them becomes the current line.
e file	edit - deletes buffer contents and loads "file". The current line is the last one in the buffer. If the buffer has changed since the last save, **ed** prompts with "?" to verify that you want to delete it.
E file	edit - works like e but does not check for changes made to the buffer.
f [file]	file - changes the default filename. If none is specified, it prints the current value.
[#,#]g/pat/com	global - marks every line that matches the pattern "pat", then executes command "com" for each one. "com" can include other commands.
f#,#]G/pat	interactive global - moves to and displays the first line that matches pattern "pat", and waits for a command. After executing the command, it moves to and displays the next matching line.
[#]i	insert - inserts text before the addressed line
[#,#+1]j	join - joins contiguous lines by removing intervening newline characters
[#]kx	mark - marks addressed line with the name "x" (must be lowercase). Using 'x then addresses it directly. Does not change the current line number.
[#,#]l	list - displays the addressed lines

[#,#]m#	move - moves addressed lines to the third address
[#,#]n	number - displays the addressed lines preceded by their numbers and a tab character. Does not change the current line number.
[#,#]p	print - displays the addressed lines and sets the current line to the last one displayed
P	prompt - turns the **ed** prompt "*" on or off
q	quit - exits **ed**. If the buffer has not been saved, it prompts with "?". A second q quits without saving the buffer.
Q	quit - exits **ed** without checking the buffer
[#]r file	read - reads "file" into the buffer without destroying its current contents
[#,#]t#	transfer - copies addressed lines to the third address. Sets the current line to the last one copied.
u	undo - restores the buffer to its state before the last command
[#,#]v/pat/com	executes command "com" for each line that does not contain the pattern "pat" (complement to the g command)
[#,#]V/pat	displays the first line that does not contain the pattern "pat" and waits for a command. It then searches for the next non-match, and displays it (complement to the G command).
[#,#]w file	write - copies the addressed lines from the buffer to "file"
=	displays the current line number
! com	executes the system command "com"
+/-[#]	moves the current line by the specified number of lines, and displays the new current line

Notes

ed imposes several restrictions, including 512 bytes per line, 256 bytes per global command list, and 128kB buffer size. The maximum number of lines you can edit depends on available memory.

edit

Description:
Line editor with a simplified command set

Compatibility:

OSF/1	Yes
SCO Unix	Yes
SCO Xenix	Yes
System V Release 3.2	Yes
System V Release 4	Yes
X/Open	Yes

Syntax:
edit [-l] [-R] [-v] [-r file] [-t tag] [-w number] [+command] [-] [file]

Versions:
Option support varies considerably, depending on the implementation.

Options:
- `-` suppresses interactive feedback. Does not generate any error messages
- `+` begins the edit with execution of "command"
- `-l` indents for LISP programs
- `-r` recovers "file" after an editor or system crash. If no filename is provided, it displays all saved files.
- `-R` sets the "readonly" option, preventing alterations to the file
- `-t` loads the file containing "tag", moving to the line that contains it
- `-v` invokes **vi**
- `-w` sets the window size to "number" lines

See Also:

ed; vi

Discussion

edit is based on **ed**. It supports the following commands:

[#]a	append - enters text mode from command mode. Appends lines to the last addressed one if no number is specified. If a line is specified, text is appended after it.
[#,#]c	change - removes the addressed lines and replaces them with new input
[#,#]d	delete - removes the addressed lines. The line after the last one deleted becomes the current line.
e file	edit - deletes buffer contents and loads "file". The current line is the last one in the buffer. If the buffer has changed since the last save, **edit** prompts with "?" to verify that you want to delete it.
f [file]	file - changes the default filename. If none is specified, it prints the current value.
[#,#]g/pat/com	global - marks every line that matches the pattern "pat", then executes command "com" for each one. "com" can include other commands.
[#,#]m#	move - moves addressed lines to the third address
[#,#]p	print - displays the addressed lines and sets the current line to the last one displayed
pre	preserve - saves the current edit buffer as though the system had just crashed (used when w produces an error)
[#,#]put[buf]	retrieves the contents of a buffer identified by a lowercase letter
q	quit - exits **edit**. If the buffer has not been saved, it prompts with "?". A second q quits without saving the buffer.

rec file	recover - recovers "file" from the system save area
u	undo - restores the buffer to the state before the last command
[#,#]w file	write - copies the addressed lines from the buffer to "file".
[#,#]ya[buf]	yank - places the addressed lines in a buffer identified by a lowercase letter

egrep

Description:
Searches a file for a pattern

Compatibility:

OSF/1	Yes
SCO Unix	Yes
SCO Xenix	Yes
System V Release 3.2	Yes
System V Release 4	Yes
X/Open	Yes

Syntax:
egrep [-bchilnv] [-e expr] [files]

Versions:
OSF/1: does not support the -i option, adds the -s option.

SCO Unix and Xenix: do not support the -i option.

Options:

-b	puts block number ahead of each line
-c	displays only a count of matching lines
-h	suppresses display of file name
-i	ignores case distinctions
-l	displays only the names of files with matching lines
-n	displays each line with its number in the file
-s	suppresses output except error messages (OSF/1 only)
-v	displays all lines except ones that match
-e expr	form required for expressions that start with a dash

Returns:

0 if it finds any matches

1 if it finds no matches

2 if it encounters a syntax or file error

See Also:

ed; fgrep; grep

Discussion

egrep searches files for lines that match a pattern. The pattern can be any regular Unix expression. It displays lines of up to 256 characters and truncates longer ones.

egrep supports expressions in **ed**'s style plus the following:

+	matches one or more occurrences of an expression
?	matches zero or one occurrence of an expression
|	matches either of two expressions
()	around regular expressions for grouping

egrep does not support **ed**'s "\(" and "\)" operators or extended ranges. To allow them, use **grep** instead.

To avoid misinterpretation by the shell, you should place expressions inside single quotation marks.

Examples

Unix provides three commands for pattern matching. **fgrep** matches fixed strings, **grep** matches limited expressions, and **egrep** matches full expressions.

The simplest use of **egrep** is to search a file for a string. The command

```
egrep 'duplicate entries' chapter.1
```

searches the file chapter.1 for all occurrences of the string "duplicate entries", and displays each matching line. The -y option makes it ignore case. A typical result is

```
You can remove duplicate entries easily.
This approach will help you avoid duplicate entries.
The following method eliminates duplicate entries:
```

Each line that matches the expression or string appears in full.

Patterns and expressions used with **egrep** follow **ed**'s format. The command

```
grep '[CK]ramer' chapter.1
```

matches "Cramer" or "Kramer" in chapter.1.

egrep provides other options for expressions. One followed by a plus sign matches one or more occurrences on a line. A vertical bar is treated as "or", and matches either expression. Parentheses may surround groups of strings for evaluation. For example, the command

```
egrep 'Theat(re|er)' chapter.1
```

matches either "Theatre" or "Theater". Similarly,

```
egrep 'Jo(hn|n|nn)son' chapter.1
```

matches "Johnson", "Jonson", or "Jonnson".

enable

Description:

Turns printers or terminals on

Compatibility:

OSF/1	Yes
SCO Unix	Yes
SCO Xenix	Yes
System V Release 3.2	Yes
System V Release 4	Yes
X/Open	No

Versions:

OSF/1, SVR3.2, and SVR4: applies only to printers.

Syntax:

enable printer ...

enable tty...

Files:

/etc/conf/init.base (SCO Unix)	devices
/etc/ttys (SCO Xenix)	devices
/usr/spool/lp/*	temporary files

See Also:

disable; lp; lpstat

Discussion

For terminals, **enable** sets the /etc/conf/init.base (Unix) or /etc/ttys (Xenix) file to allow logins. It invokes **init** to initiate them.

For printers, **enable** activates them and allows print requests to be submitted.

To disable terminals or printers, use **disable**.

Security considerations may restrict the use of **enable**.

Examples

The command

```
enable tty8a
```

allows the terminal on port tty8a to accept logins. It also initiates the login message.

The command

```
enable laser
```

activates the printer “laser” and allows print requests.

env

Description:
Sets environment for command execution

Compatibility:

OSF/1	Yes
SCO Unix	Yes
SCO Xenix	Yes
System V Release 3.2	Yes
System V Release 4	Yes
X/Open	Yes

Syntax:
env [-] [name=value ...] [command]

Options:
- \- ignore the current environment completely

Discussion
env modifies the current environment according to the arguments, then executes the command. Arguments take the form "name=value", and are merged into the environment before command execution.

If no command is specified, **env** prints the modified environment with one name=value pair per line.

expand

Description:
Replaces tabs with spaces

Compatibility:

OSF/1	Yes
SCO Unix	No
SCO Xenix	No
System V Release 3.2	No
System V Release 4	No
X/Open	No

Syntax:
expand [-tabstop] [-tab1, tab2, ...] [file]

Options:
- sets tab stops to tabstop
- sets tabs at specified columns

Defaults:
8 spaces per tab

See Also:
unexpand

Discussion
expand converts all tab characters to their equivalent in space characters. If no value is specified, it replaces them with eight spaces. If a single argument appears, tabs use it. If several appear, **expand** assumes they are tab values. **expand** preserves and counts backspace characters.

Examples

To replace all tabs in "MobyDisk" with three spaces, enter

```
expand -3 MobyDisk
```

"He piled upon the whale's white hump the sum of all the general rage and hate felt by his whole race from Adam down . . ." (Melville)

expr

Description:
Evaluates arguments as an expression

Compatibility:

OSF/1	Yes
SCO Unix	Yes
SCO Xenix	Yes
System V Release 3.2	Yes
System V Release 4	Yes
X/Open	Yes

Syntax:
expr argument(s)

Returns:
expr returns exit values from an evaluation, besides the expression result itself. The exit codes are:

0 expression is neither null nor zero

1 expression is null or zero

2 expression is invalid

You can use them for diagnostics in a shell script.

Discussion
expr takes any arguments specified, evaluates them, and writes the result to standard output. Argument terms must be separated by spaces, and special characters must be written as escape sequences using backslashes.

expr supports the following operators (in order of increasing precedence):

arg | arg	returns the first arg if it is not null or 0, otherwise the second
arg & arg	returns the first arg if neither is null or 0, otherwise the second
arg {=,>,>=,<,<=,!=} arg	returns the integer comparison of integers or the lexical comparison of strings
arg {+,-} arg	returns the sum or difference of integer arguments
arg {*,/,%} arg	returns the product, quotient, or remainder (modulus) of integer arguments
arg : arg	compares the two arguments as regular expressions

Strings that contain blanks or escape characters should be inside quotation marks. If the expressions evaluate to null, no output is generated. An output of zero refers only to a numerical value.

Examples

expr is useful primarily in shell programming. The command

```
VAL='expr $VAL + 3'
```

adds three to the numeric value of VAL. The quoted part of the command uses **expr** to add the number, and the sum is then reassigned to the variable.

factor

Description:

Factors a number

Compatibility:

OSF/1	No
SCO Unix	Yes
SCO Xenix	Yes
System V Release 3.2	Yes
System V Release 4	Yes
X/Open	No

Syntax:

factor [number]

Warnings:

factor cannot handle numbers larger than 2^46.

It produces no output if the number is not an integer.

SVR3.2 and SVR4: return the message "Ouch" for invalid input. So much for those who think computers are insensitive!

Discussion

factor displays a number's prime factors. If no argument appears, it waits for you to type a number, then factors it and waits for another. To exit, use the break key or enter zero or any non-numeric character.

Notes

factor can take a long time. Its execution time is proportional to the square root of its argument.

Examples

You can use **factor** in two ways: interactively or with an argument. With an argument, **factor** displays the prime factors, then exits:

```
factor 14
14
    2
    7
```

A recurring factor appears the requisite number of times:

```
factor 24
24
    2
    2
    2
    3
```

indicating three 2's as factors.

false

Description:

Returns a nonzero exit value

Compatibility:

OSF/1	Yes
SCO Unix	Yes
SCO Xenix	Yes
System V Release 3.2	Yes
System V Release 4	Yes
X/Open	Yes

Syntax:

false

See Also:

true

Discussion

false always returns a nonzero exit value. Its primary use is in shell programs to allow a loop to continue forever.

The opposite is **true**, which returns a zero exit value.

Note that the logic convention is the opposite of C's, where zero is false and nonzero true.

Examples

The most common use of **false** is to provide a loop in a shell program that continues until interrupted. For example,

```
until false
do
    date
done
```

executes the **date** command continually until the break sequence interrupts it.

fgrep

Description:

Searches a file for a pattern

Compatibility:

OSF/1	Yes
SCO Unix	Yes
SCO Xenix	Yes
System V Release 3.2	Yes
System V Release 4	Yes
X/Open	Yes

Syntax:

fgrep [-bcilnvxy] [-f exprfile] [files]

Versions:

OSF/1: adds the -h and -s options.

SCO Unix and Xenix: do not support the -i option. They add -y instead.

Options:

-b	puts block number ahead of each line
-c	displays only a count of matching lines
-h	suppresses filename reporting (OSF/1 only)
-i	ignores case
-l	displays only the names of files with matching lines
-n	displays each line with its number in the file
-s	suppresses output except for error messages (OSF/1 only)
-v	displays all lines except ones that match
-x	displays only exact matches of an entire line
-y	matches any case (SCO Unix and Xenix only)
-f exprfile	reads the matching expression from the file "exprfile"

Returns:

0 if it finds any matches

1 if it finds no matches

2 if it encounters a syntax or file error

See Also:

egrep; grep

Discussion

fgrep searches files for lines that match a fixed string. The default settings display each matching line. **fgrep** displays lines of up to 256 characters and truncates anything longer.

To avoid misinterpretation by the shell, you should put single quotation marks around the strings.

Examples

Unix provides three commands for pattern matching. **fgrep** matches fixed strings, **grep** matches limited expressions, and **egrep** matches full expressions.

fgrep searches a file for a string. The command

```
fgrep 'printer error' chapter.1
```

searches the file chapter.1 for all occurrences of the string "printer error", and displays each matching line in full.

file

Description:

Determines file types

Compatibility:

OSF/1	Yes
SCO Unix	Yes
SCO Xenix	Yes
System V Release 3.2	Yes
System V Release 4	Yes
X/Open	Yes

Syntax:

file [-c] [-h] [-m [filename]] file ...

file [-c] [-h] [-m [filename]] -f filelist

Versions:

SCO Unix and Xenix: do not support the -c or -h options. The -m option has a different function.

SVR4: adds the -h option.

Options:

-c checks the "magic file" for format errors

-f takes the list of files from filelist

-h does not follow symbolic links

-m SCO Unix and Xenix: sets the file's access time to the current time
Others: uses a trailing filename instead of /etc/magic

Discussion

file tries to classify each argument. If the file seems to be ASCII, it examines the first 512 bytes and tries to guess the source language.

With the -f option, **file** takes the list of files to be classified from the argument.

file uses /etc/magic to identify files in which a numeric or string constant indicates the type. Comments in the file usually explain the format. The -c option (not supported by SCO Unix or Xenix) checks it.

The -m option differs for SCO Unix and Xenix. Under them, **file** does not normally change the access times for files. But -m makes it set the access time to the current time. With SVR3.2, SVR4, and X/Open, the -m option is followed by a filename to be used instead of /etc/magic.

Examples

file tries to guess the language in which a file was written by matching identification strings in /etc/magic. It can help identify unfamiliar files. For example, the command

```
file script_file
```

produces the output

```
script_file:    commands text
```

indicating it seems to be script language.

Text files are identified as "English text". C files are identified either as "c program text" or "English text", depending on the amount of comments appearing in their first 512 bytes.

file often confuses text, C programs, and script files. It can use only English language character data to identify text. If it finds an 8-bit character, it identifies the file as "8 bit text". The process is like trying to determine what is in an unlabeled can bought from a grocery store's bargain shelf.

find

Description:

Finds files

Compatibility:

OSF/1	Yes
SCO Unix	Yes
SCO Xenix	Yes
System V Release 3.2	Yes
System V Release 4	Yes
X/Open	Yes

Syntax:

find pathname expression

Versions:

OSF/1: adds the arguments -fstype and -prune.

SVR4: adds the arguments -follow, -fstype, -local, -mount, -nogroup, -nouser, and -prune.

Arguments:

pathname — pathnames

expression — Boolean expression containing arguments from the following list:

-atime n	true if the file was last accessed "n" days ago
-cpio dev	writes the file on device "dev" in cpio format
-ctime n	true if the file was created or modified "n" days ago

-depth	acts on all directory entries before acting on the directory itself
-exec cmds	executes the shell commands “cmds”. They must terminate with an escaped semicolon. The current pathname replaces the argument “{}”.
-follow	causes symbolic links to be followed (always true) (SVR4 only)
-fstype type	true if the file belongs to a filesystem of type “type” (OSF/1 and SVR4 only)
-group gname	true if the file belongs to the group “gname”. A numeric argument is checked against /etc/group.
-inum num	true if the file’s inode is “num”
-links n	true if the file has “n” links (integer only)
-local	true if the file resides on the local system (SVR4 only)
-mount	restricts the search to the filesystem containing the specified directory (always true) (SVR4 only)
-mtime n	true if the file was last modified “n” days ago
-name file	true if the filename matches “file”. Supports shell metacharacters (such as * and ?)
-newer file	true if the current file has been modified more recently than “file”
-nogroup	true if the file belongs to a group not in /etc/group (SVR4 only)
-nouser	true if the file belongs to a user not in the /etc/passwd file (SVR4 only)

-ok cmds	similar to -exec except "cmds" is displayed on the terminal and the user is asked whether to execute it.
-perm perms	true if file's permissions (read, write, and execute) match "perms". If a minus sign appears ahead of "perms", all modes (file type, setgid, setuid, sticky bits) are significant.
-print	prints current pathname
-prune	does not examine any files or directories in the directory structure below the pattern just matched (always true) (OSF/1 and SVR4 only)
-size n	true if file is "n" blocks long (assuming 512 bytes per block)
-type x	true if file's type is "x". Valid values are "b" (block special file), "c" (character special file), "d" (directory), "f" (regular file), and "p" (pipe).
-user name	true if file belongs to "name". Checks numeric argument against /etc/passwd.
(expr)	true if expression is true.
!	used in expressions to indicate the negation of the next option
-o	used in expressions to indicate an "inclusive or" operator (true if either argument is true or both are true).

Files:

/etc/group	group names and IDs
/etc/passwd	user names and IDs

See Also:

cpio; test

Discussion

find locates filenames matching a pattern. It recursively searches directories specified in the pathnames, and lists all matching files. To display the results on the terminal, use the -print option.

The -depth option is usually used with the -cpio option to transfer files from directories that lack write permission.

Examples

The simplest form of **find** locates a file. The command

```
find / -name letter.4 -print
```

finds all occurrences of files named letter.4 and displays their full pathnames. If there are no matches, it generates no output. The backslash makes the search begin at the root directory and continue through the entire tree.

find allows wildcards. For example,

```
find . -name chapt* -print
```

finds all files that begin with "chapt" in the current directory and all its subdirectories.

The other options work similarly. To find all files that have not been accessed in the past year, enter

```
find / -atime +365 -print
```

You can combine **find** with other shell commands using the -exec option. For example, to find all occurrences of files named "core" and remove them automatically, enter

```
find / -name core -exec rm {} \;
```

The -exec option has curly braces to indicate that it should substitute the current pathname. The backslash escapes the trailing semicolon as **find** requires.

The operators ! and -o indicate negation and inclusive "or"ing, respectively. You could use negation in a command such as

```
find / ! -atime +1 -print
```

It prints all files that are less than one day old (i.e., created in the last 24 hours). The command

```
find / \(-name *.c -o -name *.pas\) -print
```

displays all files with the suffix .c or .pas.

finger

Description:

Finds information about users

Compatibility:

OSF/1	Yes
SCO Unix	Yes
SCO Xenix	Yes
System V Release 3.2	No
System V Release 4	Yes
X/Open	No

Syntax:

finger [-bfhilmpqsw] [login ...]

Versions:

OSF/1 and SVR4: add the -h and -m options.

Options:

-b brief output format

-f suppresses printing of header lines

-h suppresses printing of the ".project" file in long format (OSF/1 and SVR4 only)

-i quick list of users and idle times

-l forces long output

-m matches arguments only on the user name (i.e., not first or last names) (OSF/1 and SVR4 only)

-p suppresses printing of the .plan file

-q quick list of users (displays login, TTY, and login time)

-s forces short output

-w forces narrow output

See Also:

last; listusers; who

Discussion:

finger displays information about users. It reports login name, full name, terminal name, terminal write status, idle time, login time, office location, and telephone number.

The idle time is in minutes if only a single integer appears, or hours and minutes if a colon appears. A "d" indicates a display in days and hours. Idle time is calculated from the last activity that occurred on the terminal.

An asterisk before the terminal name indicates that write permission is denied.

The long format occupies several lines. It provides the name of any plan given in the user's home directory .plan file, the project name given in the home directory .project file, and full account information.

Options can be combined.

Examples

A basic **finger** command has no arguments. It produces output like

Login	Name	TTY	Idle	When	Office
root	Superuser	*01		Mon 10:33	
tim	Tim Parker	*02	4	Mon 11:36	
bill	Bill Smith	*002	25	Mon 13:45	

The names and office information come from the /etc/passwd file. If they are missing, question marks appear.

The -i option (for idle time) provides the following typical output:

Login	TTY	When	Idle
root	*tty01	Mon Feb 18 10:33	
tim	*tty02	Mon Feb 18 11:36	18 minutes 6 seconds
bill	*tty001	Mon Feb 18 13:45	40 minutes 3 seconds

fixhdr

Description:

Changes headers in executable binary files

Compatibility:

OSF/1	No
SCO Unix	Yes
SCO Xenix	Yes
System V Release 3.2	No
System V Release 4	No
X/Open	No

Syntax:

fixhdr option file ...

Options:

-5x[-n]	changes the Unix 5.2 a.out format to the x.out format. The -n option passes leading underscores on symbol names unchanged.
-86x	adds x.out format to the "86rel" object module format
-ax -c [11,86]	changes the a.out format to the x.out format. The -c option specifies the target CPU type. "11" indicates a DEC PDP-11 CPU, and "86" indicates the 80x86 family CPUs.
-A num	adds or changes the load address in the x.out format to "num". "num" must be hexadecimal.
-bx	changes the b.out format to the a.out format
-C CPU	sets the CPU type. CPU can be "186", "286", "386", "8086". Some Unix versions support other CPUs.

-F num	adds or changes the fixed stack size in the x.out format to "num". "num" must be hexadecimal.
-M[smlh]	changes the memory model of the x.out or 86rel format to small (s), medium (m), large (l), or huge (h).
-r	ensures that the resolution table has a nonzero size
-s s1=s2 [-s s3=s4]	changes symbol names. s1 changes to s2, and s3 to s4.
-v[2,3,5,7]	changes the Xenix version in the header
-xa	changes the x.out format to the a.out format
-xb	changes the x.out format to the b.out format
-x4	changes the x.out format to 4.2BSD a.out format
-x5[-n]	changes the x.out format to Unix 5.2 a.out format. The -n option passes leading underscores on symbol names unchanged.

Discussion

fixhdr lets you change the format information of binary executable files. This is useful when you want to run a file from another system without modifying the source code and recompiling.

fixhdr changes the header of files created by link editors or compilers. Changes can include header format, fixed stack size, load address, and symbol names.

When making multiple modifications, do them one at a time.

Notes

fixhdr is an extension supplied by the Santa Cruz Operation.

fmt

Description:
Formats mail messages

Compatibility:

OSF/1	Yes
SCO Unix	No
SCO Xenix	No
System V Release 3.2	No
System V Release 4	No
X/Open	No

Syntax:
fmt [-width] file ...

Option:
- sets line width to "width"

Defaults:
Line width of 72 characters

See Also:
mail

Discussion
fmt reads input files and writes a copy to standard output that has lines as close to a specified width as possible. It will join and split lines to achieve this width, but it never joins paragraphs. It retains spaces. The most common use of **fmt** is to format a mail message before sending it.

Examples

To reformat letter.1 to a 30 character line width, enter

```
fmt -30 letter.1
```

fold

Description:
Sets maximum width for lines

Compatibility:

OSF/1	Yes
SCO Unix	No
SCO Xenix	No
System V Release 3.2	No
System V Release 4	Yes
X/Open	No

Syntax:
fold [-w width | -width] [file ...]

Option:
-w sets line width to "width"

Defaults:
Line width of 80 characters

Discussion
fold breaks lines that are longer than "width". It assumes standard input if no filenames are specified. The "width" should be a multiple of 8 if tabs are present. To use other values, expand tabs first.

Notes

fold accepts the width argument without the -w option. Future releases will require -w.

fold may not work correctly if the text contains underlining.

Examples

To display a file with lines broken at a width of 48, the command is

```
fold -w 48 file
```

format

Description:
Formats floppy disks and mini cartridge tapes

Compatibility:
OSF/1	No
SCO Unix	Yes
SCO Xenix	Yes
System V Release 3.2	No
System V Release 4	No
X/Open	No

Syntax:
format [-f][-n][-q][-v] [device] [-i interleave]

Options:
-f suppresses interactive formatting

-i specifies the interleave factor

-n does not verify

-q suppresses track and head output display

-v verifies format

Defaults:
The default device is /dev/rfd0.

Files:
/etc/default/device specifies the default device and whether to verify disks

See Also:
dosformat

Discussion

format lets you format floppy disks and mini cartridge tapes for Unix. You can use it interactively or from the command line.

The -f option suppresses the interactive mode. Usually, **format** waits for you to confirm that the disk is ready. The -f option initiates formatting without waiting. It still displays head and track information as it formats and verifies the disk. The -q (quiet) option suppresses this output. Using -q and -f together causes no terminal output, and proceeds with the formatting immediately. The combination is ideal for those who are completely confident and unconcerned with what is actually happening.

Notes

The **format** command formats disks for Unix only; you must format MS-DOS disks with another command (**dosformat** for SCO Unix and Xenix).

Examples

To run **format** for a specific device, put its name on the command line, as in

```
format /dev/rfd096ds15
```

This command formats a disk to quad density format. It displays the message

```
insert diskette in drive; press <RETURN> when ready
```

and waits for you to press Return. The **format** command then displays track and head numbers as it runs. If verification is active, it also displays the numbers as it verifies the disk.

from

Description:
Shows who sent a mail message

Compatibility:

OSF/1	Yes
SCO Unix	No
SCO Xenix	No
System V Release 3.2	No
System V Release 4	No
X/Open	No

Syntax:
from [-s sender] [user]

Option:
-s prints headers of all mail from sender

user examines user's mailbox instead of your own

See Also:
biff; mail

Discussion
from displays the mail header lines in your mailbox. If another user is specified (and you have permission to access the mailbox), his or her header is displayed. To select mail from only a single sender, use the -s option. You can thus find, review, or discard messages from a particular source.

Examples

The command

```
from -s bill
```

displays the headers from all mail sent from user "bill". To display all mail in your mailbox, enter

```
from
```

grep

Description:

Searches a file for a pattern

Compatibility:

OSF/1	Yes
SCO Unix	Yes
SCO Xenix	Yes
System V Release 3.2	Yes
System V Release 4	Yes
X/Open	Yes

Syntax:

grep [-bchilnqsvy] [-e expr] [-p separator] pattern [files]

Versions:

OSF/1: does not support the -h or -y option. Adds the -p, -q, and -w options.

SCO Unix and Xenix: do not support the -i option. They add the -y option.

Options:

-b	precedes each line with its block number
-c	displays only a count of matching lines
-h	suppresses the display of the filename
-i	ignores case
-l	displays only the names of files with matching lines
-n	displays each line with its number in the file
-p	displays the entire paragraph. If an argument is provided, it is used as the paragraph separator. The default is a blank line. (OSF/1 only)

-q	suppresses all output except error messages (OSF/1 only)
-s	suppresses error messages
-v	displays all lines except ones that match
-w	searches for the expression as a word, not a partial word (OSF/1 only)
-y	matches any case (SCO Unix and Xenix only)
-e expr	form required for expressions that start with a dash

Returns:

0 if it finds any matches

1 if it finds no matches

2 if it encounters a syntax or file error

Warnings:

The -y option may be inaccurate when ranges are specified in brackets.

See Also:

ed; egrep; fgrep

Discussion

grep searches files for lines that match a pattern. The patterns are limited regular expressions based on **ed**'s style. **grep** displays lines of up to 256 characters and truncates anything longer.

When searching multiple files, **grep** displays the name of the one in which the match occurs with the line (unless you use the -h option).

grep uses patterns that are limited regular expressions (i.e., it does not support all expression commands) for speed. To match full expressions, use **egrep**.

Expressions can use any valid wildcard, but be sure to avoid misinterpretation by the shell. You should place expressions inside single quotation marks.

Examples

Unix provides three commands for pattern matching. **fgrep** matches fixed strings, **grep** matches limited expressions, and **egrep** matches full expressions.

grep searches a file for a string or pattern. The command

```
grep 'Ols[e|i|o]n' chapter.1
```

matches “Olsen”, “Olsin”, or “Olson” in chapter.1.

groups

Description:

Displays a user's group memberships

Compatibility:

OSF/1	Yes
SCO Unix	No
SCO Xenix	No
System V Release 3.2	No
System V Release 4	Yes
X/Open	No

Syntax:

groups [user]

Defaults:

/etc/group is the default group file.

/etc/passwd is the user file.

See Also:

chgrp; newgrp

Discussion

groups displays all groups to which you (or a specified user) belongs.

Examples

To display all groups to which you belong, issue

```
groups
```

grpcheck

Description:
Checks group files

Compatibility:

OSF/1	Yes
SCO Unix	Yes
SCO Xenix	Yes
System V Release 3.2	No
System V Release 4	No
X/Open	No

Syntax:
grpcheck [file]

Defaults:
/etc/group is the default group file.

Files:

/etc/group	group names, numbers, and members
/etc/passwd	user names and numbers

Discussion

grpcheck verifies the group file to ensure that its entries have the proper format. If a filename is specified, it is checked instead of the default.

Groups with no logins attached (i.e., empty ones) are indicated as empty on the output.

Examples

Use **grpcheck** to verify that modifications to the group file are in the proper format, and will not prevent Unix from using them. It usually has no arguments.

hashcheck

Description:

Generates hash codes from compressed or hashed spelling lists

Compatibility:

OSF/1	No
SCO Unix	Yes
SCO Xenix	No
System V Release 3.2	Yes
System V Release 4	Yes
X/Open	No

Syntax:

[/usr/lib/spell/]hashcheck list

Arguments:

list   compressed or hashed spelling list

See Also:

hashmake; spell; spellin

Discussion

hashcheck reads compressed or hashed words and recreates the nine-digit hash codes for them. It is used with the **spell** utility.

hashcheck can be used with the **hashmake**, **spell**, and **spellin** commands to maintain spelling lists.

Examples

To read the file /usr/lib/spell/hlista (consisting of one word per line) and write the hash codes to file "hashcodes", issue

```
cat /usr/lib/spell/hlista | /usr/lib/spell/hashcheck
  >hashcodes
```

See **spellin** for an example of using **hashcheck** when adding words to a spelling list.

hashmake

Description:

Creates hash codes for spelling lists

Compatibility:

OSF/1	No
SCO Unix	Yes
SCO Xenix	No
System V Release 3.2	Yes
System V Release 4	Yes
X/Open	No

Syntax:

[/usr/lib/spell/]hashmake

See Also:

hashcheck; spell; spellin

Discussion

hashmake reads words from standard input and writes their corresponding nine-digit hash codes to standard output.

To add words to the spelling list, you must use the **spellin** command to read the hash codes. For an example, see **spellin**.

hd

Description:
Displays files in hexadecimal format

Compatibility:

OSF/1	No
SCO Unix	Yes
SCO Xenix	Yes
System V Release 3.2	No
System V Release 4	No
X/Open	No

Alternative:
In non-SCO versions, use **od** instead.

Syntax:
hd [-format] [-s offset] [-n count] [file ...]

Options:
-n count "count" is the number of bytes to process. Units appear in the table below.

-s offset starts the output at the specified "offset". It may be decimal, hexadecimal, or octal. Units appear in the table below. The offset and multiplier units may have an asterisk in-between to avoid interpretation as a "b" option.

-format valid flags are:

a	addresses
A	ASCII
b	bytes
c	characters
l	longs
w	words

For both offset and count, the default is bytes. Other valid options are:

b	half kilobytes
k	kilobytes
l	long words
w	words

Output base specifiers are:

d	decimal
o	octal
x	hexadecimal

Defaults:

The default arguments are "-abx -A".

If no output format appears, "bx" is assumed. If no base specifier appears, all three are used ("xdo"). If no output format appears, but a base specifier does, the format is set to "abclw" (all options).

See Also:

od

Discussion

hd displays a file's contents in hexadecimal, decimal, octal, or character format. The default setting shows addresses and bytes in hexadecimal, with characters printed.

Several format and base specifiers can appear in a single command.

Notes

hd is an extension supplied by the Santa Cruz Operation.

head

Description:

Prints the first lines of a file

Compatibility:

OSF/1	Yes
SCO Unix	Yes
SCO Xenix	Yes
System V Release 3.2	Yes
System V Release 4	Yes
X/Open	No

Syntax:

head [-count] [file ...]

Options:

-count number of lines to print

Defaults:

Prints 10 lines

See Also:

tail

Discussion

head displays the first few lines of the specified file. It can help you identify the contents.

Examples

The command

```
head 5 chapter.1 chapter.2 chapter.3
```

displays the first five lines of the three files.

hello

Description:

Sends a message to another user

Compatibility:

OSF/1	No
SCO Unix	Yes
SCO Xenix	Yes
System V Release 3.2	No
System V Release 4	No
X/Open	No

Syntax:

hello user [tty]

Arguments:

tty sends the message to the device if the user is logged onto more than one terminal

user valid user name

See Also:

mesg; who

Discussion

hello transmits messages between users. When one is sent, a line appears on the recipient's terminal. He or she can then send text back. Communications continue until someone sends a break (usually via the Del key).

You should use the **who** command to identify currently active users. Anyone can prohibit **hello** messages by using the **mesg** command.

If an exclamation mark starts a line of text, the shell is called to interpret it.

Notes

hello is an extension supplied by the Santa Cruz Operation.

Examples

To initiate a conversation with user "bill", enter

```
hello bill
```

Bill's terminal will display a message similar to

```
Message from tim! tty8a
```

You can then type text that is echoed to Bill's screen, and vice versa, until one of you presses Del. When this happens, the other terminal shows

```
"(end of message)"
```

The generally accepted protocol for using **hello** is to end each transmission with "o" (for over) and terminate the conversation with "oo" (over and out). Another convention uses a few line feeds to indicate that the message has ended and the sender is waiting for a reply.

help

Description:

Displays help for commands and SCCS error messages

Compatibility:

OSF/1	Yes
SCO Unix	No
SCO Xenix	Yes
System V Release 3.2	Yes
System V Release 4	No
X/Open	No

Syntax:

help [command] [errornumber]

Options:

command	command name
errornumber	SCCS message number

Files:

/usr/lib/help	files of message texts

Discussion

help displays on-screen explanations of common commands or error messages generated by SCCS.

You can specify several arguments. If you do not provide any, **help** prompts for one.

Examples

To display help for the **tar** command, enter

```
help tar
```

Nowadays Macbeth would simply type

```
help kill
```

to learn how to dispose of (process) Duncan. The computer would not even have any dramatic sieges of guilt or see blood dripping from its keyboard.

id

Description:

Prints user's name, group ID, and group name

Compatibility:

OSF/1	Yes
SCO Unix	Yes
SCO Xenix	Yes
System V Release 3.2	Yes
System V Release 4	Yes
X/Open	Yes

Syntax:

id [-a]

Versions:

SVR4: adds the -a option.

Options:

-a reports all groups to which the invoking process and user belong (SVR4 only)

See Also:

getuid; groups; logname

Discussion

id displays a person's user and group names, derived from the files /etc/passwd and /etc/group.

Examples

You can enter the **id** command at the shell prompt, or use it inside a shell script. It displays the user and group names, as in

```
uid=200(tim)    gid=51(programmers)
```

The person who issued the command is user 200 "tim", who belongs to group ID 51, called "programmers". How much more identity could a person want?

join

Description:

Joins two relations

Compatibility:

OSF/1	Yes
SCO Unix	Yes
SCO Xenix	Yes
System V Release 3.2	Yes
System V Release 4	Yes
X/Open	Yes

Syntax:

join [-a] [-e] [-j] [-o] [-t] file1 file2

Options:

-ax	besides normal output, produces a line for each unpaired line in filex (x=1,2)
-e str	replaces all empty output fields with string "str"
-jx y	joins on the yth field of filex (x=1,2). If no x appears, uses the yth field of each file.
-o list	uses the fields specified in "list" for the output line. Each entry takes the form x,y where x is the file number (x=1,2), and y the field number.
-tx	uses character x as the field separator

Defaults:

The first column is the join field.

Warnings:

Both files to be **join**ed must be in ascending ASCII sequence based on the key field, or **join** will not work properly.

See Also:

awk; comm; sort

Discussion

join displays a joining of two files. It uses standard input if one filename is a dash. Both files must be sorted on the field to be joined in increasing ASCII order, or the join will not work properly.

If no field is specified, **join** uses the first one. Fields are normally separated by spaces, tabs, or newlines. **join** ignores leading separators and multiple ones.

The output consists of a line for each pair of lines from the two files that have identical join fields. The line displays the common field and the rest of the lines.

Examples

join displays lines from two files that have the join field in common. For example, if file1 contains:

```
1  Allen
2  Brown
3  Chase
```

and file2 contains:

```
1  carpenter
2  accountant
4  clerk
```

the command

```
join file1 file2
```

produces the output:

```
1  Allen     carpenter
2  Brown     accountant
```

Only lines with the common key field (the default is the first one) appear.

kill

Description:

Terminates a process

Compatibility:

OSF/1	Yes
SCO Unix	Yes
SCO Xenix	Yes
System V Release 3.2	Yes
System V Release 4	Yes
X/Open	Yes

Syntax:

kill [-number] processid...

kill -l

Versions:

OSF/1 and SVR4: add the -l option.

Options:

number	send signal "number" instead of terminate signal
-l	displays a list of symbolic signal names (OSF/1 and SVR4 only)

Defaults:

Sends signal 15 (terminate)

See Also:

ps

Discussion

kill sends a terminate signal (signal 15) to the specified process. Its ID number must appear, or the command has no effect. You can determine process IDs from a list command, such as **ps**. Advocates of non-violence may prefer to alias the name, even though it terminates only abstractions.

A user can only **kill** a process he or she owns. The superuser can **kill** any process. So looking at the situation from a cheerful point of view, users can **kill** their children, whereas superusers can **kill** anyone (divine right of kings). Unix is hardly a modern democratic society.

Examples

Use **ps** to determine process IDs. To kill process 1127, enter

```
kill 1127
```

"Even nowadays a man can't step up and kill a woman without feeling just a bit unchivalrous." (Robert Benchley)

l

Description:

Lists directory contents with file information

Compatibility:

OSF/1	No
SCO Unix	Yes
SCO Xenix	Yes
System V Release 3.2	No
System V Release 4	No
X/Open	No

Syntax:

l [-aAbcCdfFgilnopqrRstu] dir ...

Options:

- -a lists all entries including "." (current directory) and ".." (parent directory)
- -A displays all files, including those beginning with ".", except "." (current directory) and ".." (parent directory)
- -b prints non-graphic characters in octal in "\ddd" format
- -c uses time of last modification of the inode (can be sorted with -t)
- -C forces columnar output
- -d does not list contents if argument is a directory
- -f forces arguments to be interpreted as directories (turns off -l, -r, -s, -t; turns on -a)
- -F marks directories with a trailing /, and executable files with a trailing *
- -g same as -l but does not display the owner field
- -i prints the inode number in the first column

- -l long format (includes mode, links, owner, group, size, and modification time). Lists major and minor numbers for special files.
- -n same as -l, but displays owner ID instead of owner name. When used with -g, displays group ID instead of group name.
- -o same as -l, but does not display group names
- -p puts a slash after directory names
- -q prints non-graphic characters in filenames as "?"
- -r reverses sort order
- -R lists subdirectories recursively
- -s gives size in 512-byte blocks
- -t sorts by modification time (latest first)
- -u uses last modification time (can be sorted with -t)

Defaults:

If no arguments appear, **l** displays the current working directory.

It sorts the output alphabetically by filename.

See Also:

lc; ls

Discussion

l lists the contents of each directory given as an argument. If several arguments appear, it sorts them alphabetically first.

l produces output in the same format as **ls -l**. It formats all output to 80 columns. Similar commands are **lc** and **ls**.

The mode displayed with the long format consists of 10 characters. The first one indicates the type of file:

- \- ordinary file
- b block type special file
- c character type special file
- d directory
- m shared data
- p named pipe
- s semaphore

The next nine characters are the permissions (read, write, execute) for owner, group, and others.

Examples

The command

```
l /usr/tim
```

lists the directory /usr/tim. The command

```
l -r /usr/tim
```

displays the same directory, but sorted in reverse alphabetical order.

last

Description:

Displays last logins of users or terminals

Compatibility:

OSF/1	No
SCO Unix	Yes
SCO Xenix	Yes
System V Release 3.2	No
System V Release 4	Yes
X/Open	No

Syntax:

last [-h] [-n limit] [-t tty] [-w file] [name]

Versions:

SCO Unix: adds the -h option.

Options:

-h	no headers (SCO Unix only)
-n limit	restricts the report to “limit” lines
-t tty	specifies the tty line
-w file	uses “file” instead of /etc/wtmp

Defaults:

last without arguments prints all logins and logouts in reverse chronological order.

Files:

/etc/wtmp	login database

See Also:

finger; listusers; who

Discussion

last displays a record of logins and logouts for all users or serial devices.

The output for a serial device includes login name, tty line used, device name, process ID, start time, and elapsed time.

Examples

last by itself displays the login and logout record maintained in the /etc/wtmp file. Due to the length of the display, you should pipe its output to **more** or a file. The command

```
last
```

displays the user name, line, device, process ID, login time, elapsed time, and comments. Each column has a header unless you use the -h option (SCO Unix only).

To determine activity for a specific terminal, specify its line number. For example, the command

```
last -t 02
```

lists all activity for /dev/tty02.

With a user name supplied, **last** displays only his or her activity. The command

```
last -t 02 tim
```

shows all activity by user tim on /dev/tty02. Now you can see if tim has actually been working away on his computer (even so he may have been playing Star Trek!).

lc

Description:

Lists directory contents in columns

Compatibility:

OSF/1	No
SCO Unix	Yes
SCO Xenix	Yes
System V Release 3.2	No
System V Release 4	No
X/Open	No

Syntax:

lc [-1aAbcCdfFgilmnopqrRstux] dir ...

Options:

-1 forces output to have one entry per line

-a lists all entries, including "." (current directory) and ".." (parent directory)

-A displays all files, including those beginning with ".", except "." (current directory) and ".." (parent directory)

-b prints non-graphic characters in octal in "\ddd" format

-c uses time of file creation (can be sorted with -t)

-C forces columnar output

-d does not list contents if argument is a directory

-f forces arguments to be interpreted as directories (turns off -l, -r, -s, and -t; turns on -a)

-F marks directories with a trailing /, and executable files with a trailing *

-g same as -l, but does not display the owner field

- -i prints the inode number in the first column
- -l long format (includes mode, links, owner, group, size, and modification time). Lists major and minor numbers for special files.
- -m uses stream output format
- -n same as -l, but displays owner ID instead of owner name. When used with -g, displays group ID instead of group name.
- -o same as -l, but does not display group names
- -p pads output with spaces
- -q prints non-graphic characters in filenames as ?
- -r reverses sort order
- -R lists subdirectories recursively
- -s gives size in 512-byte blocks
- -t sorts by modification time (latest first)
- -u uses last modification time (can be sorted with -t)
- -x columnar output with entries sorted across instead of down

Defaults:

If no arguments appear, **lc** displays the current working directory.

lc sorts the output alphabetically by filename.

See Also:

l; ls

Discussion

lc lists the contents of each directory specified as an argument. If several appear, it sorts them alphabetically first.

It formats the output to 80 columns.

Shorthand versions of **lc** include:

lf	same as lc -F
lr	same as lc -R
lx	same as lc -x

The mode displayed with the long format consists of 10 characters. The first one indicates the type of file:

-	ordinary file
b	block type special file
c	character type special file
d	directory
m	shared data
p	named pipe
s	semaphore

The next nine characters are the permissions (read, write, execute) for owner, group, and others.

Examples

The command

```
lc /usr/tim
```

lists the directory /usr/tim. The command

```
lc -r /usr/tim
```

displays the same directory, but sorted in reverse alphabetical order.

line

Description:

Reads one line

Compatibility:

OSF/1	Yes
SCO Unix	Yes
SCO Xenix	Yes
System V Release 3.2	Yes
System V Release 4	Yes
X/Open	Yes

Syntax:

line

Discussion

line reads a line from standard input and writes it to standard output. A newline character terminates it. Shell scripts commonly use **line** to read from a user's terminal.

line always prints a newline character on completion.

listusers

Description:

Displays user login information

Compatibility:

OSF/1	No
SCO Unix	No
SCO Xenix	No
System V Release 3.2	No
System V Release 4	Yes
X/Open	No

Syntax:

listusers [-g groups] [-l logins]

Options:

-g lists all user logins belonging to the group

-l lists all user logins

Files:

/etc/passwd user logins

See Also:

finger; last; who

Discussion

listusers with no options displays a list of all user logins. With the -g or -l option, it displays only ones belonging to the argument. It allows multiple arguments separated by commas. It sorts all displays alphabetically by login.

The -g and -l options can be combined, with logins listed just once even if they belong to more than one group. Duplicates are displayed with the first group.

Notes

listusers assumes that a user login has a UID of 100 or more.

Examples

To list all logins belonging to group “admin”, enter

```
listusers -g admin
```

ln

Description:

Links files

Compatibility:

OSF/1	Yes
SCO Unix	Yes
SCO Xenix	Yes
System V Release 3.2	Yes
System V Release 4	Yes
X/Open	Yes

Syntax:

ln [-f] [-n] [-s] file1 [file2 ...] file3

Versions:

OSF/1: supports the -f and -s options.

SVR4: supports the -n and -s options.

Options:

-f suppresses interactive prompt for mode errors (OSF/1 only)

-n does not overwrite an existing file if the linkname exists (SVR4 only)

-s creates a symbolic link (OSF/1 and SVR4 only)

See Also:

cp; mv; rm

Discussion

ln allows several directory entries to refer to the same file. A file may thus have several links. Each name is treated as the same file.

If the file to be linked does not allow writing, its name appears with a user message asking whether to proceed. You can suppress this with the -f option (OSF/1 only).

OSF/1 and SVR4 allow symbolic links to be created. A symbolic link contains the name of the file to which it is linked, and can be across filesystems.

Examples

Assume you have a file /usr/tim/chapter.1, and you want to also refer to it as /usr/book/chapter.1, the command

```
ln /usr/tim/chapter.1 /usr/book/chapter.1
```

links the two names. There is no “original” file; both names refer to the same file, and changes in either affect both.

lock

Description:

Locks a terminal using a password

Compatibility:

OSF/1	Yes
SCO Unix	Yes
SCO Xenix	Yes
System V Release 3.2	No
System V Release 4	No
X/Open	No

Syntax:

lock [-v] [-mins]

Versions:

SCO Unix and Xenix: add the -v option.

Options:

-v	verbose operation (SCO Unix and Xenix only)
-mins	sets the time limit for the lock to "mins" minutes

Discussion

lock allows a user to lock his or her terminal until a password is entered. It requests a password from the user, validates it by asking again, and then locks the terminal until that password is entered.

If a number of minutes is specified on the command line, it is how long the lock stays in force. The user is then logged out and the terminal freed. A default from the file /etc/default/lock applies if no value is specified. If the time for which the lock is requested exceeds the maximum set by the system, a message is sent to the user.

The user or the superuser may terminate a lock with a **kill** command.

Examples

To lock your terminal when you leave it, without logging out, enter

```
lock
```

lock requests a password, verifies it, then waits for you to retype it to regain control of the terminal. It ignores attempts to enter an invalid password.

To specify a ten minute lock before logging off the terminal, enter

```
lock -10
```

After ten minutes, you are logged off, and the terminal is available to others.

lock can save you from having to log back on when leaving the terminal for a few minutes, while keeping others from using it or your account. A popular command among curmudgeons, misers, and those who turn off the television set and take the remote tuner with them when they have to go to the bathroom.

login

Description:

Allows access to the system

Compatibility:

OSF/1	Yes
SCO Unix	Yes
SCO Xenix	Yes
System V Release 3.2	Yes
System V Release 4	Yes
X/Open	Yes

Syntax:

login [-d device] [name [envvar ...]]

login [-p] [name] (OSF/1 only)

login [-p] [-h host] [-f name] (OSF/1 only)

Versions:

OSF/1: Adds the -f, -h, and -p options.

SVR4: Adds the -d option.

Options:

-d	pathname of the tty port (SVR4 only)
-f	suppresses password requests (OSF/1 only)
-h	indicates the host name used by **telnet** (OSF/1 only)
-p	preserves the environment (OSF/1 only)
name	login name to be used
envvar	sets environment variables to other than default values

Defaults:

The basic environment is set to:

HOME	login directory
LOGNAME	login name
MAIL	~/mail/login
PATH	/usr/bin
SHELL	last field in /etc/passwd entry
TZ	system timezone default

See Also:

env; telnet

Discussion

login is used at the beginning of every terminal session to allow access to the system. It identifies you as a system user, and sets access permissions. **login** is usually performed automatically when a terminal is enabled.

login asks for your user name and a password, and compares your entries to those in /etc/passwd. If they match, it invokes the commands in the last field of /etc/passwd (usually a shell).

When a password is entered on a terminal, **login** turns echoing off. If you do not complete your login within a specified amount of time (usually one minute), it will disconnect silently.

login accepts the user name as an argument, as well as environment settings if they differ from the defaults or those in your initialization file (.profile or .login). When you log in successfully, **login** updates system audit files.

Users do not generally invoke **login**. The system runs it automatically for all active terminals, and starts it for all modem sessions when connected. To execute **login** as a command, you must first replace the original command interpreter by using the **exec** command.

Examples

To execute **login** for user "tim", enter

```
exec login tim PATH=/usr/bin;/bin;/usr/lib/;./
```

This command also changes the default PATH to the new value given as an argument.

logname

Description:
Gets the login name

Compatibility:

OSF/1	Yes
SCO Unix	Yes
SCO Xenix	Yes
System V Release 3.2	Yes
System V Release 4	Yes
X/Open	Yes

Syntax:
logname

See Also:
env; id; login

Discussion
logname returns the user's login name. If there is no name in the file /etc/utmp, it returns the user's ID number.

Examples
Use **logname** by typing it at the shell prompt, or from a script. The command

```
logname
```

returns the output

```
tim
```

This is useful in shell scripts, when you want to use the user's login name in a command. It resembles the marvelous mail/merge facilities that allow advertising or solicitation letters to refer to you by name as if you were an old friend.

look

Description:
Finds lines in sorted lists

Compatibility:

OSF/1	Yes
SCO Unix	No
SCO Xenix	No
System V Release 3.2	No
System V Release 4	No
X/Open	No

Syntax:
look [-d] [-f] [-tchar] string [file ...]

Options:
-d uses dictionary order with only letters, numbers, spaces, and tabs being significant in comparisons

-f ignores case

-t ignores "char" and characters following it in the search string

Defaults:
If no file is specified, **look** assumes the -d and -f options, and searches the system word list in /usr/share/dict/words.

Discussion
look searches a sorted file and displays all lines that begin with a string.

To use the -f flag (ignore case), the file must have been sorted with the **sort -f** option, too. Otherwise, **look** will display only lowercase matches.

Examples

To examine the sorted file mail.list for all lines beginning with "Parker", enter

```
look Parker mail.list
```

To search the system word list for words beginning with "error", use the command

```
look error
```

To ignore part of a search string, you can use the -t option. The command

```
look -tER PRINTER test.file
```

will search test.file for the string "PRINT". The search will ignore the letter "E" and everything after it. This option is usually used in shell scripts when several strings may appear.

lp

Description:

Sends a print request to a printer

Compatibility:

OSF/1	Yes
SCO Unix	Yes
SCO Xenix	Yes
System V Release 3.2	Yes
System V Release 4	Yes
X/Open	Yes

Syntax:

OSF/1: lp [-c] [-d dest] [-m] [-n num] [-s] [-t title] [-w] file ...

SCO Unix and SVR4: lp [-c] [-d dest] [-f form] [-H arg] [-m] [-n num] [-o opt] [-P pages] [-q level] [-s] [-S charset] [-t title] [-T] [-w] [-Y] file ...

SCO Xenix: lp [-c] [-d dest] [-m] [-n num] [opt] [-r] [-s] [-t title] [-T] [-w] file ...

SVR3.2: lp [-c] [-d dest] [-m] [-n num] [-o opt] [-s] [-t title] [-w] file ...

Arguments:

id print request number

Options:

-c copies the file and uses the copy for output

-d prints on printer "dest"

-f uses the form "form"

-H prints using one of the following options:

hold do not print until notified

	immediate	print the request next
	resume	print a held request
-L	sends request to local printer (SCO Unix only)	
-m	sends mail after printing the file	
-n	prints "num" copies of the file	
-o	uses one of the following options:	
	cpi	characters per inch
	length	page length
	lpi	lines per inch
	nobanner	no banner page
	nofilebreak	no form feeds between files
	stty	use options for the **stty** command
	width	page width
-P	prints specified pages	
-q	assigns the request to the specified priority level	
-r	deletes file after sending it to the queue	
-s	suppresses messages	
-S	uses the character set or printwheel "set"	
-t	prints "title" on the banner page	
-T	specifies the types of files to be printed	
-w	sends a message to the user after printing the file	
-y	prints using the specified mode list	

Defaults:

Uses the default printer if no destination is specified (with -d). If the destination is a class of printers, it uses the first available member.

Prints one copy of each file, unless you use the -n option.

Does not print a title unless you use -t.

Files:

/etc/default/lpd	default **lp** settings
/usr/spool/lp	print requests

See Also:

cancel; lprm; lpstat; stty

Discussion

lp sends files to be printed. A print command, coupled with options, forms a print request. Unix prints files in the order specified on the command line. If no filenames appear, it uses standard input.

Unix assigns each request a unique number, or *print request id.* It identifies the request for purposes such as cancelling, rerouting, or status reporting. When a request is sent, **lp** responds with a message such as "request id is laser-1234". -s suppresses these messages.

To change a print request, use the **lp -i** command. It uses the number to change options. If the request has been printed, the changes are ignored. If it is being printed currently, the print is cancelled, and the request is resent with the new options.

The -c option instructs **lp** to copy the file and use the copy for output. Normally, **lp** does not make a copy. Without -c, if the file is deleted before the request finishes, it will not print. Note that -c also means that changes made to the file before the request finishes are not printed. Its primary use is to obtain an interim printout of the file you are currently editing.

The -f option ensures that a specified form is in the printer. It can be a preprinted form, letterhead, overhead transparency, or any other output media. If a form is specified, **lp** will request that it be readied if it is not in place. If the destination printer does not support the specified form, the request is denied. You can combine -f with -d to print on any printer that has the correct form (see Examples).

The -S option instructs **lp** to use either the character set or the printwheel specified as an argument. **lp** rejects the request if the administrator has not defined the set. -S combined with the **-d any** option prints the request on any printer with the specified character set or printwheel.

-m sends a mail message when the print request has been completed. It is useful on systems with long print queues to avoid having to check the status of requests.

-o controls print output format according to options. The nobanner option suppresses the banner page that identifies the user and the print request id. The administrator may override this. The nofilebreak option prints files with no page break between them. The "length", "width", "lpi", and "cpi" options have arguments that specify lines, columns, inches ("i"), or centimeters ("c"). When neither "i" nor "c" appears, **lp** assumes lines or columns. The stty option uses commands that are valid for the **stty** command. You cannot combine the -o option with the -f forms option.

-R deletes the specified files after submitting them to the print queue.

-w writes a message to the user's terminal after the file has been printed. If the user is not logged in, **lp** sends mail instead. Use the -w option when print queues are long to avoid having to wait for the output.

Notes

The -H option is usually restricted to system administrators.

Examples

The -d option requires the name of either a specific printer or a class of printers. A class is a group of printers identified as a single type. When output is sent to a class, the first available printer of the type is used. If the destination is unavailable, a diagnostic message will appear. The request must be resubmitted if this occurs. To send "file" to the printer HPLaser, enter

```
lp -d HPLaser file
```

The -f option allows the use of specific types of paper, formfed preprints, or other types of material. The system administrator must have set up the printer to accept the type of form requested, or the request is cancelled and must be resubmitted. When the form is not currently on the machine, a message will appear requesting a change. When using the **-d any** option with the -f option, you can force the output to the first printer with the form mounted. The command to print "file" on any printer with the form "lhead" mounted is

```
lp -f lhead -d any file
```

The special handling options given by -H are seldom used for routine work, but both the "hold" and "resume" options are available to everyone. The "hold" command places a file in the print queue, but does not print it until a "resume" command is given. The "hold" file is kept at the end of the queue until the "resume" occurs, at which time it moves to the front. You can use the "hold" command to queue a print request (but not activate it) until you are ready to collect the output. The "immediate" option, available only to administrators, prints the request next, regardless of the queue.

The -o option provides control over the output page's appearance. You cannot use it with the -f option for forms. You can suppress the banner page with the nobanner option. The nofilebreak option is useful for printing files one after another without a page eject in-between. The size of the printed page is controlled by the "length", "width", "cpi" (characters per inch), and "lpi" (lines per inch) options. The argument should be followed by "i" for inches or "c" for centimeters.

You can combine several -o options. To print "file" with no banner page and a page length of 66 lines, enter

```
lp -o nobanner -o length=66 file
```

The command

```
lp -o length=11i -o width=8i file
```

uses a page length of 11 inches and a width of 8 inches.

The -P option prints specified pages. A filter must determine page numbers, or the entire request is ignored. You can specify the pages to be printed individually or as a range. The command

```
lp -P 1-5,8 file
```

prints pages 1 through 5, and page 8.

The -S option resembles the -f option. It allows selection of a character set or a printwheel (depending on printer type). If the specified set or wheel is not on the printer, a message prompts for a change. You can use the **-d any** option to route the print request to any printer with the specified set. If the -S option is omitted, the current printwheel or character set is used. To identify the character set or printwheel currently mounted on a printer, use the **lpstat -p -l** command.

The -t option prints a title on the banner page. For example,

```
lp -t Test file
```

prints the title "Test" on the banner page. The -T option sends special instructions to appropriate printers. For example, if a file contains commands that only an HP LaserJet can understand, it forms a special type that can be routed only to LaserJets. The system administrator can specify the types each printer can support. If no printer can support a type, a filter is used to try to print it. A -r option after -T suppresses the filter, and rejects the print request.

lpq

Description:

Displays the printer spool queue

Compatibility:

OSF/1	Yes
SCO Unix	No
SCO Xenix	No
System V Release 3.2	No
System V Release 4	No
X/Open	No

Alternative:

lpstat

Syntax:

lpq [+][number] [-l] [-Pprinter] [ID ...] [user ...]

Options:

+ displays the spool queue until it empties. **lpq** sleeps "number" seconds between scans.

-l displays information about each file in the printer request

-P specifies a particular printer

Discussion

lpq examines the printer spool queue and displays the status of requests for the system, a specified printer, or specified user. If a request ID is specified, only it is reported.

Examples

The command

```
lpq -Plaser
```

displays the spool queue for the printer "laser".

To watch the queue change, use the + option. The command

```
lpq +120 tim
```

displays the queue for all requests submitted by "tim". It will display a new report every 2 minutes (120 seconds) until the queue is empty. This format can burden the system, so use it judiciously. Besides, watching a print queue change is almost as exciting as watching ice cream melt.

lpr

Description:

Sends files to the spooling daemon for printing

Compatibility:

OSF/1	Yes
SCO Unix	No
SCO Xenix	No
System V Release 3.2	No
System V Release 4	No
X/Open	No

Alternative:

lp

Note: Many versions use **lp** and **lpr** as equivalent commands. OSF/1 separates their functions. If **lpr** is not available, use **lp**.

Syntax:

lpr [-c|d|f|g|l|n|p|t|v] [-C class] [-h] [-i number] [-j] [-J name] [-m] [-P printer] [-r] [-s] [-T title] [-wnumber] [-#number] [-1|2|3|4font] file ...

Options:

-c	assumes the files contain data from a **cifplot** filter
-C	specifies the class of printer
-d	assumes the files contain data from **tex**
-f	interprets the first character of each line as a FORTRAN carriage control character
-g	assumes the files contain plot data from **plot**
-h	suppresses the header page
-i	indents output by "number" of spaces. Defaults to 8.

-j	displays the request ID
-J	specifies the request name to appear on the header page
-l	prints control characters and suppresses page breaks
-m	sends mail after completion
-n	assumes the files contain data from **ditroff**
-p	formats the files using the **pr** filter
-P	specifies the printer to use
-r	deletes the files after completion
-s	uses symbolic links instead of copying the file to a spool area
-t	assumes the files contain data from **troff**
-T	specifies the title to be used by **pr** (used with -p)
-v	assumes the files contain raster images
-w	defines the page width for **pr**
-#	specifies the number of copies to print
-1...-4	specifies the font

See Also:

lp; lpstat; pr

Discussion

lpr uses a spooling daemon to print files when a printer becomes available. The options -c, -d, -f, -g, -l, -n, -p, -t, and -v indicate that the files are not standard text. The options are mutually exclusive.

Example

To print five copies of the files new.c and newone.c, with the title "Programs" on the header page, enter

```
lpr -#5 -T Programs new.c newone.c
```

lprint

Description:
Prints on a printer attached to the terminal

Compatibility:
OSF/1	No
SCO Unix	Yes
SCO Xenix	Yes
System V Release 3.2	No
System V Release 4	No
X/Open	No

Syntax:
lprint [-] [file]

Options:
- uses standard input

Files:
/etc/termcap terminal definitions and printer codes

See Also:
lp; lpr

Discussion
lprint accepts print requests sent to a printer attached directly to a terminal, instead of one attached to the system. Not all terminals support local printers. The printer sequences must be in the file /etc/termcap.

Notes

lprint is an extension by the Santa Cruz Operation.

lprm

Description:
Removes requests from the print spool queue

Compatibility:

OSF/1	Yes
SCO Unix	No
SCO Xenix	No
System V Release 3.2	No
System V Release 4	No
X/Open	No

Alternative:
cancel

Syntax:
lprm [-Pprinter] [-] [request-ID ...] [user ...]

Options:
- \- removes all requests from the user issuing the command
- -P specifies the printer queue to use

See Also:
cancel; lp; lpr

Discussion
lprm removes requests from the printer spooling daemon. It is usually used with a request ID or a user name as arguments. To remove all your print requests, use the - option by itself.

Examples

To remove printer request 1254 from the spool queue, enter

```
lprm 1254
```

lpstat

Description:

Provides information about print services

Compatibility:

OSF/1	Yes
SCO Unix	Yes
SCO Xenix	Yes
System V Release 3.2	Yes
System V Release 4	Yes
X/Open	Yes

Syntax:

lpstat [-a] [-c list] [-d] [-f list [-1]] [-o list [-1]] [-p list [-D] [-1]] -r [-R] [-s] [-S list [-1]] [-t] [-u users] [-v list]

Versions:

OSF/1: supports only the -a, -d, -o, -p, -r, -s, -t, -u, and -v options.

SVR4: adds the -R option.

Options:

-a displays acceptance status of printers in "list". The default is all printers.

-c displays class names and their members. The default is all classes.

-d displays the default printer

-f verifies that forms in "list" are recognized. Displays form details if -l appears.

-o displays the status of output requests. Displays more details if -l appears.

-p displays the status of printers in "list". Adds a brief description with -D or more details with -l.

-r displays the status of the print scheduler

-R displays a number showing the position of the print request in the queue (SVR4 only)

-s displays a summary including default printer, class names and members, devices, current forms, and recognized character sets and printwheels

-S displays a verification of supported character sets and printwheels recognized by the system. With -l specified, the display also shows which printers can handle the sets.

-t displays all status information

-u displays the output requests for the specified users (default is all users)

-v displays the names of specified printers and their devices. The default is all printers.

See Also:

lp

Discussion

lpstat provides information about the status of print services. Alone, it reports the status of all print requests. When used with arguments, it determines if they are valid options. If not, it assumes they are print request IDs or printer names and classes.

Examples

lpstat by itself displays a list of all print requests, and their order in the print queue. **lpstat -s** displays information about the printers and their classes, forms, and character sets. The more detailed **lpstat -t**, which provides complete information about print services, is the most common form.

The -p option displays more details about printers. The -D suboption provides brief descriptions, whereas -l gives detailed ones. The -v option displays the names and paths of printers. With no argument, it includes all printers.

-a displays the status of all printers, unless you specify a list of them. Each line indicates whether the particular printer is accepting requests. To list all printers and their classes, use the -c option. With an argument, it shows only the specified class' members.

When using forms, you should ensure that the print service recognizes their names. You can do this with the **lpstat -f** command, followed by the names to be verified. A -l after them prints the form descriptions. A similar option is -S, which displays the character sets and printwheels supported. The trailing -l option displays the printers that support each character set or printwheel, and are currently mounted.

ls

Description:

Lists directory contents with file information

Compatibility:

OSF/1	Yes
SCO Unix	Yes
SCO Xenix	Yes
System V Release 3.2	Yes
System V Release 4	Yes
X/Open	Yes

Syntax:

ls [-1ACFLRabcdfgilmnopqrstux] [names]

Versions:

OSF/1 and SVR4: add -1 and -L options.

Options:

-1 displays one entry per line (OSF/1 and SVR4 only)

-a lists all entries, including "." (current directory) and ".." (parent directory)

-A displays all files, including ones beginning with ".", except "." (current directory) and ".." (parent directory)

-b prints non-graphic characters in octal in "\ddd" format

-c uses time of last modification of the inode (can be sorted with -t)

-C forces columnar output

-d does not list contents if argument is a directory

-f forces arguments to be interpreted as directories (turns off -l, -r, -s, and -t; turns on -a)

-F marks directories with a trailing /, and executable files with a trailing *

-g same as -l, but does not display the owner field

-i prints the inode number in the first column

-l long format (includes mode, links, owner, group, size, and modification time). Lists major and minor numbers for special files.

-L if the file is a symbolic link, lists the reference, not the link (OSF/1 and SVR4 only)

-m sends output in the stream command format

-n same as -l, but displays owner ID instead of owner name. When used with -g, displays group ID instead of group name.

-o same as -l, but does not display group names

-p puts a slash after directory names

-q prints non-graphic characters in filenames as "?"

-r reverses sort order

-R lists subdirectories recursively

-s gives size in 512-byte blocks

-t sorts by modification time (latest first)

-u uses last modification time (can be sorted with -t)

-x multicolumn output with entries sorted across instead of down

Defaults:

If no arguments appear, **ls** displays the current working directory.

It sorts the output alphabetically by filename unless specified otherwise.

See Also:

dosdir; dosls; l; lc

Discussion

ls lists the contents of each directory given as an argument. If several appear, they are sorted alphabetically first. **l** and **lc** are similar.

ls formats all output to 80 columns.

The mode displayed with the long format consists of 10 characters. The first one indicates the type of file:

-	ordinary file
b	block type special file
c	character type special file
d	directory
m	shared data
p	named pipe
s	semaphore

The next nine characters are the permissions (read, write, and execute) for owner, group, and others (world).

Examples

The command

```
ls -l /usr/tim
```

produces a detailed directory listing of the contents of /usr/tim.

mail, mailx, Mail, rmail

Description:

Sends and receives messages

Compatibility:

OSF/1	Yes
SCO Unix	Yes
SCO Xenix	Yes
System V Release 3.2	Yes
System V Release 4	Yes
X/Open	Yes

Syntax:

mail [-e] [-f mailfile] [-F] [-h number] [-H] [-i] [-n] [-N] [-p] [-r address] [-R] [-s subject] [-t] [-u user] [-U] [user ...]

Versions:

The **mail**, **Mail**, **mailx**, and **rmail** commandss differ greatly even within versions. Not all options may be available despite claimed compliance to standards. There is also frequently confusion between **mail** and **Mail**. Both are often aliased.

OSF/1: adds the -H, -p, and -t options. The -r option differs.

SCO Unix: adds the -F, -h, -H, -n, -N, and -U options.

SCO Xenix: supports the -R option.

X/Open: **mail** simply displays a user's mail. **Mail** usually sends and handles mail.

Options:

- -e tests for mail. Exits with a nonzero return code if there is any and with zero if not.
- -f reads mail from filename instead of default mailbox. If no filename is specified, uses “mbox”.
- -F records messages in files named after the recipient (SCO Unix and SVR4 only)
- -h reports the number of network transfers made so far (SCO Unix only)
- -H prints header summaries only
- -i ignores interrupts (usually the Del key)
- -n does not initialize the mail system from the default “mailrc” file (SCO Unix only)
- -N does not display initial header summary (SCO Unix only)
- -p displays mail without prompting for action. Does not allow deletion, copying, or forwarding. (OSF/1 only)
- -r passes *address* to the network mail software
- -r displays mail in first-in, first-out order (OSF/1 only)
- -R causes the current session to be read-only. No changes are made to the mailbox. (SCO Xenix only)
- -s sets the mail Subject field to *subject*
- -t prefixes messages with names of all recipients (OSF/1 only)
- -u reads user’s mailbox (must have read access)
- -U converts uucp addresses to Internet standards (SCO Unix only)

Files:

/usr/lib/mail/mailrc	global startup file
$HOME/.mailrc	user’s startup file
$HOME/mbox	secondary mail file
/usr/spool/mail	primary mailbox files

See Also:

biff; mailq; uucp

Discussion

The mail commands may have slightly different names in different Unix versions. The mail facility may be **mail, mailx, Mail, rmail,** or the like. They all work similarly, but idiosyncracies often occur. Some systems have two mail programs: a full-featured version, and a stripped down one that lets users examine unread mail quickly. Your system administrator can tell you what your system has.

mail lets you send and receive electronic messages. Incoming mail is stored in a file for each user. The mailbox file is checked when you call **mail**. You also have a secondary mail file in your home directory where you can store messages for future use without cluttering your main mailbox.

When you start **mail**, you can specify options that control its behavior. The -f option lets you read your secondary mail file instead of the primary one. You can also read any other mail file you have created.

To read mail, enter **mail** and any options by itself on the command line. **mail** starts in command mode. It displays the headers of messages in your mailbox, and waits for you to enter a command.

To send mail, you specify the destination on the command line. It may include network addresses, as long as the **uucp** system is aware of the first network name. Recipients can be login names or aliased groups (see the alias command below). **mail** then switches to input mode, and waits for you to type your message. You can enter commands by beginning a new line with the escape character (usually the tilde), followed by the command. If your mail cannot be sent successfully (due to a bad recipient address, for example), the contents are saved in your home directory in the file "dead.letter". Sometimes Unix is surprisingly direct and graphic!

mail supports the following commands:

!cmd	executes the shell command "cmd" and return
#comment	null command (used for comments in .mailrc)
=	prints the current message number
?	prints a summary of available commands

alias alias name [...]	creates an alias for the given names. When alias is the recipient, the names are substituted. There may be several names to an alias. Aliases are usually set in the .mailrc file.
alt[ernates] [name...]	provides alternate names for your login. The names are removed from the list of recipients when responding to mail. With no argument, displays the current alternates.
cd [dir]	changes directory. With no argument, uses the home directory.
ch[dir] [dir]	same as cd
copy [filename]	copies current message to filename without marking the messages as saved
copy [msgs] filename	copies msgs to filename without marking the messages as saved
Copy [msgs]	saves msgs in a file named after the author. Copied messages are not marked as saved.
d[elete] [msgs]	deletes msgs. With no argument, deletes current message.
di[scard] [field]	suppresses display of header field when displaying messages
dp [msgs]	deletes specified msgs and displays the one after the last one deleted. With no argument, deletes the current message and displays the next one.
dt [msgs]	same as dp
ec[ho] string	echoes string
e[dit] [msgs]	edits msgs. With no argument, edits the current message. Places messages in a temporary file and calls the default editor.
ex[it]	exits **mail** without changing the mailbox
fi[le] [filename]	leaves the current message file and loads filename. Supports the following special characters:

	% current mailbox (default)
	%user user's mailbox
	# previous file
	& current mbox
fold[er] [filename]	same as fi
folders	displays the names of the files in the directory set by the FOLDER environment variable
fo[rward] [msg] name [...]	forwards msg to the specified users, shifting the text right by one tab stop
Fo[rward] [msg] name [...]	forwards msg to the specified users without altering text
f[rom] [msgs]	displays the header summary for msgs
g[roup] alias name [...]	same as alias
h[eaders] [+|-|msgs]	displays the current range of headers. "+" displays the next page, and "-" the previous one. Both can have a number to indicate the number of pages to skip.
hel[p]	same as ?
ho[ld] [msgs]	holds msgs in the mailbox
ig[nore] [field]	same as discard
li[st]	displays all commands without descriptions
l[pr] [msgs]	prints msgs on the default printer
m[ail] name [...]	mails a message to the specified users
M[ail] name [...]	mails a message to the specified users and keeps a copy of it in a file named after the user
mb[ox] [msgs]	sends msgs to mbox when **mail** terminates normally
n[ext] [msg]	displays the next message matching msg
pi[pe] [msgs] [cm] | [msgs] [cmd]	pipes msgs through shell command cmd. Marks the messages as read.
pre[serve] [msgs]	same as hold

P[rint] [msgs]	displays msgs on the screen, including all header fields. Overrides fields suppressed by the ignore command.
p[rint] [msgs]	displays the specified messages. Long ones can be paged through the default environment variable PAGER (default is **more**).
q[uit]	exits from **mail**, storing all marked messages in mbox
R[eply] [msgs]	replies to the specified messages. Sends reply to all recipients.
r[eply] [msg]	replies to the specified message. The Subject field is the same as the original message. Sends reply to all recipients.
S[ave] [msgs]	saves msgs in a file named after the message's author
s[ave] [msgs] [filename]	saves msgs in filename. Creates the file if it does not exist. Deletes msgs from the mailbox when **mail** terminates normally.
sh[ell]	invokes an interactive shell
si[ze] [msgs]	displays the size (in characters) of msgs
so[urce] [filename]	reads commands from filename and returns to command mode
to[p] [msgs]	displays the top few lines (default is 5) of msgs
tou[ch] [msgs]	**touch**es msgs. Will save any non-specified file in mbox.
T[ype] [msgs]	same as Print
t[ype] [msgs]	same as print
u[ndelete] [msgs]	cancels deletion of msgs
ve[rsion]	displays the current **mail** version and release date
v[isual] [msgs]	edits msgs with a screen editor (default is **vi**)
w[rite] [msgs] filename	saves msgs in filename, removing headers and trailing blank lines
x[it]	same as exit

z [+|-]	scrolls the header display forward or backward one screen

Input mode supports the following tilde escapes:

~! cmd	executes the shell command cmd
~.	terminates current message input
~:cmd	performs the command mode cmd (valid only when sending a message while reading mail)
~?	displays a list of tilde escape commands
~~< filename	reads filename into the current text
~~< !cmd	executes shell command cmd, and reads output into the current text
~|cmd	pipes the message through the shell command cmd. If the operation succeeds, the output replaces the message.
~A	inserts the Sign environment variable's autograph string
~a	same as ~A
~b name [...]	adds names to the blind carbon copy list
~c name [...]	adds names to the carbon copy list
~d	reads the dead.letter file
~e	invokes the editor
~f [msgs]	forwards msgs
~h	prompts for header fields (Subject, To, Cc, Bcc, Return-Receipt)
~i var	inserts the value of var into the text
~M [msgs]	inserts msgs into the text (valid only when sending a message while reading mail)
~m [msgs]	inserts msgs into the text, shifting the new text right one tab stop (valid only when sending a message while reading mail)
~p	prints the message
~q	quits input mode by simulating an interrupt. Saves any text in dead.letter.
~r filename	reads filename into the text

~s string	sets the Subject field to string
~t name [...]	adds names to the To list (recipients)
~v	invokes the screen editor (default is **vi**)
~w filename	saves the message in filename without header information
~x	exits input mode. Does not save contents.

Notes

Command line options are version dependent. Some may be unavailable.

Entering a subject field longer than 1024 characters causes a core dump in most **mail** versions.

Examples

To send a message to user "bill" on your own system, enter

```
mail bill
```

To send a message through **uucp** to another network, add its address (using **uucp**, Internet, or other addressing formats). For example, to send a message to tparker on system "tpci" through UUNET, enter

```
mail uunet!tpci!tparker
```

Please try this; I love getting mail (even bills, contest announcements, solicitations, and threats). **mail** asks you for the subject, then lets you enter your message. You can use any tilde escape to issue commands while composing it. You terminate the message with "." on a line by itself, or by pressing Ctrl-D.

To read mail, enter **mail** by itself. If there is mail waiting, it displays the headers of all messages. You can read from first to last by pressing Return (or typing "p").

mailq

Description:

Displays the mail queue

Compatibility:

OSF/1	Yes
SCO Unix	No
SCO Xenix	No
System V Release 3.2	No
System V Release 4	No
X/Open	No

Syntax:

mailq [-v]

Options:

-v adds priority information to the display

See Also:

mail

Discussion

mailq displays a list of messages in the mail queue. Each message appears with its identifying number, size (in bytes), the date it entered the queue, and the sender's name.

Examples

To display your mail queue, issue **mailq** by itself. The output will resemble:

```
Mail Queue (1 request)
—QID— -Size- —Q-Time———— —Sender/Recipient—
AA102365  512  Tues May 14 15:39    bill
```

The exact format varies among systems.

man

Description:

Prints documentation pages from the reference guide

Compatibility:

OSF/1	Yes
SCO Unix	Yes
SCO Xenix	No
System V Release 3.2	Yes
System V Release 4	No
X/Open	No

Syntax:

man [-abcfw] [-t format] [-p pager] [-d dir] [-T term] [section] [title]

man [-] [-f|-k key ...] [-M path] [-t] [section] [title ...] (OSF/1 only)

Options:

-	suppresses pipe through **more** (OSF/1 only)
-a	displays all matching titles
-b	leaves blank lines in output
-c	uses **col** with **man**
-d	dir adds directory "dir" to search path for entries
-f	displays only the first matching title (default mode)
-k	locates references by keyword (OSF/1 only - same as **apropos**)
-M	specifies the alternate search path (OSF/1 only)
-p pager	formats the pages using "pager" (default is pg)
-t format	passes to "format" command for formatting (except OSF/1)
-t	uses **troff** to format pages (OSF/1 only)

-T term	formats and passes to terminal definition "term"
-w	displays only the pathnames of the entries

Valid sections for **man** are:

ADM	System Administration
C	Commands
CP	Programming Commands
DOS	DOS Subroutines and Libraries
F	File Formats
HW	Hardware Dependent
LOCAL	Local Utilities
M	Miscellaneous
S	Subroutines and Libraries

See Also:

apropos; catman; more; whatis

Discussion

man locates and displays reference guide pages. With a title given (in lowercase), it searches all sections of the guides unless specified otherwise. You can separate sections by colons. **man** displays the first matching entry unless you use the -a option (except in OSF/1).

The **man** command usually filters out blank lines. The default is to display no more than two of them. The -b option suppresses the filter (except in OSF/1).

You can process the output from **man** in several ways. For example, you can specify a formatting command (such as **nroff**) with the -t option, or a page display program (such as **more**). OSF/1 uses **nroff** as the default filter unless the -t option is used, in which case it invokes **troff**.

You can search more subdirectories for custom applications by specifying them with the -d option (or -M for OSF/1).

Notes

The manual pages are in the directory /usr/man and its subdirectories. OSF/1 uses the directory /usr/share/man. Each section has two directories, called "man" and "cat" with the section name as a suffix.

Except for OSF/1, a "bin" directory relates to programs and scripts. An index file called "index" is maintained in /usr/man.

Examples

To display the reference page for the command **cat**, enter

```
man cat
```

To format the display for paging output using **more**, the command (for all versions except OSF/1) is

```
man -pmore cat
```

mesg

Description:
Allows or forbids messages to be sent to a terminal

Compatibility:

OSF/1	Yes
SCO Unix	Yes
SCO Xenix	Yes
System V Release 3.2	Yes
System V Release 4	Yes
X/Open	Yes

Syntax:
mesg [n | y]

n forbids messages

y allows messages

Returns:
0 if messages can be received

1 if they cannot

2 if there is an error

See Also:
talk; wall; write

Discussion

mesg toggles a terminal between allowing and forbidding the **write** command to display messages. Without an argument, it displays the toggle's current state. The superuser can still send messages even if you have issued **mesg n**. Some people are impossible to discourage, and the system administrator must ensure perfect attendance at his (or her) weekly birthday party and testimonial dinner (gift required!).

Examples

To prevent messages from being displayed on your terminal (by others using the **write** or **wall** command, for example), enter

```
mesg n
```

A subsequent

```
mesg y
```

allows messages.

You may want to turn messages off in full-screen applications as they can ruin displays. However, remember that you may lose important system messages. This is the Unix equivalent of silencing the bell on your telephone or unplugging it when you do not want to be disturbed. Perhaps the latest Captain Marvel comic book just reached your desk.

mkdir

Description:

Creates a directory

Compatibility:

OSF/1	Yes
SCO Unix	Yes
SCO Xenix	Yes
System V Release 3.2	Yes
System V Release 4	Yes
X/Open	Yes

Syntax:

mkdir [-m mode] [-p] directory ...

-m specifies mode

-p creates the directory and any nonexistent parent directories

Versions:

SCO Xenix: does not support the -m and -p options.

Defaults:

All new directories have mode 777 (read, write, and execute) unless changed by **umask**. The -m option lets you specify some other mode.

The directory owner and group are those of the user who issues the command.

Returns:

mkdir returns an exit code of 0 if it succeeds, and nonzero if it fails. In the case of failure, it displays a diagnostic message and stores the error code in errno.

See Also:

dosmkdir; rm; rmdir; umask

Discussion

mkdir creates a new directory. You can create several at a time by specifying them on the command line. Use the shorthand "." for the current directory, and ".." for the current parent directory. If the parent directory lacks write permission, **mkdir** will fail. It sets the owner and group IDs of the new directory to the user's.

The -p option creates nonexistent parent directories required for the specified directory.

Examples

To create two new directories called book1 and book2 under /usr/tim, enter

```
mkdir /usr/tim/book1 /usr/tim/book2
```

If you are currently in /usr/tim, the command reduces to

```
mkdir book1 book2
```

To create a new directory tree with automatic creation of parent directories, use the -p option. If /usr/tim has no subdirectories, the command

```
mkdir -p /usr/tim/book/chapter1/diagrams
```

creates /usr/tim/book and /usr/tim/book/chapter1 as well as the specified directory.

more

Description:

Displays text a screen at a time

Compatibility:

OSF/1	Yes
SCO Unix	Yes
SCO Xenix	Yes
System V Release 3.2	No
System V Release 4	Yes
X/Open	No

Alternative:

cat; page; pg

Syntax:

more [-cdflprsuvw] [-n] [+line] [+g|+/pattern] [name ...]

Versions:

OSF/1: adds the -g, -p, and -v options; does not support -r.

SCO Unix: adds the -v option.

Options:

-c	draws each new line after erasing the previous one; avoids scrolling
-d	displays verbose messages
-f	uses logical instead of screen lines (does not wrap long ones)
+g	starts at the last screen in the file (OSF/1 only)
-l	ignores form feeds
-n	uses "n" lines per screen

-p	sets the mode to no scrolling, with a screen clear between displays (equivalent to invoking **page**) (OSF/1 only)
-r	prints carriage returns as "^M"
-s	reduces multiple blank lines to one
-u	suppresses underlining
-v	displays control characters preceded by a caret (^) (OSF/1 and SCO Unix only)
-w	prompts before exiting
+line	starts at line "line"
+/pattern	starts two lines before matching "pattern"

Commands supported inside **more** include:

d, Ctrl-D	displays 11 more lines
h,?	displays help
n/string	searches for the nth occurrence of "string"
n<spacebar>	displays n more lines
n:n	skips to the nth file given in the command line
n:p	skips to the nth previous file
nf	skips n screens and displays the next one
nn	searches for the last string entered
ns	skips n lines and displays the next screen
nz	same as using the space bar but n becomes the new window size
q,Q,:q,:Q	quits **more**
v	starts **vi** at the current line
=	displays the current line number
'	returns to the point where the last search started
!cmd	executes the command "cmd"
:f	displays current filename and line number

See Also:

cat; page; pg

Discussion

more is a filter that displays text on a screen by screen basis. After each screen, it pauses and waits for the user to indicate what to do next. The message "—More—" appears at the bottom of the screen unless the end of the file has been reached. It also reports the percentage of the file that has been displayed, unless it was called by a pipe.

Pressing the Enter key makes a new line scroll at the bottom. Pressing the space bar displays the next screen.

more is similar to **page** and **pg**. They differ only in options. You can use any of them for screen-oriented file browsing.

Notes

more uses the /etc/termcap file to determine terminal characteristics. The default window size is two lines less than the total number supported, so that a 24-line display will have 22 lines of text, a header line, and a command line at the bottom. You can set the number of lines displayed with the -n option.

more tries to determine whether the file to be displayed is non-printing binary. If so, it will exit. The test is not always accurate.

Examples

more displays a large file one screenful at a time. You can use it directly on the command line, or redirect input from another command. For example

```
more file
```

displays the contents of "file", whereas

```
ls | more
```

displays the output from the **ls** command in a screen-oriented format.

mv

Description:

Moves or renames files or directories

Compatibility:

OSF/1	Yes
SCO Unix	Yes
SCO Xenix	Yes
System V Release 3.2	Yes
System V Release 4	Yes
X/Open	Yes

Syntax:

mv [-f] [-i] [--] file1 [file2 ...] target

Versions:

OSF/1: adds the -i and -- options.

SVR4: adds the -i option.

Options:

- -f suppresses interaction
- -i confirms overwrites interactively (OSF/1 and SVR4 only)
- -- interprets arguments as filenames. Allow filenames to start with a dash. (OSF/1 only)

See Also:

copy; cp; dosrm; mvdir; rm

Discussion

mv lets you either rename or move files (equivalent in Unix). The simplest form renames a file or directory by specifying the old and new names. If the destination already exists, it is overwritten without warning.

The **mv** command also moves files to another directory, retaining their original names. It cannot physically move files around filesystems, but only renames them. To move directories, use the **mvdir** command. **mv** will not move or rename anything if the target directory does not allow writing.

If the source and destination are on different filesystems, **mv** copies the file and deletes the original. It sets the copy's owner ID to that of the person initiating the command. Links attached to the original file are lost in moving across filesystems.

Examples

The command

```
mv tim.file backup.file
```

renames the file tim.file to backup.file in the current directory. If tim.file does not exist, **mv** looks for a directory by that name. If one exists, it renames it to backup.file.

An example of moving files between directories is

```
mv *.c /usr/tim/c
```

It moves all files with extension ".c" to the directory /usr/tim/c.

mvdir

Description:
Moves or renames directories

Compatibility:

OSF/1	Yes
SCO Unix	No
SCO Xenix	No
System V Release 3.2	No
System V Release 4	No
X/Open	No

Alternative:
mv

Syntax:
mvdir dir1 dir2

Arguments:

dir1	original name
dir2	new name or parent directory

See Also:
copy; cp; mv; rm

Discussion
mvdir renames directories. To use it, you must have write permission for both directories. If the second one does not exist, the first is renamed to it. If the second already exists, the first becomes a subdirectory of it (see Examples). You cannot use **mvdir** across filesystems.

Examples

The command

```
mvdir /usr/tim/books /usr/tim/handbook
```

renames /usr/tim/books to /usr/tim/handbook if /usr/tim/handbook does not already exist. If it does, then /usr/tim/books becomes a subdirectory of it (i.e., it becomes /usr/tim/handbook/books).

newform

Description:

Changes a text file's format

Compatibility:

OSF/1	No
SCO Unix	Yes
SCO Xenix	Yes
System V Release 3.2	Yes
System V Release 4	Yes
X/Open	No

Syntax:

newform [-s] [-an] [-bn] [-cchar] [-en] [-f] [-itabspec] [-ln] [-otabspec] [-pn] [file ...]

Options:

-an appends "n" characters to the end of a line. Default is the number of characters required to reach the effective line length (see -l).

-bn truncates "n" characters from the beginning of the line if the length is greater than the effective line length (see -l). Default is to truncate the number of characters necessary to reach that length when "n" is omitted.

-cchar changes the prefix and append character to "char". Default is a space (see -a and -p)

-en truncates "n" characters from the end of the line

-f writes the tab specification format line to standard output before writing any other lines

-i input tab specification: expands tabs to spaces (see tabspec below). "tabspec" may be "--", in which case tab specifications appear in the first line read. A tabspec of 0 assumes no tabs: any found are treated as -1. Default is -8.

-ln sets effective line length to "n" characters. Default is 80 if -l is not present. If -l has no argument, 72 is assumed.

-o output tab specification: expands tabs to spaces (see tabspec below). A tabspec of 0 assumes no tabs: any found are treated as -1. Default is -8.

-pn prefixes "n" characters (see -c) to the beginning of the line. Default is the number of characters required to reach the effective line length (see -l).

-s removes leading characters up to the first tab, and places up to 8 of them at the end of the line. If more than 8 were removed, the eighth one appended is an asterisk. The first tab is discarded.

tabspec four types of specification are accepted: canned, repetitive, arbitrary, and file. Column numbering always starts with 1.

Canned tabspecs appear as -code with one of the following values:

-a 1,10,16,36,72
Assembler, IBM S/370 first format

-a2 1,10,16,40,72
Assembler, IBM S/370 second format

-c 1,8,12,16,20,55
COBOL normal format

-c2 1,6,10,14,49
COBOL compact format

-c3 1,6,10,14,18,22,26,30,34,38,42,46,50,54,58,62,67
COBOL compact format

-f 1,7,11,15,19,23
FORTRAN

-p 1,5,9,13,17,21,25,29,33,37,41,45,53,57,61
PL/I

-s 1,10,55
SNOBOL

-u 1,12,20,44
Assembler, UNIVAC 1100

Repetitive tabspecs occur regularly. -n places tabs at 1+n, 1+2*n, 1+3*n, etc. The normal setting is -8.

Arbitrary tabspecs are a list of column numbers separated by commas. Up to 40 numbers can appear.

File tabspecs have a format specification in their first line. If one exists, tabs are set accordingly. Otherwise, they are set as -8.

Returns:

0 for completed execution

1 for any error

Errors:

newform errors are self-explanatory. All errors are fatal.

See Also:

dd; translate

Discussion

newform reads lines from an input file and reproduces them on standard output reformatted according to command arguments. Its common use is to change or remove language-specific formats (such as line numbers or forced tabs). Another use is to convert files from an application such as a word processor to standard ASCII format or to a form required for input into another application. For example, we might want to replace tabs with spaces. Arguments can be in any order, except for -s.

Examples

The command

```
newform -a -e -i -l text_file > new_file
```

converts text_file into a new format by expanding tabs (-i), appending spaces (-a), and truncating (-e) to a line length of 72 characters (-l). It stores the converted file as new_file.

newgrp

Description:
Changes the user's current group

Compatibility:

OSF/1	Yes
SCO Unix	Yes
SCO Xenix	Yes
System V Release 3.2	Yes
System V Release 4	Yes
X/Open	Yes

Syntax:
newgrp [-] group

Options:
- forces a new login

Defaults:
newgrp by itself switches to the user's default group in the password file.

See Also:
chgrp; groups; login

Discussion
A user can belong to several groups. However, only one is the default group he or she belongs to on login. It is assigned in the /etc/passwd file by the system administrator. **newgrp** allows the user to change to another group of which he or she is a member. The new group's permissions can then be used to control file access.

Examples

To change groups, use **newgrp** with the new group's name. The command

```
newgrp programming
```

changes you to the group "programming," assuming you are a member. If you are not, it has no effect. As Groucho Marx wrote, "I don't want to belong to any club that will accept me as a member."

To return to your default group, use **newgrp** by itself.

news

Description:

Prints news items

Compatibility:

OSF/1	Yes
SCO Unix	Yes
SCO Xenix	Yes
System V Release 3.2	Yes
System V Release 4	Yes
X/Open	Yes

Syntax:

news [-a] [-n] [-s] [item(s)]

Options:

-a prints all items

-n prints just the names of current items

-s displays how many current items exist

Discussion

news keeps users up to date with news items, usually entered by administrators. With no arguments, it displays the contents of all current files from latest to oldest.

The **news** command maintains a "currency time" in your home director. It displays only more recent items.

By default, news items are stored in files in the /usr/news directory.

To interrupt **news**, press the interrupt key. It cancels the current item, and moves to the next one. Maybe you simply don't want to see the system administrator's weekly gift registry. Two interrupts within a second of each other terminate **news**.

You can display a specific item by putting its name on the command line.

Examples

The command **news** by itself displays all system news since the last time you accessed it. Using the -a option lets you examine all news items.

The command

```
news -s
```

displays the number of unexamined news items. **news -n** displays the names of all items you have not read. “All the news that’s fit to print,” as the New York Times would say. Plus other items that are display-only.

nice

Description:

Runs a command with a specified scheduling priority

Compatibility:

OSF/1	Yes
SCO Unix	Yes
SCO Xenix	Yes
System V Release 3.2	Yes
System V Release 4	Yes
X/Open	No

Syntax:

nice [-increment] command [argument(s)]

Discussion

nice lets you execute a command with a scheduling priority other than your default value. You can use it to execute an unimportant command at a low priority. The command is uncommon; legend says that no one has ever used it (except perhaps Ralph Nader or Mother Teresa).

Each Unix process has a "nice value" set by the administrator between 0 (highest) and 39 (lowest). The default value is 20. To execute a command at a different priority, give the increment from the default. The default is 10.

Only the superuser may execute commands at higher priorities than the default. Users can specify only lower ones.

The increment cannot bring the priority below 39 or above 0.

nice is a program under the Bourne shell, but an intrinsic command of the C shell. The two differ in implementation, but do the same job.

Examples

If the default nice value is 20, and you want to execute a command at priority 25, enter

```
nice +5 command
```

The command may have arguments. If you do not specify an increment, **nice** assumes +10, so the priority is 30.

The superuser can run processes at higher priorities by using a double negative. The command

```
nice --5
```

runs a process with a nice value of 15. It will run before ones at priority 20.

nl

Description:

Adds line numbers to a file

Compatibility:

OSF/1	Yes
SCO Unix	Yes
SCO Xenix	Yes
System V Release 3.2	Yes
System V Release 4	Yes
X/Open	Yes

Syntax:

nl [-btype] [-ddelimit1 delimit2] [-ftype] [-htype] [-iincrement] [-lnum] [-nformat] [-p] [-ssep] [-vstart] [-wwidth] file

Versions:

OSF/1: adds the -d option.

Options:

-b specifies the numbering rules. Valid types are:

a	all lines
n	no line numbering
pstring	number only lines containing "string"
t	printable text only (default value)

-d uses delimit1 and delimit2 as delimiters for a logical page section (OSF/1 only)

-f same as -b but applies only to footers. The default type is "n".

-h same as -b but applies only to headers. The default type is "n".

-i numbers pages using the increment specified. The default is 1.

- -l treats "num" as the number of blank lines to be treated as a single line. The default is 1.
- -n uses the specified format for line numbering. Valid options are:
  - ln left justified with leading zeros suppressed
  - rn right justified with leading zeros suppressed (default)
  - rz right justified, keeping leading zeros
- -p does not restart numbering at page delimiters
- -s uses the specified character as a separator between the line number and the text line. The default is a tab.
- -v initial page number. The default is 1.
- -w number of characters used for the page number. The default is 6.

See Also:

pr

Discussion

nl is used to read lines from a file (or standard input if no file is specified) and display them on standard output with numbers to the left. You can control the numbering format with the -b option.

nl treats text as pages, resetting line numbers at the top of each one unless you specify the -p option. Each page has a header, body of text, and footer. You can suppress numbering of headers with the -h option, and of footers with the -f option.

Examples

The **nl** command generates output with the lines numbered. For example

```
nl -ba -p file
```

displays "file" with all lines numbered continuously (including non-text ones). The numbering is not reset on each page.

nohup

Description:

Does not allow a hangup to interrupt a process

Compatibility:

OSF/1	Yes
SCO Unix	Yes
SCO Xenix	Yes
System V Release 3.2	Yes
System V Release 4	Yes
X/Open	Yes

Syntax:

nohup command [args]

See Also:

ct; nice; signal

Discussion

nohup's usual purpose is to keep commands going on a remote system. Any specified with it will not terminate if the line connection to the terminal is broken. The process ignores hangups and quit commands.

If the terminal is not available as standard output, **nohup** redirects output to a file named nohup.out. If the current directory lacks write permission, the file goes in the user's home directory.

Examples

Use **nohup** to avoid having a process terminated by a failed terminal or modem connection. To execute the command **lp file**, for example, without interruption by a terminal disconnect, enter

```
nohup lp file
```

The command is also useful for stopping marching bands, drill teams, and football plays.

od

Description:

Displays a file in octal format

Compatibility:

OSF/1	Yes
SCO Unix	Yes
SCO Xenix	Yes
System V Release 3.2	Yes
System V Release 4	Yes
X/Open	Yes

Syntax:

od [-bcdosx] [file] [+offset[.|b]]

od [-abBcCdDefFhHiIlLopPvxX] [-s number] [-w number] [file] [+] [offset] [.] [label] (OSF/1 only)

Versions:

SCO Unix and Xenix: do not support -s option.

SVR4: adds -D, -F, -f, -O, -S, -v, and -X options.

Options:

- -a displays bytes as characters with their ASCII names (OSF/1 only)
- -b interprets bytes as octal values
- -B displays short words as octal values (OSF/1 only)
- -c interprets bytes as ASCII
- -C displays extended characters as ASCII using escape sequences (OSF/1 only)
- -d interprets words in unsigned decimal
- -D interprets long words in unsigned decimal (OSF/1 and SVR4 only)

-e displays long words as double precision floating point (OSF/1 only)

-f interprets long words in floating point (OSF/1 and SVR4 only)

-F interprets double long words in extended precision (OSF/1 and SVR4 only)

-h displays short words as unsigned hex values (OSF/1 only)

-H displays long words as unsigned hex values (OSF/1 only)

-i displays short words as signed decimal values (OSF/1 only)

-I displays long words as signed decimal values (same as -l and -L) (OSF/1 only)

-l displays long words as signed decimal values (same as -I and -L) (OSF/1 only)

-L displays long words as signed decimal values (same as -i and -l) (OSF/1 only)

-o displays short words as octal values

-O interprets long words in unsigned octal (OSF/1 and SVR4 only)

-p indicates even parity when used with -a (OSF/1 only)

-P indicates odd parity when used with -a (OSF/1 only)

-s interprets 16-bit words in signed decimal (except OSF/1)

-s looks for strings of number characters terminated with a null (OSF/1 only)

-S interprets long words in signed decimal (SVR4 only)

-v displays all data (SVR4 only)

-w specifies number of bytes to be displayed (OSF/1 only)

-x interprets words in hexadecimal

-X interprets words in hexadecimal (OSF/1 and SVR4 only)

offset specifies an offset for displaying the file. The default is octal bytes unless a period (decimal) or a “b” (blocks) is included.

See Also:

hd

Discussion

od displays a file (or standard input) in octal using a specified format. If no file name is specified, you must put a plus sign ahead of the offset.

The display terminates at an end of file character.

In practice, most users now prefer hexadecimal over the older octal format.

Examples

To display the contents of "file", interpreting words as hexadecimal values, enter

```
od -x file
```

To start at the hundredth line in the file, enter

```
od -x file +100
```

pack

Description:

Compresses files

Compatibility:

OSF/1	Yes
SCO Unix	Yes
SCO Xenix	Yes
System V Release 3.2	Yes
System V Release 4	Yes
X/Open	Yes

Syntax:

pack [-] [-f] file ...

Versions:

SCO Unix and Xenix: do not support the -f option.

Option:

-	shows diagnostic information
-f	forces packing of the file

Warning:

pack does not work on a file that is already compressed (i.e., has a ".z" suffix), has more than twelve characters in its name, has links, is a directory, or for which a ".z" file already exists.

See Also:

compress; pcat; unpack

Discussion

pack stores a file in a compressed format. It adds ".z" to the filename, preserving its permissions, date, and owner, then deletes the original file. **pack** displays a message indicating the number of files it failed to compress. It does not work on directories.

pack displays information about the compression if you include the - argument. Typically, it reduces text files by one third, but binary files little if any. Compression is effective only for files larger than three blocks.

unpack restores a packed file to its original format.

pcat displays packed files.

pack differs from **compress** in its compression algorithm (it uses Huffman rather than Lempel-Ziv coding). **pack** is more efficient.

Notes

For information about compression methods, see M. Nelson, *The Data Compression Book* (San Mateo, CA: M & T Books, 1991).

Examples

Packing is useful for seldom accessed files.

To pack a large file called (colorfully) "file", enter

```
pack file
```

This creates a new file called file.z and deletes the original. The -f option allows a set of files to be packed automatically (by a script, for example). This is useful for distribution or for creating archive floppies.

page

Description:

Displays text a screen at a time

Compatibility:

OSF/1	Yes
SCO Unix	No
SCO Xenix	No
System V Release 3.2	No
System V Release 4	Yes
X/Open	No

Syntax:

page [-cdflpsuvw] [-n] [+line] [+g|+/pattern] [name ...]

Versions:

OSF/1: adds the +g, -p, and -v options.

SVR4: adds the -r option.

Options:

-c draws each new line after erasing the previous one; avoids scrolling

-d displays verbose messages

-f uses logical instead of screen lines (does not wrap long ones)

+g starts at the last screen in the file (OSF/1 only)

-l ignores form feeds

-n uses "n" lines per screen

-p sets the mode to no scrolling, with a screen clear between displays (equivalent to invoking **page**) (OSF/1 only)

-r prints carriage returns as "^M" (SVR4 only)

-s reduces multiple blank lines to one

-u suppresses underlining

-v displays control characters preceded by a caret (^) (OSF/1 only)

-w prompts before exiting

+line starts at line “line”

+/pattern starts two lines before matching “pattern”

Commands supported inside **page** include:

d, Ctrl-D	displays 11 more lines
h,?	displays help
n/string	searches for the nth occurrence of “string”
n<spacebar>	displays n more lines
n:n	skips to the nth file given in the command line
n:p	skips to the nth previous file
nf	skips n screens and displays the next one
nn	searches for the last string entered
ns	skips n lines and displays the next screen
nz	same as using the space bar but n becomes the new window size
q,Q,:q,:Q	quits **page**
v	starts **vi** at the current line
=	displays the current line number
‘	returns to the point at which the last search started
!cmd	executes the command “cmd”
:f	displays current filename and line number

See Also:

more; pg

Discussion

page is similar to **more** and **pg**. It is a filter for displaying text on a screen by screen basis. After each screen, it pauses and waits for the user to indicate what to do next. The message "—More—" appears at the bottom of the screen unless the end of the file has been reached. It also reports the percentage of the file that has been displayed, unless it was called by a pipe.

If the user presses the Return key, another line scrolls at the bottom of the screen. Pressing the space bar displays another full screen.

Notes

page uses the /etc/termcap file to determine terminal characteristics. The default window size is two lines less than the total number supported, so that a 24 line display will have 22 lines of text, a header line, and a command line at the bottom. You can set the number of lines displayed with the -n option.

page tries to determine whether the file to be displayed is non-printing binary. If so, it exits. The test is not always accurate.

Examples

page displays a large file one screenful at a time. You can use it directly on the command line, or redirect input from another command. For example

```
page file
```

displays the contents of "file", whereas

```
ls | page
```

displays the output from **ls** in a screen-oriented format.

passwd

Description:

Changes passwords

Compatibility:

OSF/1	Yes
SCO Unix	Yes
SCO Xenix	Yes
System V Release 3.2	Yes
System V Release 4	Yes
X/Open	Yes

Syntax:

passwd [-s] [-a] [name]

passwd [-fsystem] [-rretries] [-ddialname]

passwd [-l | -d] [-f] [-nmin] [-xmax] [-w warn] name

Versions:

OSF/1: supports only the -f and -s options.

SCO Xenix: does not support arguments other than “name”.

SVR4: adds the -w option.

Options:

-a shows attributes for all entries

-d deletes the password and prevents login

-f forces the user to change passwords at next login

-F changes the password for the filesystem “system”

-l locks the password entry

-m changes the password for a dialup shell called “dialname”

-n sets minimum number of days between password changes

-r sets the number of tries the user has to change the password

-s shows password attributes (name, status, date, min, max)

-w sets number of days before a password expires to "warn". When true, a warning is displayed to the user (SVR4 only)

-x sets maximum number of days between password changes

See Also:

pwcheck

Discussion

passwd lets you change passwords, typically your own (unless you specify a user name). It asks for your old password, then the new one. It verifies the new password by asking for it again, changing passwords only upon confirmation.

Administrators can change anyone's passwords. Users cannot change others' passwords. The administrator can also control whether users can pick their own passwords, or the system chooses them.

To prevent users from simply changing their passwords back to the original values (thus subverting system requirements for new passwords), the administrator can specify a minimum time between changes. The administrator can also force all new passwords to be checked to prevent obvious words, combinations of login names, or examples from the system manual.

All passwords are valid until their expiration time is reached. Expiration dates are set by the administrator, or on the command line. If your password expires, the system will prompt you to change it the next time you log on. If you do not change it within a certain time after expiration, the system considers it to be "dead". The system locks out logins from users with dead passwords until the administrator resets them. Perhaps a modern-day Gogol would have a hero who collects expired passwords.

Some users can use the -s option to display password information, namely login name, status, last password change date, and minimum and maximum number of days for changes. Valid status values are PS for passworded or locked, LK for locked, and NP for no password.

Notes

Most **passwd** options are available only to the system administrator.

Examples

Most users will employ the simplest form of **passwd** to change their own passwords. The administrator must allow them to choose passwords, instead of having the system assign them. Also, the time must be between the minimum and maximum number of days for password changes.

To change your password, enter

```
passwd
```

and follow the command prompts to enter your new password twice.

paste

Description:
Merges lines from several files

Compatibility:

OSF/1	Yes
SCO Unix	Yes
SCO Xenix	Yes
System V Release 3.2	Yes
System V Release 4	Yes
X/Open	Yes

Syntax:
paste [-d] [-s] file1 file2 ...

Options:
- \- indicates redirection when used instead of a filename
- -d replaces joining character with specified characters
- -s merges subsequent lines instead of taking one from each file

Limitations:
Output lines are limited to 511 characters. Exceeding this causes an error message. **paste** allows a maximum of 12 input files unless you use the - option for redirection.

See Also:
cat; cut

Discussion
paste concatenates lines of input files. It considers each file as a table of columns, and connects files horizontally. Output is to standard output

unless redirected or piped. Input can be from a redirection if a hyphen appears instead of a filename on the command line.

The tab character separates columns in the new file. **paste** converts newlines to tabs except in the last column of each line, unless you use the -d option.

With the -d option, it replaces newlines with the specified characters. They immediately follow the option. If you specify several of them, **paste** uses the list in rotation repeatedly. The last character of each line is a newline, unless you specify the -s option. The list should be inside quotation marks if the shell could misinterpret it. The list of valid separators includes the sequences:

\n	newline
\t	tab
\\	backslash
\0	null string

The -s option merges subsequent lines instead of taking one from each input. It defaults to using a tab as a separator (unless you specify the -d option) and a newline at the end of each line.

paste resembles **cat**. **cat** connects files vertically, whereas **paste** connects them horizontally. The **cut** command separates columns.

Examples

The most common use of **paste** involves redirection. The command

```
ls | paste -
```

indicates that **paste** is to take its input from the pipe. It will list the output of **ls** in one column. The hyphen specifies input from the pipe.

A variation is

```
ls | paste - - -
```

which displays the directory in three columns separated by tabs.

Each hyphen tells paste to create a column of data from standard input. The first line will be in the first column, the second in the second column, etc. The result can be very confusing.

pcat

Description:

Displays packed (compressed) files

Compatibility:

OSF/1	Yes
SCO Unix	Yes
SCO Xenix	Yes
System V Release 3.2	Yes
System V Release 4	Yes
X/Open	Yes

Syntax:

pcat file ...

See Also:

cat; pack; unpack

Discussion

pcat displays packed files much as **cat** does ordinary ones. It expands them and sends them to standard output unless redirected. It does not modify the originals.

You can compress files with **pack** and expand them with **unpack**.

Examples

To display the compressed (packed) file file.z, enter

```
pcat file.z
```

The ".z" extension is assumed if not specified. To route the unpacked output to the printer, for example, enter

```
pcat file | lp
```

pg

Description:

Displays files a screen at a time

Compatibility:

OSF/1	Yes
SCO Unix	Yes
SCO Xenix	Yes
System V Release 3.2	Yes
System V Release 4	Yes
X/Open	Yes

Syntax:

pg [-number] [-cefnrs] [-pstring] [+line] [+/string/] [file ...]

Versions:

SVR4: adds the -r option.

Options:

-number	specifies the number of lines per screen
-c	homes the cursor and clears the screen before each new display
-e	eliminates the pause at the end of each file
-f	prevents line splitting
-n	eliminates the need to press the Return key after entering a command
-r	restricted mode: shell escapes not allowed (SVR4 only)
-p	string uses "string" as the prompt. %d indicates the page number
-s	displays all messages and prompts in standard mode

+line	starts at line number "line"
+/string/	starts display at the first line containing "string"

Warnings:

The **pg** command assumes tab stops set every eight characters. If they are not set, the screen may appear jumbled.

See Also:

cat; more; page

Discussion

Like **more** and **page**, **pg** displays a file on a terminal one screen at a time. It differs from other filters in that it allows both backward and forward movement. It follows each screen with a prompt. Pressing Return by itself displays the next screen.

If the output device is not a terminal, **pg** acts like **cat**, except that it displays a header at the top of each file. It treats each screen as a "page" of text.

You can move screens forward and backward with several commands. They specify the number of screens or lines involved. If no number is specified, the default is 1. To move backward, put a minus sign ahead of the number.

Commands that you may use at the prompt are:

1 or Return	displays next screen
n	displays "n"th following screen
nl	displays the next "n" lines
nd or Ctrl-D	displays next "n"th half screen
. or Ctrl-L	redisplays current screen
$	displays the last page in the file
n/string/	searches for the "n"th occurrence of "string"
n?string? or n^string^	searches backwards for the "n"th occurrence of "string"

s file	saves the output from the current file in "file"
h	displays abbreviated help screen
q or Q	quits
!cmd	executes the command "cmd"

You can modify the search commands by specifying "m" or "b" afterward. **pg** defaults to showing the line with the matching pattern at the top of the screen. The "m" argument shows it in the middle, and "b" at the bottom.

You can append modifiers for the search command after the number of matches. Valid ones are:

xn	searches the "x"th subsequent file in the command line (default is 1)
xp	searches the "x"th previous file in the command line
xw	displays a screen of text. "x" is the number of lines per screen.

The user can stop output to the screen with the interrupt key. It lets the user enter a valid **pg** command. Some output may be lost due to the flushing of buffers.

Examples

To display a large file a screen at a time, enter

```
pg filename
```

You can change the prompt **pg** displays with the -p option. The command

```
ls | pg -p"Page %d"
```

pipes the output from **ls** to **pg**, and changes the prompt to display "Page" with the page number after it.

pr

Description:

Prints files

Compatibility:

OSF/1	Yes
SCO Unix	Yes
SCO Xenix	Yes
System V Release 3.2	Yes
System V Release 4	Yes
X/Open	Yes

Syntax:

pr [z] [-adfhmprt] [-exy] [-F] [-ixy] [-ln] [-n|xy] [-on] [-sn] [-wn]

Versions:

OSF/1: adds the -x option.

SVR4: adds the -F option.

Options:

+/-z	begins printing at page "z"
-a	multicolumn output across the page
-d	double spaces
-exy	expands input tabs to positions y+1, 2y+1, 3y+1, etc. Default spacing is eight characters. If "x" appears, use it as the input tab character.
-f	uses form feeds for new pages (default is a set of line feeds)
-F	folds input lines to fit column width (set with -a or -m), or 80 columns if not specified (SVR4 only)
-h	uses the argument as the header

-ixy replaces whitespace with tabs at positions y+1, 2y+1, 3y+1, etc. If "x" appears, use it as the output tab character (default is tab).

-ln sets the length of each page to "n" lines

-m merges and prints all files together, one per column

-nxy uses line numbering of length "y" (default is 5). If "x" appears, append it to each line number.

-on offsets each line by "n" characters (default is 0)

-p pauses before printing each page

-r no diagnostic output of errors

-sn separates columns with the character "n" (default is tab)

-wn sets the line width to "n" (default is 72)

-x same as -n (OSF/1 only)

See Also:

cat; more; page; pg

Discussion

pr prints files to standard output with headers giving the file name, page number, and date and time.

pr is used to format printer output. To format screen output, use **more** or **page**.

Examples

To display two files double spaced on standard output, enter

```
pr -d file1 file2
```

The command

```
pr -2dh "Project Wombat" file1 file2
```

displays the files double spaced with two columns. The header is "Project Wombat".

ps

Description:

Process status report

Compatibility:

OSF/1	Yes
SCO Unix	Yes
SCO Xenix	Yes
System V Release 3.2	Yes
System V Release 4	Yes
X/Open	Yes

Syntax:

ps [-adefgjlmnpstu] [-oO specifier]

Versions:

OSF/1: adds the -j, -m, -o, and -O options, does not support the -n option.

Options:

-a	displays all processes except group leaders and ones attached to no terminal
-d	displays all processes except group leaders
-e	displays all processes
-f	displays a full listing with expanded details
-g list	displays processes whose leaders appear in "list"
-j	displays job control information (OSF/1 only)
-l	displays a long listing
-m	displays all threads in a task (OSF/1 only)
-n name	uses "name" as the alternate namelist (default is /unix) (not in OSF/1)

-o	uses specifier to format output (OSF/1 only)
-O	same as -o with added information (OSF/1 only)
-p list	displays processes that have their PIDs in "list"
-s dev	uses the "dev" file instead of /dev/swap
-t list	displays processes associated with terminals in "list"
-u list	displays processes whose user IDs or login names are in "list"

See Also:

kill; nice

Discussion

ps displays information about active processes. Without arguments, it displays information only about ones started by the user.

The administrator controls access to the **ps** command. Users can typically see only information about their own processes.

You can change the display's format with the -f and -l options. The columns have the following titles and meanings:

all formats:

PID	process ID	unique process ID number

full and long formats only:

C	process utilization	used for scheduling
CMD	command name	(full name and arguments given with "-f" option)
PPID	parent process ID	process ID of the parent
TIME	cumulative execution time	
TTY	controlling terminal	
UID	user ID number	displays the user ID number of the process' owner. The "-f" option displays the login name (truncated to seven characters).

long format only:

ADDR1, ADDR2		memory address of u-area processes or the disk address if nonresident. ADDR1 is the frame number for the first half of the u-area, and ADDR2 for the second half.
F	status word	indicates bits in the status word. The values are summed to form an octal number. Valid bits are: 01 in core 02 system process 04 locked in core 10 being swapped 20 being traced by another process
NI	nice value (for priority)	
PRI	priority of the process	
S	process status	Valid values are: B waiting I intermediate O nonexistent R running S sleeping T stopped Z terminated

SZ size in blocks of the core image

WCHAN event the process is waiting for. If blank, process is running.

full format only:

STIME start time of process

Notes

If a process has terminated but has a parent that is still running, **ps** will display "<defunct>". Such a process is sometimes called a *zombie*, a colorful name well-known to readers who actually have children and have asked them to wash the dishes.

The **ps** command gives only a summary, and may not reflect constant activity loads.

pwcheck

Description:
Checks the password file

Compatibility:

OSF/1	No
SCO Unix	Yes
SCO Xenix	Yes
System V Release 3.2	No
System V Release 4	No
X/Open	No

Syntax:
pwcheck [file]

Defaults:
Checks /etc/passwd unless a filename argument appears

See Also:
groups; passwd

Discussion
pwcheck checks the password file for validity and integrity. It verifies that each line has the correct number of fields, a login name, user ID, and group ID. It also verifies that a login directory is specified.

pwd

Description:

Prints working directory

Compatibility:

OSF/1	Yes
SCO Unix	Yes
SCO Xenix	Yes
System V Release 3.2	Yes
System V Release 4	Yes
X/Open	Yes

Syntax:

pwd

See Also:

cd

Discussion

pwd prints the name of the current (working) directory.

quot

Description:

Summarizes file ownership

Compatibility:

OSF/1	No
SCO Unix	Yes
SCO Xenix	Yes
System V Release 3.2	No
System V Release 4	No
X/Open	No

Syntax:

quot [-c] [-f] [-n] [filesystem]

Options:

-c displays three columns containing file size (in blocks), number of files of that size, and the cumulative total number of blocks.

-f counts the number of files and amount of disk space for each user

-n reads standard input

Limitations:

The totals for files of 499 blocks include all larger ones.

Defaults:

Examines all files in /etc/mnttab if no filesystem is specified.

Files:

/etc/mnttab	mounted filesystems
/etc/passwd	user names

See Also:

du; quota

Discussion

quot displays the number of blocks in the filesystem that each user owns.

Notes

Systems may restrict access to **quot** to administrators.

quot reports all sizes in 512-byte blocks.

Examples

quot produces a lot of output, so you should pipe it to a paging program. Typical output of

```
quot -c
```

is:

```
/dev/root
0    18    0
2    963   1966
4    257   2994
6    127   3756
etc.
```

quota

Description:

Displays disk usage and limits

Compatibility:

OSF/1	Yes
SCO Unix	No
SCO Xenix	No
System V Release 3.2	No
System V Release 4	No
X/Open	No

Syntax:

quota [-g group] [-q|-v] [-u user]

Options:

- -g displays quotas for groups of which you are a member, besides your user quotas. If a group is specified, only its quotas are displayed.
- -q displays information only for filesystems over quota. Overrides -v.
- -u displays only your quotas. If a user is specified, displays his or her quotas.
- -v displays user quotas on filesystems with no storage allocated

See Also:

du; groups; quot

Discussion

quota displays the amount of disk space you are currently using and are allowed to use (if set). You can display quotas for your groups with the -g argument. Only the superuser can display someone else's quotas.

random

Description:
Generates a random number

Compatibility:

OSF/1	No
SCO Unix	Yes
SCO Xenix	Yes
System V Release 3.2	No
System V Release 4	No
X/Open	No

Syntax:
random [-s] [scale]

Options:

-s	silent option, returns the random number as an exit value
scale	generates a number between 1 and scale

Defaults:
random by itself generates a number between 0 and 1.

Warnings:
You cannot use a scale exceeding 255. Trying to do so generates an error message, and the command terminates. (For a larger scale, use a multiplier.)

Discussion
random generates a random number to standard output. It also returns the number as the exit value. The -s option causes it to generate no output; the exit value holds the number.

To generate numbers over a wider range than the default 0 to 1, you can specify the upper limit. It cannot exceed 255.

Notes

random uses the time of day as a seed to generate the number.

Examples

To generate a random number between 1 and 10, issue

```
random 10
```

To generate a random number between 0 and 1000, issue

```
1000*random
```

rcp

Description:

Copies files across systems

Compatibility:

OSF/1	Yes
SCO Unix	Yes
SCO Xenix	Yes
System V Release 3.2	No
System V Release 4	Yes
X/Open	No

Syntax:

OSF/1 and SVR4:

rcp [-p|-r] [source:]file1 [destination:]file2

SCO Unix and Xenix:

rcp [-m] [-u [machine:]user] [source:]file1 [destination:]file2

Arguments:

source	source machine
destination	destination machine

Options:

-	indicates standard input when used instead of a source filename
-m	sends mail on completion (SCO Unix and Xenix only)
-p	tries to give copies the same modification time, access time, and modes as the original (OSF/1 and SVR4 only)
-r	copies subtrees rooted at file1: destination must be a directory (OSF/1 and SVR4 only)
-u	sends mail to "user" on the system "machine" (SCO Unix and Xenix only)

Defaults:

The -u option defaults to the user who issued the command.

Limitations:

The source machine must have read permission for the file to be copied.

The destination machine must have write permission for the directory to which the file is copied.

See Also:

remote; uupick; uuto

Discussion

rcp copies files between systems on a Micnet network (Micnet is used with SCO Unix and Xenix). It copies file1 (on machine "source") to file2 (on machine "destination"). If a machine name is omitted, the current one is assumed.

rcp handles binary files.

Remote machines require full pathnames and no wildcards.

Notes

Do not use **rcp** to copy a file onto itself, as you will corrupt it.

SCO Unix and Xenix: To set the environment properly, the network must have one of the following two lines:

```
rcp=/usr/bin/rcp
executeall; execpath=PATH=path
```

in /etc/default/micnet. "path" must contain /usr/bin.

Examples

You can use **rcp** to transfer files across a Micnet network. To transfer /usr/bob/letter.doc from the system "remote", issue

```
rcp -m remote:/usr/bob/letter.doc /usr/tim
```

This copies the file into /usr/tim on the current system.

reject

Description:

Prevents print requests from being sent to a specific printer or class of printers

Compatibility:

OSF/1	No
SCO Unix	No
SCO Xenix	Yes
System V Release 3.2	No
System V Release 4	No
X/Open	No

Syntax:

/usr/lib/reject [-r[reason]] dest

Arguments:

dest   printer name or a class of printers

Options:

-r   displays "reason" in the message to users

Files:

/usr/spool/lp/*   printer spool directories

See Also:

accept; disable; enable; lp; lpstat

Discussion

reject prevents a particular printer, or class of printers, from accepting print requests.

Notes

reject is separate only for SCO Xenix. It is incorporated into **lpstat** for other versions.

reject is usually accessible only to the system administrator.

Examples

To prevent a printer hplaser from accepting print requests, issue

```
reject -r "Toner change required" hplaser
```

When a user tries to send a print request, the message is displayed and the request rejected.

To make an entire class of printers reject commands, use its name.

remote

Description:
Executes commands on remote systems

Compatibility:

OSF/1	No
SCO Unix	Yes
SCO Xenix	Yes
System V Release 3.2	No
System V Release 4	No
X/Open	No

Syntax:
remote [-] [-f file] [-m] [-u user] machine command [arguments]

Options:
- \- uses standard input for the commands
- -f reads commands from "file" on the local system
- -m sends mail when completed
- -u sends mail to "user"

See Also:
rcp; uux

Discussion
remote allows execution of Unix commands on a remote system. It does not support wildcards.

Examples

The command

```
remote nethost lpstat -t
```

issues the command **lpstat -t** on the remote system nethost.

reset

Description:

Initializes terminals

Compatibility:

OSF/1	No
SCO Unix	No
SCO Xenix	No
System V Release 3.2	Yes
System V Release 4	No
X/Open	No

Alternative:

stty; tset

Syntax:

reset [-] [-e[c]] [-E[c]] [-i[c]] [-k[c]] [-IQrs] [-m [identity] [port][baud]:type]] [type ...]

Options:

-	prints the terminal type on the standard output
-e	uses the character "c" as the erase character. The default is Ctrl-H.
-E	same as -e except used on terminals that can backspace
-i	uses "c" as the interrupt character. The default is Ctrl-C.
-I	suppresses output of the terminal initialization string
-k	uses "c" as the kill character. The default is Ctrl-U.
-m	mapping flag for terminal port, baud, and type
-Q	suppresses **tset** messages
-r	displays the terminal type on the diagnostic output
-s	sets the shell environment variables for the terminal type

See Also:

stty; tset

Discussion

reset is similar to **tset**, and is used frequently when a program dies and leaves the terminal unresponsive. See **tset** for more details.

restor, restore

Description:

Incremental file system restorer

Compatibility:

OSF/1	No
SCO Unix	No
SCO Xenix	Yes
System V Release 3.2	No
System V Release 4	No
X/Open	No

Syntax:

restore [c|C|r|R|t|T|x|X] [k] [f|F] [arguments]

Options:

c,C verifies the tape for I/O or checksum errors. C is a more rigorous check than c.

f uses the device appearing as the next argument

F reads the specified file on the tape as the first to restore. Skips all files before it.

k size of the backup volume (next argument)

r,R adds the archive into the filesystem appearing as the next argument. R causes **restore** to ask which archive of a multivolume set to begin with.

t prints the archive date

T prints the full listing of the archive contents

x,X extracts the files named in the next argument. X retains their original names and paths. x assigns numbers to them instead.

See Also:

backup; mkfs; sddate

Discussion

restore is used to read media created with the **backup** command. You should use the r option only to restore a complete backup or add an incremental one to a newly restored filesystem.

You cannot restore an entire active root filesystem.

Notes

restore and **restor** are equivalent.

Examples

To restore from a backup, enter

```
restore
```

It assumes the default backup device. To use something else, add the f option followed by its name.

Use **restore** with the r option only with a new filesystem, using **mkfs** to create it first. A typical sequence is:

```
/etc/mkfs /dev/hd1
restore r /dev/hd1
```

rev

Description:

Reverses characters on a line

Compatibility:

OSF/1	Yes
SCO Unix	No
SCO Xenix	No
System V Release 3.2	No
System V Release 4	No
X/Open	No

Syntax:

rev [file ...]

Defaults:

Assumes standard input if no filename appears

Discussion

rev reverses the order of the characters on every line. Output is to standard output.

rev is seldom used, except to create confusing displays on a terminal.

rlogin

Description:

Remote login on TCP network services

Compatibility:

OSF/1	Yes
SCO Unix	No
SCO Xenix	No
System V Release 3.2	No
System V Release 4	Yes
X/Open	No

Alternative:

cu

Syntax:

rlogin [-e char] [-L] [-l username] [-8] hostname

Versions:

SVR4: adds the -L option.

Options:

-8 uses 8-bit data

-e uses "char" as the escape character to disconnect from the remote system

-l uses "username" for the remote login

-L allows session to be run in litout mode (SVR4 only)

Defaults:

~ as the escape (disconnect) character

Local username for remote login

7-bit data

See Also:

cu; rcp; remote; uucp

Discussion

rlogin lets you log in remotely to another machine. The hostname must be a valid machine name defined by the system administrator (usually in /etc/hosts). Several files are involved in security, and must be configured for the network and local access permissions.

Notes

rlogin works only with a TCP network service.

Examples

To remotely log in to system “merlin” as “tparker”, enter

```
login -l tparker merlin
```

rm

Description:
Deletes (removes) files or directories

Compatibility:

OSF/1	Yes
SCO Unix	Yes
SCO Xenix	Yes
System V Release 3.2	Yes
System V Release 4	Yes
X/Open	Yes

Syntax:
rm [-efir] file ...

Versions:
OSF/1: adds the -e option.

Options:
-e displays a message after deleting each file (OSF/1 only)

-f deletes files for which the user lacks write permission without prompting for confirmation

-i requests confirmation interactively for each file or directory before deleting it

-r deletes the entire contents of directories recursively along with the directories themselves

Limitations:
The file ".." cannot be deleted.

The root directory of a filesystem cannot be deleted with the -r option.

The -r recursion is limited to 17 levels of subdirectories.

See Also:
dosrm; rmdir

Discussion
rm deletes specified files. It supports wildcards. To delete a file, you must have write permission for its directory, but not necessarily read or write permission for the file itself. If you lack write permission for the file and you are at a terminal, **rm** will ask for permission to delete it unless you specify the -f option.

rm does not delete directories unless you specify the -r option. To prevent accidental deletion of directories, use the **rmdir** command instead to delete them.

To specify a filename with a hyphen as its first character, put "--" ahead of it (see Examples).

Examples
To delete file book1, enter

```
rm book1
```

assuming that you are in its directory. If not, specify the full pathname.

To delete file "-i" from a directory, use the double hyphen option

```
rm -- -i
```

Otherwise, **rm** interprets the filename as the -i option.

rmdir

Description:
Deletes directories

Compatibility:

OSF/1	Yes
SCO Unix	Yes
SCO Xenix	Yes
System V Release 3.2	Yes
System V Release 4	Yes
X/Open	Yes

Syntax:
rmdir [-p] [-s] dir ...

Versions:
OSF/1 and X/Open: do not support the -p or -s options.

Options:
-p deletes the directory and any empty parent directories

-s suppresses messages

Returns:
Nonzero exit code if it fails, 0 if it succeeds

See Also:
dosrmdir; rm

Discussion

rmdir deletes all files in a directory, along with the directory itself. If the sticky bit of the parent directory is set, deletion can occur only if the user owns that directory, the directory to be deleted is owned or writable by the user, or the superuser issues the command.

The -p option allows the deletion of all parent directories that become empty because of **rmdir**. A message indicates the extent of the deletion, unless you use the -s option.

rmdir will not delete the root directory of a mounted filesystem.

Examples

The command

```
rmdir -p /usr/tim/book/chapter1/tables
```

deletes all files in /usr/tim/book/chapter1/tables and deletes the directory "tables". If the deletion empties any parent directories, it removes them also.

rwho

Description:
Lists users logged into hosts on the local network

Compatibility:

OSF/1	Yes
SCO Unix	No
SCO Xenix	No
System V Release 3.2	No
System V Release 4	No
X/Open	No

Syntax:
rwho [-a]

Options:
-a include all users

See Also:
who

Discussion

rwho displays the user name, host name, and start date and time for each user on the local network who is logged into a host. It displays only those who have been active in the past hour unless you specify the -a option.

rwho displays status information every three minutes for each network host until it is cancelled.

rwho uses a lot of system resources, so the system administrator may restrict access to it. In any case, use it carefully.

sddate

Description:

Displays and sets backup dates

Compatibility:

OSF/1	No
SCO Unix	Yes
SCO Xenix	Yes
System V Release 3.2	No
System V Release 4	No
X/Open	No

Syntax:

sddate [name level date]

Arguments:

name	last component of the device pathname
level	backup level (0-9)
date	date in the form "mmddhhmm[yy]"

Files:

/etc/ddate	backup dates

See Also:

backup; restore

Discussion

If no arguments appear, **sddate** displays the contents of /etc/ddate.

If you specify arguments, **sddate** makes or replaces the entry in /etc/ddate for the device.

Examples

To set the backup date for the root hard disk (rhd0) to December 25th at 8:00 am, enter

```
sddate rhd0 0 12250800
```

This sets the backup level to 0 (full backup). That should keep Bob Cratchit and his computer busy all day. Bah, humbug!

sdiff

Description:
Compares files side by side

Compatibility:

OSF/1	Yes
SCO Unix	Yes
SCO Xenix	Yes
System V Release 3.2	Yes
System V Release 4	Yes
X/Open	No

Syntax:
sdiff [-losw] file1 file2

Options:
-l prints only the left side of identical lines

-o uses the next argument as the name of a file containing identical lines from the merged files. Prints differences. After each line, the user must enter one of the following commands:

- e calls the editor with a zero length file
- e b calls the editor with a concatenation of both columns
- e l calls the editor with the left column
- e r calls the editor with the right column
- l appends left column to output
- q quits **sdiff**
- r appends right column to output
- s does not print identical lines
- v prints identical lines

-s does not print identical lines

-w uses the next argument as the output width. Default is 130 characters.

See Also:

diff

Discussion

sdiff uses **diff** to produce a side by side display of all lines in two files. Each appears with a space between the sides if it is in both files, a "<" character if it is only in the first file, or a ">" character if it is only in the second file.

The -o option sends output to another file. **sdiff** copies all identical lines to the output automatically; it displays ones that differ on the terminal and uses a % to indicate that it is waiting for a command (see Options). If you call the editor from this prompt, the resulting file is appended to the output file.

sdiff and **diff** have similar purposes, but many users find **sdiff**'s output easier to understand.

Examples

Suppose two files contain the following lines:

```
Allen       Allen
Cramer      Drew
Drew        Jones
```

and you compare them with

```
sdiff file1 file2
```

the output is

```
file1    |   file2
Allen        Allen
Cramer   <
Drew         Drew
         >   Jones
```

sed

Description:
Edits a file according to a command script

Compatibility:

OSF/1	Yes
SCO Unix	Yes
SCO Xenix	Yes
System V Release 3.2	Yes
System V Release 4	Yes
X/Open	Yes

Syntax:
sed [-e script] [-f file] [-n] [file ...]

Options:
-e specifies the command script

-f uses file to obtain script commands

-n suppresses output

See Also:
awk; ed; egrep; fgrep; grep

Discussion
sed uses a "stream editor" to edit an input file according to a series of script commands. Usually, it copies each input line into a "pattern space" (buffer) and executes all commands that affect it. It then copies the resulting line to the output (unless -n appears) and deletes the pattern space.

Script commands have the form:

```
[address [, address]] function [arguments]
```

where address is either a decimal number specifying the input lines, the symbol $ referring to the last line, or a pattern to be matched. Patterns are specified as with the **ed** command.

sed is a text processing command, and most Unix reference material describes it in both the User's Guide and the Text Processing Guide.

Examples

To perform a global search for the string "1991" in file AnnRpt91 and replace it with the string "1992", the command is

```
sed "s/1991/1992/g" AnnRpt91 > AnnRpt92
```

The pattern follows the format for **ed** ("s" triggers the search, and "g" causes it to be global), and here the output is saved in a file AnnRpt92. Similarly you could replace "Second" with "Third" in a quarterly report or "Stinky Steve's Garbage Haulers" with "Adelson Solid Waste Disposal" to make a business sound more respectable.

You can use **sed** to display lines that match a criteria. The command

```
sed -n "/Unix/p" Chapter_1
```

displays all lines in Chapter_1 that contain the string "Unix". The -n option prevents **sed** from displaying non-matching lines. Without it, **sed** would display all lines in Chapter_1, repeating the matches.

size

Description:

Displays section sizes of binary files

Compatibility:

OSF/1	Yes
SCO Unix	No
SCO Xenix	No
System V Release 3.2	Yes
System V Release 4	No
X/Open	No

Syntax:

size [-d|-o|-x] [-f] [-V] [file ...]

Versions:

OSF/1: adds the -d and -f options.

Options:

-d displays in decimal (OSF/1 only)

-f displays the section name after its size (OSF/1 only)

-o displays in octal

-V displays version information

-x displays in hexadecimal

Defaults:

Decimal display

Discussion

size displays size information for each section (text, data, and uninitialized data) of a binary file. It also displays the file's total size. If the input is an archive file, all its components appear.

sleep

Description:

Suspends execution

Compatibility:

OSF/1	Yes
SCO Unix	Yes
SCO Xenix	Yes
System V Release 3.2	Yes
System V Release 4	Yes
X/Open	Yes

Syntax:

sleep time

Discussion

sleep suspends execution for a specified number of seconds. It is used primarily in shell script programming to execute a command after a certain amount of time, or to repeat a command at regular intervals.

The amount of time should not exceed 65,536 seconds. If it does, **sleep** reduces it arbitrarily below that value.

Examples

sleep usually appears in shell scripts. The simple program:

```
while true
do
        who
        sleep 600
done
```

displays who is on the system (using the command **who**) every ten minutes (600 seconds) until terminated.

sleep can delay the processing of a background command. The command

```
(sleep 600; cmd)&
```

uses the ampersand to submit the commands in parentheses to the shell. It executes “cmd” ten minutes after submission.

sort

Description:

Sorts or merges files

Compatibility:

OSF/1	Yes
SCO Unix	Yes
SCO Xenix	Yes
System V Release 3.2	Yes
System V Release 4	Yes
X/Open	Yes

Syntax:

sort [-cmu] [-dfiMnr] [-ooutput] [-ymem] [-zrec] [-b|tx] [+pos1] [-pos2] [file ...]

OSF/1:

sort [-Abcdfimnru] [-ooutput] [-tchar] [-Tdir] [-ymem] [-zrec] [+pos1] [-pos2] [file ...]

Options:

-A uses each character's value for the sort (OSF/1 only)

-b ignores leading spaces and tabs in key comparisons

-c checks if the input file is already sorted. If so, it generates no output.

-d uses collating sequence (letters, digits, and spaces)

-f ignores case

-i sorts only characters in the octal range 040-0176 (printing characters and space, ignores nonprinting ones)

-m merges only with no sorting (files are presumably already sorted)

-M compares as months, using the first three nonblank characters converted to uppercase. Invalid fields precede "JAN".

-n sorts an initial numeric string in arithmetic order. Implies the -b option.

-o sends output to the argument. The default is standard output. The input and output filenames may be the same.

-r reverses the specified sort order

-t uses "char" as the field separator

-T places temporary files in "dir" (OSF/1 only)

-u produces unique entries only, suppressing duplicates

-y takes the argument as the memory in kilobytes to use for the sort (unless it exceeds system limits). The default is the maximum amount. Without the -y option, **sort** starts with a default amount of RAM and uses more as needed.

-z uses the argument as the buffer size for a merge. The default is the longest line from the sort. Longer ones cause an abort.

Defaults:

All **sort** comparisons use a single default key specified on the input line. Without it, **sort** uses the entire line and sorts according to a specified default (set by the system administrator). It is usually dictionary order.

See Also:

comm; join; uniq

Discussion

sort sorts lines in a file, and merges sorted files. It organizes lines of input files into a specified order and writes the results to standard output. If "-" appears instead of a filename, **sort** uses standard input. The -o option directs output to a file.

The sort orders are:

dictionary sort: uses letters, numbers, and spaces or tabs. Case is significant. The -b option causes leading spaces or tabs to be ignored, but all others remain significant.

folded order: ignores case for letters, assuming them to be uppercase for comparisons.

months:	interprets the first three non-blank characters of each line as a month abbreviation. It uses calendar order, so JAN precedes FEB, MAR, etc. DEC is the highest value. It treats non-matching abbreviations as coming before January, so errors such as "FEV', "FBR", or "SPT" appear at the start of the list (or at the end if reversed).
numeric:	assumes that the line contains an initial numeric string on which to base the sort order. This option ignores leading blanks. The string can include a sign and a decimal point.
reverse:	reverses the order of comparison

The -i option instructs **sort** to ignore nonprinting characters in comparisons.

The sorting option specified on the command line applies throughout the file unless you specify a local key using the +pos1 and -pos2 options. The local key applies to all entries between pos1 and pos2 (usually column numbers) inclusive. If pos2 is omitted, the end of the line is assumed.

To check if a file is already sorted, use the -c option. If it is, no output is generated. This is handy when using the -m (merge only) option.

The -u option suppresses duplicate entries with the same key.

Examples

To sort a file of several lines into alphabetical order, ignoring case, enter

```
sort -f filename
```

To sort a file with several columns into order based on the third one, enter

```
sort +2 -3 filename
```

spell

Description:
Finds spelling errors

Compatibility:

OSF/1	Yes
SCO Unix	Yes
SCO Xenix	No
System V Release 3.2	Yes
System V Release 4	Yes
X/Open	Yes

Syntax:
spell [-b] [-i] [-l] [-v] [-x] [-d hash] [-s stop] [-h history] [+local_file] [file ...]

Versions:
OSF/1: adds the -d, -h, and -s options.

Options:
-b British spelling (“colour”, “synchronise”, “theatre”, etc.)

-d uses “hash” as the alternate spelling list (OSF/1 only)

-h uses “history” as the alternate history list (OSF/1 only)

-i ignores all chains of included files

-l follows all chains of included files

-s uses “stop” as the alternate stop list (OSF/1 only)

-v displays words not in the spelling list with plausible derivatives

-x displays plausible stems for each word

+local_file removes words in the list from the output

Defaults:

Uses standard input if no file is specified.

spell follows all chains of included files except ones beginning with /usr/lib. -l forces it to follow them also.

See Also:

hashcheck; hashmake; spellin; spellout

Discussion

spell collects words from input files and checks them against a spelling list. It displays all words that are not in the list and not derivable from it.

spell ignores most constructions from the **eqn**, **tbl**, and **troff** programs.

You can create a file of words that **spell** is to ignore and specify it on the command line. The file should be sorted alphabetically, with one word per line.

Spelling lists on most systems are in /usr/lib/spell/hlista or /usr/lib/spell/hlistb. On OSF/1 systems, they are in /usr/lbin/spell.

spellin

Description:

Reads hash codes and writes a compressed spelling list

Compatibility:

OSF/1	Yes
SCO Unix	Yes
SCO Xenix	No
System V Release 3.2	Yes
System V Release 4	Yes
X/Open	No

Syntax:

spellin x

Arguments:

x   number of codes to read

See Also:

hashcheck; hashmake; spell

Discussion

spellin reads hash codes from standard input and writes a compressed spelling list for use with **spell**.

Examples

To add the words in "newwords" to the dictionary /usr/lib/spell/hlista, enter the following commands:

```
cd  /usr/lib/spell
cat newwords | ./hashmake | sort -u > newwords.codes
cat hlista | ./hashcheck > hashcodes.old
cat newwords.codes hashcode.old | sort -u > hashcodes.new
cat hashcodes.new | ./spellin 'cat newhash | wc -l' > hlist
```

After you switch to the /usr/lib/spell directory (to shorten pathnames), **hashmake** generates a set of hash codes that are sorted by **sort** and saved as newwords.codes. **hashcheck** converts the existing spelling list to hash codes, and saves them as hashcodes.old. The lists are then combined, resorted, and saved as hashcodes.new. **spellin** generates the spelling list hlist, which can be copied over the original hlista.

spellout

Description:
Displays words missing from the spelling list

Compatibility:

OSF/1	Yes
SCO Unix	No
SCO Xenix	No
System V Release 3.2	No
System V Release 4	No
X/Open	No

Syntax:
spellout [-d] list

Options:
-d displays words that are in the spelling list (reverses command)

See Also:
hashcheck; hashmake; spell

Discussion
spellout looks up words from the input and compares them to the spelling hash list. It displays any missing ones unless you use the -d option.

spline

Description:

Interpolates a smooth curve

Compatibility:

OSF/1	No
SCO Unix	Yes
SCO Xenix	No
System V Release 3.2	Yes
System V Release 4	No
X/Open	Yes

Syntax:

spline [-aknpx] [file ...]

Options:

- -a supplies abscissas automatically with spacing given by an argument (default is 1)
- -k uses the constant k in the boundary value computation
- -n spaces the output points so n intervals occur between the x limits. The default value is 100.
- -p makes the output periodic
- -x next argument(s) are lower (and upper) x limits. They are normally determined from the data.

Discussion

spline takes pairs of numbers from a file or standard input and treats them as abscissas and ordinates of a function. The input points are completed with Ctrl-D. **spline** produces a set of coordinates that are approximately equally spaced and include the input values.

The **spline** command generates two continuous derivatives. It provides enough points to make the curves appear smooth when plotted. This is important in graphics applications such as font generation.

With the -p option, **spline** matches derivatives at both ends (so the first and last values agree under normal conditions).

If the input data is not monotonic, **spline** reproduces it without interpolating extra points. There is a limit of 1000 input points.

Examples

For a simple example, enter

```
spline
1,1
2,4
3,9
4,16
5,25
Ctrl-D
```

spline will generate 100 points lying on the curve y=x^2. To save the output in a file, redirect it, as in

```
spline > points
```

When redirected, no output appears on the terminal.

split

Description:
Divides a file into pieces

Compatibility:

OSF/1	Yes
SCO Unix	Yes
SCO Xenix	Yes
System V Release 3.2	Yes
System V Release 4	Yes
X/Open	Yes

Syntax:
split [-n] [file [outname]]

Options:
-n specifies the length in lines of each piece. The default is 1000.

See Also:
bfs; csplit

Discussion
split reads a specified file or standard input, and divides it into pieces of 1000 lines (or the length specified with the -n option).

split stores the first piece in the file "outname" if specified, or "x" if not, with the letters "aa" appended. Subsequent pieces have names with the appended letters increasing alphabetically.

Examples

If the file "points" consists of 1000 lines, to break it into smaller files of 200 lines each, issue

```
split -200 points
```

The new files have the obscure names "xaa", "xab", "xac", "xad", and "xae" unless you specify a more meaningful base, as in

```
split -200 points out
```

which saves the output in "outaa", "outab", etc.

strings

Description:
Finds printable strings in an object file

Compatibility:

OSF/1	Yes
SCO Unix	Yes
SCO Xenix	No
System V Release 3.2	Yes
System V Release 4	Yes
X/Open	No

Syntax:
strings [-] [-a] [-o] [-num] file ...

Versions:
OSF/1 and SVR4: use the -a option instead of - (not supported).

Options:

-	examines all of a file (SCO Unix and SVR3.2 only)
-a	looks everywhere in the file, otherwise looks only in initialized data space of object files (OSF/1 and SVR4 only)
-o	precedes strings with their decimal offset in the file
-num	uses "num" as the minimum string length. Default is 4.

Discussion
strings searches a binary file for ASCII strings. It considers a "string" to be any sequence of four (unless changed with the -num option) or more printing characters ending with a newline or null character.

strings examines only the initialized data space unless you use the "-" option to specify the entire file.

stty

Description:

Sets options for a terminal

Compatibility:

OSF/1	Yes
SCO Unix	Yes
SCO Xenix	Yes
System V Release 3.2	Yes
System V Release 4	Yes
X/Open	Yes

Syntax:

stty [-a] [-f device] [-g] [options]

Versions:

OSF/1: adds the -f option.

Options:

-a reports all option settings

-f uses "device" as an alternate output device (OSF/1 only)

-g reports option settings as hexadecimal codes

Discussion

stty sets terminal options. Without an argument, it reports the current settings of some options. The -a option reports all settings.

Valid options are:

Control Modes:

0	hangs up the telephone line
50 75 110 134 150 200 300 600 1200 1800 2400 4800 9600 19200	sets the terminal baud rate
clocal (-clocal)	assumes a line without (with) modem control
cread (-cread)	enables (disables) the receiver
cs5, cs6, cs7, cs8	selects the size of characters in bits
cstopb (-cstopb)	uses two (one) stop bits per character
ctsflow (-ctsflow)	enables (disables) CTS protocol
hup (-hup)	hangs up (does not hang up) line on closing
hupcl (-hupcl)	hangs up (does not hang up) line on closing
ispeed 50 75 110 134 150 200 300 600 1200 1800 2400 4800 9600 19200	sets terminal input baud rate
ospeed 50 75 110 134 150 200 300 600 1200 1800 2400 4800 9600 19200	sets terminal output baud rate
parenb (-parenb)	enables (disables) parity
parodd (-parodd)	selects odd (even) parity
rtsflow (-rtsflow)	enables (disables) RTS signalling

Input Modes:

brkint (-brkint)	signals (does not signal) Interrupt on break
icrnl (-icrnl)	maps (does not map) carriage return to newline
ignbrk (-ignbrk)	ignores (does not ignore) break
igncr (-igncr)	ignores (does not ignore) carriage return
ignpar (-ignpar)	ignores (does not ignore) parity errors
inlcr (-inlclr)	maps (does not map) newline to carriage return
inpck (-inpck)	enables (disables) input parity checking
istrip (-istrip)	strips (does not strip) input characters to 7 bits
iuclc (-iuclc)	maps (does not map) uppercase to lowercase
ixany (-ixany)	allows (prohibits) any character to restart output
ixoff (-ixoff)	requests the system send (not send) DC1/DC3 characters when the input queue is nearly empty or full.

ixon (-ixon)	enables (disables) DC1/DC3 (STOP/START)
parmrk (-parmrk)	marks (does not mark) parity errors

Output Modes:

bs0 bs1	type of delay for backspaces
cr0 cr1 cr2 cr3	type of delay for carriage returns
ff0 ff1	type of delay for form feeds
nl0 nl1	type of delay for line feeds
ocrnl (-ocrnl)	maps (does not map) carriage return to newline
ofdel (-ofdel)	fill characters are DELETEs (NULs)
ofill (-ofill)	uses fill characters (uses timing) for delays
olcuc (-olcuc)	maps (does not map) lowercase to uppercase
onlcr (-onlclr)	maps (does not map) newline to carriage return and newline
onlret (-onlret)	newline performs (does not perform) carriage return function
onocr (-onocr)	does not (does) write carriage returns in column zero
opost (-opost)	postprocesses (ignores all output modes)
tab0 tab1 tab2 tab3	selects type of delay for tabs
vt0 vt1	type of vertical tabs

Local Modes:

echo (-echo)	echoes (does not echo) every character
echoe (-echoe)	echoes (does not echo) ERASE character as spaces
echok (-echok)	echoes (does not echo) newline after KILL
echol (-echol)	echoes (does not echo) newline
icanon (-icanon)	enables (disables) canonical input
iexten (-iexten)	enables (disables) extended implementation function
isig (-isig)	enables (disables) checking of characters against INTERRUPT and QUIT
ixany (-ixany)	allows (prohibits) any character to restart output

ixoff (-ixoff)	requests the system send (not send) DC1/DC3 characters when the input queue is nearly empty or full.
ixon (-ixon)	enables (disables) DC1/DC3 (STOP/START)
noflsh (-noflsh)	disables (enables) flush after INTERRUPT or QUIT
parmrk (-parmrk)	marks (does not mark) parity errors
tostop (-tostop)	disables (enables) background process to write to terminal only if job control is supported
xcase (-xcase)	unprocessed case maps (does not map) uppercase to lowercase

Control Assignments:

Ctrl-Char C	sets a control character (erase, eof, eol, interrupt, kill, quit, suspend, or switch) to C. If C is preceded by a caret and escaped from the shell, the sequence is the corresponding control character.
min x, time x	used with -icanon to set read request or timeout delays. x is between 0 and 127.

Combination Modes:

ek	resets ERASE and KILL characters to Ctrl-H and Ctrl-U
evenp, parity	enables parenb and cs7
lcase, LCASE (-lcase, -LCASE)	sets (unsets) iuclc, olcuc, and xcase
nl (-nl)	unsets (sets) icrnl, onlcr. -nl also unsets igncr, inlcr, ocrnl, and onlret.
oddp	enables cs7, parenb, and parodd
-parity, -evenp, -oddp	disables parenb and sets cs8
raw (-raw, cooked)	enables (disables) raw I/O
sane	resets all modes to default values
tabs (-tabs, tab3)	preserves tabs (expands tabs to spaces)
term	sets all modes suitable for specific terminals

Notes

stty does not check whether combinations make sense.

Examples

A frequent use of **stty** is to reset a terminal that has its attributes scrambled (is displaying garbage or not printing properly). Issuing

```
stty sane
```

resets the terminal to standard values.

su

Description:

Makes the user another user or superuser

Compatibility:

OSF/1	Yes
SCO Unix	Yes
SCO Xenix	Yes
System V Release 3.2	Yes
System V Release 4	Yes
X/Open	Yes

Syntax:

su [-] [-f] [name [args ...]]

Versions:

OSF/1: adds the -f option.

Options:

-	changes environment to the new user's
-f	prevents **csh** (the C shell) from executing .cshrc (OSF/1 only)
name	user to log in as
args	passes "args" to shell

Discussion

su allows a user with the proper permissions to log in as another user without logging off. If no "name" is specified, **su** assumes you want to log in as "root".

Users cannot use **su** to indiscriminately log in under other identities. It primarily allows the following:

- the superuser to log in as anyone
- a user with administrator permission to log in as “root”
- a system daemon to use a user’s account

su asks for a password when invoked, unless you are logged in as superuser. It then starts a new shell. To return to your original login, use Ctrl-D. If more arguments appear on the command line, they are passed to the new shell.

su is a much easier way to become superuser (provided you have the password) than the traditional method of finding an old-fashioned telephone booth and struggling into the timeworn blue and red costume.

Examples

If you have access to the “root” login, you can log in by issuing

```
su
```

and providing the password. To return to your original login, press Ctrl-D.

To execute the command **chmod +rwx** with the temporary permissions of the “bin” login, issue

```
su - bin -c "chmod +rwx"
```

sum

Description:

Calculates a checksum and counts blocks in a file

Compatibility:

OSF/1	Yes
SCO Unix	Yes
SCO Xenix	Yes
System V Release 3.2	Yes
System V Release 4	Yes
X/Open	Yes

Syntax:

sum [-o] [-r] file

Versions:

OSF/1: adds the -o option.

Options:

-o computes the checksum with a word-by-word computation (OSF/1 only)

-r uses an alternate algorithm

Discussion

sum calculates the 16-bit checksum for the file names, and displays it and the number of 512-byte blocks the file occupies. The -r option makes **sum** use an alternate algorithm for the checksum.

Examples

sum is used primarily when a filesystem is becoming damaged or corrupted, or files are sent over an error-prone medium (such as telephone lines).

To determine the checksum of sent_data, issue

```
sum sent_data
```

If you have sent the file via a modem, the destination can perform a similar **sum**, and you can compare the two to ensure a match.

sync

Description:
Updates the super block (the block containing control information for a filesystem)

Compatibility:

OSF/1	Yes
SCO Unix	Yes
SCO Xenix	Yes
System V Release 3.2	Yes
System V Release 4	Yes
X/Open	Yes

Syntax:
sync

Discussion
sync executes a system primitive that flushes all unwritten system buffers to disk. Its common use is when the system must be stopped rapidly. Executing **sync** ensures that all file modifications are saved to disk.

Only a system administrator usually executes **sync**. System users may not have access to it.

Notes
sync cannot be used to flush buffers on a remote machine.

Examples

sync is usually used when an immediate shutdown must be performed, or there is a fear of a system failure (during an electrical storm or extraterrestrial invasion, for example). To rapidly shut down an SCO Unix or Xenix machine, combine **sync** with the **haltsys** command (available only to the superuser):

```
sync
haltsys
```

They flush all buffers immediately, then shut the system down in a matter of seconds.

tabs

Description:

Sets tabs on a terminal

Compatibility:

OSF/1	Yes
SCO Unix	Yes
SCO Xenix	Yes
System V Release 3.2	Yes
System V Release 4	Yes
X/Open	Yes

Syntax:

tabs [tabspec] [+mn] [-Ttype]

Options:

+mn margin: moves all tabs over "n" columns. The default is 10.

-T "type" is the terminal type

tabspec four types of tab specification are accepted: canned, repetitive, arbitrary, and file. Column numbering always starts at 1.

Canned tabspecs appear as -code, where "code" is one of the following:

a 1,10,16,36,72

Assembler, IBM S/370 first format

a2 1,10,16,40,72

Assembler, IBM S/370 second format

c 1,8,12,16,20,55

COBOL normal format

c2 1,6,10,14,49
COBOL compact format

c3 1,6,10,14,18,22,26,30,34,38,42,46,50,54,58,62,67
COBOL compact format

f 1,7,11,15,19,23
FORTRAN

p 1,5,9,13,17,21,25,29,33,37,41,45,53,57,61
PL/I

s 1,10,55
SNOBOL

u 1,12,20,44
Assembler, UNIVAC 1100

Repetitive tabspecs occur at regular intervals. A tabspec of -n places tabs at 1+n, 1+2*n, 1+3*n, etc. The normal setting is -8.

Arbitrary tabspecs are a list of column numbers separated by commas. Up to 40 numbers may appear.

File tabspecs appear in the first line of a format specification file. If one exists, tabs are set accordingly. Otherwise, they are set as -8. A file tabspec is specified with the option --file (see Examples).

Defaults:

If no terminal type is specified, **tabs** uses the current value of the TERM environment variable.

Errors:

Diagnostic and error messages are self-explanatory. All errors are fatal.

See Also:

newform; pr

Discussion

tabs sets the tab stops on your terminal according to the format given as an argument. It clears old settings.

Notes

The terminal must support remotely set tabs.

Examples

The command

```
tabs -f -Tvt100
```

sets the terminal tabs for FORTRAN. The terminal type is assumed to be a VT100 (overriding the TERM variable).

The tabspec can be read from a file using the command

```
tabs --$HOME/tabs.tim
```

which reads the file tabs.tim in the home directory.

tail

Description:

Displays the last part of a file

Compatibility:

OSF/1	Yes
SCO Unix	Yes
SCO Xenix	Yes
System V Release 3.2	Yes
System V Release 4	Yes
X/Open	Yes

Syntax:

tail [+-num] [lbcr] [-f] [file]

Versions:

OSF/1 and SVR4: add the -r option.

Options:

b	counts by blocks
c	counts by characters
-f	does not terminate after the input file has been copied
l	counts by lines
r	copies from the starting point in reverse order. If no point appears, it reverses the entire file. (OSF/1 and SVR4 only)
num	begins copying at "+num" from the start of the file, or "-num" from its end. The default is 10.

See Also:

dd; head

Discussion

tail copies a file to standard output beginning at a specified place. The copying begins “num” items from either the start or the end of the file. “Items” can be blocks, lines, or characters, as specified by the options “b”, “l”, or “c”.

With the -f option, **tail** does not terminate after reading the last line of the input file. Instead it executes a **sleep** (wait) command for a second, then samples the input again.

tail uses a buffer file. The number of items displayed is not always exact.

Notes

Nonprinting characters may cause unpredictable results.

Examples

The command

```
tail -100 file
```

displays the last 100 lines of “file”.

The -f option can monitor a continually changing file, such as a log or one being sent via modem or nework. The command

```
tail -f file
```

displays the last 10 lines of “file”, and any lines appended to it.

talk

Description:

Sends messages between users

Compatibility:

OSF/1	Yes
SCO Unix	No
SCO Xenix	No
System V Release 3.2	No
System V Release 4	Yes
X/Open	No

Alternative:

write

Syntax:

talk username [tty]

Arguments:

username user's login name

Options:

tty sends messages to the specified terminal if the user is logged on there

See Also:

mesg; write

Discussion

talk copies lines from your terminal to someone else's. You use it by specifying the recipient's login name. If he or she is logged in on several terminals, you can specify the proper one. To **talk** to someone on another host machine, you must include its name on the command line.

talk sends the following message to the other user's terminal:

> Message from TalkDaemon@ ttyXX at HH:MM
>
> talk: connection requested by your_name
>
> talk: respond with: talk your_name

If the target user issues a **talk** command with your name as the argument, you are connected. You can both type simultaneously, with your text appearing in different windows. No one ever has to listen! To interrupt **talk**, use the break character (usually Del). Ctrl-L redraws the screen at any time.

You can prevent **talk** messages from appearing on your terminal by using the **mesg** command. As Will Rogers wrote about "Silent Cal" Coolidge, ". . . he knows when not to talk, which is the biggest asset the monkey possesses over the human."

Notes

talk is hardware dependent, and may work only on machines of the same architecture.

Some commands block messages from **talk** while executing.

SCO Unix and Xenix use **write** instead.

Examples

The command

```
talk bill@merlin
```

sends a message to user "bill" on machine "merlin" saying that you want to talk. If he responds with a **talk** command with your name, you can begin typing messages to each other.

tar

Description:

Archives files

Compatibility:

OSF/1	Yes
SCO Unix	Yes
SCO Xenix	Yes
System V Release 3.2	Yes
System V Release 4	Yes
X/Open	Yes

Syntax:

tar [crtux] [AbefFklLmnpvw] [arguments] [file ...]

Versions:

OSF/1: adds the -B, -h, -i, -P, -s, and -S options.

SCO Unix and Xenix: add the -A, -e, -F, -k, -n, and -p options.

SVR4: adds the -L option.

Options:

0,...,999 selects the archive drive

A suppresses absolute filenames (SCO Unix and Xenix only)

b uses the next argument as the blocking factor

B forces blocking (OSF/1 only)

c creates a new archive

e prevents files from being split across volumes (SCO Unix and Xenix only)

f uses the next argument as the device name

F uses the next argument as the filename to take arguments from (SCO Unix and Xenix only)

h follows symbolic links (OSF/1 only)

i ignores checksum errors (OSF/1 only)

k uses the next argument as the archive size in kilobytes (SCO Unix and Xenix only)

l displays error messages if links cannot be resolved

L follows symbolic links (SVR4 only)

m does not restore modification times

n indicates the device is not magnetic tape (implied by k) (SCO Unix and Xenix only)

p extracts files with their original permissions (SCO Unix and Xenix only)

P specifies the prefix to be stripped (OSF/1 only)

r writes to the end of the existing archive

s strips leading slashes from pathnames (OSF/1 only)

S specifies the number of 512-byte blocks per volume (OSF/1 only)

t displays filenames in the archive

u updates the archive if the files are new or later than existing versions

v displays filenames as they are processed

w displays action to be taken and waits for confirmation

x extracts from the archive

Discussion

tar copies files to and from a backup medium. It uses one of the primary options c (create), t (display contents), or x (extract) to indicate its action, which the other options can then modify.

The n option added to SCO Unix and Xenix is used with floppies and other archive media that can seek. This speeds up **tar**.

Notes

tar does not verify the medium. You should display its contents using t after creating a new archive.

Examples

To create a 1.2MB diskette archive under SCO Unix with the entire /usr/tim directory on it, issue

```
tar cvfnbk /dev/rfd096ds15 4 1200 /usr/tim
```

This creates the archive, displays the actions on the terminal, uses the primary floppy drive for 1.2MB diskettes, and indicates it is not a tape and has a blocking factor of 4 and a capacity of 1200kB.

To display the directory of the archive floppy, issue

```
tar tvf /dev/rfd096ds15
```

To extract the file /usr/tim/letter.3 from the floppy, issue

```
tar xvf /dev/rfd096ds15 /usr/tim/letter.3
```

tee

Description:

Joins pipes and copies input

Compatibility:

OSF/1	Yes
SCO Unix	Yes
SCO Xenix	Yes
System V Release 3.2	Yes
System V Release 4	Yes
X/Open	Yes

Syntax:

tee [-a] [-i] [-u] [file ...]

Versions:

SCO Unix and Xenix: add the -u option.

Options:

-a appends output

-i ignores interrupts

-u unbuffered output (SCO Unix and Xenix only)

Discussion

tee moves standard input to standard output and copies it to "file". It terminates with an interrupt command unless you use the -i option. The -a option appends the output to the named files instead of overwriting them.

Examples

tee is useful for displaying redirected command output on the screen. For example,

```
grep file | tee /dev/tty1a | sort > newfile
```

displays the output from the command line on tty1a.

tee will not help your golf game in the slightest.

telnet

Description:

Provides an interface for logging into a remote host

Compatibility:

OSF/1	Yes
SCO Unix	No
SCO Xenix	No
System V Release 3.2	No
System V Release 4	Yes
X/Open	No

Syntax:

telnet [-d] [-l user] [-n file] [host] [port]

Options:

host	remote host name
port	specifies the port to use for the remote system
-d	turns debugging mode on
-l	sends *user* to the remote system as the value for the environment variable USER
-n	records network trace information in *file*

See Also:

login

Discussion

telnet uses TCP/IP to communicate with other hosts in a network. It has two modes: command mode is for entering subcommands, and input mode is for sending characters to the remote system. **telnet** supports several subcommands, which are version-dependent. See the **telnet** pages in the User Reference Guide of your Unix documentation for more details.

Examples

The command

```
telnet merlin
```

will try to log in to the system "merlin". If it succeeds, the login prompt will appear, and you can use the remote system directly.

test

Description:

Tests conditions for validity

Compatibility:

OSF/1	Yes
SCO Unix	Yes
SCO Xenix	Yes
System V Release 3.2	Yes
System V Release 4	Yes
X/Open	Yes

Syntax:

test expressions

Versions:

SVR4: adds the -L expression.

Options:

Valid primitives:

-b file	true if file is a block special file
-c file	true if file is a character special file
-d file	true if file is a directory
-f file	true if file is a regular file
-g file	true if file has its set-group-ID bit set
-k file	true if file has its sticky bit set
-L file	true if file is a symbolic link (SVR4 only)
-n str	true if the string str has nonzero length
-r file	true if file is readable
-s file	true if file is not empty

-t filedes	true if the open file is associated with a terminal device and has a file descriptor number of "filedes" (default is 1)
-u file	true if file has its set-user-ID bit set
-w file	true if file is writable
-x file	true if file is executable
-z str	true if the string str has zero length
str1 = str2	true if the strings str1 and str2 are identical
str1 != str2	true if the strings str1 and str2 are not identical
str1	true if the string str1 is not the null string
x1 -eq x2	true if integers x1 and x2 are algebraically equal
x1 -ne x2	true if integers x1 and x2 are algebraically unequal
x1 -gt x2	true if integer x1 is greater than x2
x1 -ge x2	true if integer x1 is greater than or equal to x2
x1 -lt x2	true if integer x1 is less than x2
x1 -le x2	true if integer x1 is less than or equal to x2

Valid operators:

!	unary negation
-a	binary and
-o	binary or

See Also:

find

Discussion

test evaluates an expression's validity. Its normal use is in shell programming. If the expression is true, **test** returns zero. Otherwise, it returns a nonzero value. (This is the opposite of the C convention in which zero is false and everything else is true.)

All operators and flags are separate arguments to **test**. You can use parentheses in it, but must escape them to avoid confusion from shell interpreters.

Examples

The command

```
test -f filename
```

tests whether "filename" is a regular file. If so, the return value is zero. The command

```
test -s filename
```

tests whether the file is empty (true if it is not, false if it is).

You can use **test** to evaluate expressions. The command

```
test VAR1 -gt VAR2
```

is true (zero) if VAR1 is greater than VAR2.

time

Description:

Times a command

Compatibility:

OSF/1	Yes
SCO Unix	Yes
SCO Xenix	No
System V Release 3.2	Yes
System V Release 4	Yes
X/Open	Yes

Syntax:

time command

See Also:

timex

Discussion

time measures how long a command takes to execute. It prints the elapsed time, time in the system, and time spent executing the command. All times are in seconds, and are sent to standard error.

Examples

The command

```
time data_pack
```

executes the script file or program data_pack and measures how long it takes.

timex

Description:

Times a command and reports process data and system activity

Compatibility:

OSF/1	No
SCO Unix	No
SCO Xenix	No
System V Release 3.2	Yes
System V Release 4	Yes
X/Open	No

Syntax:

timex [-ops] command

Options:

-o displays the total number of block reads and writes, and total characters transferred by "command" and its children (requires active process accounting)

-p displays process accounting records for "command" and its children (requires active process accounting). Suboptions are:

- -f displays the fork/exec flag and system exit status
- -h displays fraction of total available CPU time consumed
- -k displays total kcore-minutes
- -m displays mean core size (default setting)
- -r displays CPU factor
- -t displays separate system and user CPU times

-s displays total system activity that occurred during the execution of "command"

See Also:

time

Discussion

timex executes "command" and reports the elapsed time, user time, and system time (in seconds) spent during execution. If process accounting is active, options on the command line can provide more details.

touch

Description:
Changes a file's access and modification times

Compatibility:

OSF/1	Yes
SCO Unix	Yes
SCO Xenix	Yes
System V Release 3.2	Yes
System V Release 4	Yes
X/Open	Yes

Syntax:
touch [-acfm] [mmddhhmm[yy]] file ...

Versions:
OSF/1: adds the -f option.

Options:

-a	updates access time
-c	prevents creation of a file
-f	tries to force **touch** despite read/write permissions (OSF/1 only)
-m	updates modification time
mm	month
dd	day
hh	hour
mm	minute
yy	year

Returns:

Number of files modified (or created)

See Also:

date

Discussion

touch changes a file's access and modification time and date. It uses the current time by default and changes the date only if a new one is specified. It supports wildcards for filenames.

If the file does not exist, **touch** creates it unless you use the -c option. When **touch** creates a new file, the modification and access times can be set arbitrarily, but the creation date and time are set to the current values and cannot be changed.

Modification dates and times are in the order:

month, day, hour, minute, and (optional) year

"I will touch a hundred flowers and not pick one."—Edna St. Vincent Millay

tr

Description:

Translates characters

Compatibility:

OSF/1	Yes
SCO Unix	Yes
SCO Xenix	Yes
System V Release 3.2	Yes
System V Release 4	Yes
X/Open	Yes

Syntax:

tr [-Acds] [string ...]

Versions:

OSF/1: adds the -A option.

Options:

-A translates on a byte-by-byte basis (OSF/1 only)

-c complements the set of characters in "string" with ASCII values 001 to 377 octal

-d deletes all input characters in "string"

-s compresses all strings of repeated output characters in a second string to single characters

Discussion

tr translates or deletes characters while copying a string from standard input to standard output.

If two strings appear on the command line, **tr** maps input characters from the first to the corresponding ones in the second.

tr allows the following abbreviations:

[a-z] all characters with ASCII values between “a” and “z” inclusive

[a*x] “x” repetitions of “a”. “x” is octal if its first digit is zero, decimal otherwise.

tr deletes null characters from all inputs.

Examples

The command

```
tr -cs "[A-Z][a-z]" "[\012*]" < infile > outfile
```

takes the list of words in “infile” and creates “outfile” with one word per line (012 is ASCII newline). Note that the strings are quoted to avoid misinterpretation.

translate

Description:

Translates file formats

Compatibility:

OSF/1	No
SCO Unix	Yes
SCO Xenix	Yes
System V Release 3.2	No
System V Release 4	No
X/Open	No

Syntax:

translate [options] [file1] [file2]

Arguments:

file1	input filename
file2	output filename

Options:

-ae	ASCII to EBCDIC
-af format	ASCII to user defined format
-bm	binary/object code to mailable ASCII **uuencode** format
-ea	EBCDIC to ASCII
-ef format	EBCDIC to user defined format
-fa format	user defined format to ASCII
-fe format	user defined format to EBCDIC
-mb	mailable ASCII **uuencode** format to binary

See Also:

dd; newform

Discussion

translate converts files between formats. Conversion is usually only necessary from a hardware platform that uses a different storage format (such as EBCDIC).

true

Description:
Returns a zero exit value

Compatibility:

OSF/1	Yes
SCO Unix	Yes
SCO Xenix	Yes
System V Release 3.2	Yes
System V Release 4	Yes
X/Open	Yes

Syntax:
true

See Also:
false

Discussion
true always returns a zero exit value. The opposite of the **false** command, it is used in shell scripts to force a loop to execute forever. (Note that the convention is the opposite of the one in C in which zero is false and everything else is true.)

Examples

The command:

```
while true
do
      commands...
done
```

executes "commands" repeatedly until interrupted.

tset

Description:

Sets a terminal's characteristics

Compatibility:

OSF/1	Yes
SCO Unix	Yes
SCO Xenix	Yes
System V Release 3.2	No
System V Release 4	No
X/Open	No

Syntax:

tset -] [-hIQrsSu] [-e[c]] [-E[c]] [-k[c]] [-m [identity] [test baud]:type] [type]

OSF/1:

tset [-] [-e[c]] [-E[c]] [-i[c]] [-k[c]] [-IQrs] [-m [identity] [port][baud]:type]] [type ...]

Options:

- \- prints the terminal type on the standard output
- -e uses the character c as the erase character. The default is Ctrl-H.
- -E same as -e except used on terminals that can backspace
- -h forces **tset** to search ttytype and ignore the variable TERM
- -i uses c as the interrupt character (default is Ctrl-C) (OSF/1 only)
- -I suppresses output of the terminal initialization string
- -k uses the character c as the kill character. The default is Ctrl-U.
- -m mapping flag for using defaults in ttytype
- -Q suppresses **tset** messages

-r displays the terminal type on the diagnostic output

-s sets the shell environment variables for the terminal type

-S sends the string to be placed in the environment variable

Discussion

tset controls terminal dependent functions, including screen manipulation codes (for erasing, backspacing, etc), kill characters, and terminal responses.

The most common use of **tset** is in the .profile or .login file in your home directory to set your terminal type upon login.

The type of terminal is specified as "type" in the command line. It must be a valid entry in the /etc/termcap file, or the definition will not be accepted. If no type is specified, the value associated with the TERM environment variable is used. The -h or -m option reads the terminal type from /etc/ttytype at the entry corresponding to the device port. If that is impossible, the terminal type is set to "unknown".

Ports that **tset** recognizes are usually in the /etc/ttytype file. You can specify how to map a terminal to a port with the -m option, followed by the identifier.

Examples

The command

```
tset wy60
```

sets your terminal to be a Wyse 60, and uses its characteristics from the /etc/termcap file.

tty

Description:

Displays your terminal's pathname

Compatibility:

OSF/1	Yes
SCO Unix	Yes
SCO Xenix	Yes
System V Release 3.2	Yes
System V Release 4	Yes
X/Open	Yes

Syntax:

tty [-l] [-s]

Versions:

SVR3.2 and SVR4: add the -l option.

Options:

-l displays the synchronous line number the terminal is on (if any) (SVR3.2 and SVR4 only)

-s suppresses printed output

Returns:

0 if the standard input is a terminal

1 otherwise

Discussion

tty prints your terminal's pathname on standard output. The -s option suppresses the output (used for testing the exit code in programs).

The term "tty" is an abbreviation for the once common "teletype" (a printing terminal manufactured by Teletype Corp. of Skokie, IL). If you remember the days when teletypes were the standard printers, you can apply for membership in the Loyal and Ancient Order of Paper Tape Punchers.

Examples

The command

```
tty
```

produces output describing the port to which you are connected. For example, the output is

```
/dev/tty8a
```

if you are on device port "8a".

ul

Description:

Translates underlining for display on a terminal

Compatibility:

OSF/1	Yes
SCO Unix	No
SCO Xenix	No
System V Release 3.2	No
System V Release 4	No
X/Open	No

Syntax:

ul [-i] [-t term] [file ...]

Options:

-i indicates underlining by a separate line containing dashes

-t overrides the default terminal type with "term"

Discussion

ul translates underlining for display on a terminal lacking a built-in capability.

umask

Description:
Sets the file creation mask

Compatibility:
OSF/1	Yes
SCO Unix	Yes
SCO Xenix	Yes
System V Release 3.2	Yes
System V Release 4	Yes
X/Open	Yes

Syntax:
umask [ddd]

See Also:
chmod

Discussion
umask sets your file creation mode mask. With no argument, it displays the mask's current value.

Masks are three digit numbers representing user, group, and other permissions, respectively. Valid digits are:

0 read and write (execute for directories)

1 read and write

2 read (execute for directories)

3 read

4 write (execute for directories)

5 write

6 execute for directories

7 no permissions

Examples

The command

```
umask 022
```

changes your umask setting to remove group and other write permissions (sets them to read).

umask is also Tonto's favorite command to issue to his Lone Ranger multiuser Unix system for aiding law enforcement agencies.

uname

Description:

Prints the system name

Compatibility:

OSF/1	Yes
SCO Unix	Yes
SCO Xenix	Yes
System V Release 3.2	Yes
System V Release 4	Yes
X/Open	Yes

Syntax:

uname [-admnprsuv] [-S name]

Versions:

OSF/1: does not support the -S option.

SCO Xenix: adds the -d, -u, and -p options.

SVR4: adds the -p option.

Options:

-a	prints all information
-d	prints OEM number (SCO Xenix only)
-m	prints machine hardware name
-n	prints node name (network name)
-p	prints machine processor (SCO Xenix and SVR4 only)
-r	prints operating system release information
-s	prints system name
-S	changes system name (not in OSF/1)
-u	prints user serial number (SCO Xenix only)
-v	prints operating system version information

Defaults:

Assumes the -s option if no arguments appear.

Discussion

uname prints information about the operating system, hardware, or communications network name. By itself, it prints the system name (set by the system administrator).

The superuser can change that name using the -S option. It is limited to eight characters.

Examples

Issuing

```
uname -v -s
```

produces the output

```
Xenix
SysV
```

on an SCO Xenix machine.

uncompress

Description:

Expands compressed files

Compatibility:

OSF/1	Yes
SCO Unix	Yes
SCO Xenix	Yes
System V Release 3.2	No
System V Release 4	Yes
X/Open	No

Syntax:

uncompress [-cCdfqv] file...

Versions:

OSF/1: adds the -C, -d, and v options.

SVR4: does not support -q. Adds the -v option.

Options:

- -c writes to standard output and does not remove the original file
- -C makes the output compatible with Version 2.0 of **compress** (OSF/1 only)
- -d forces an expansion, for consistency with **compress -d** (OSF/1 only)
- -q generates error messages only (no output)
- -v verbose output

See Also:

ar; compress; pack; zcat

Discussion

uncompress restores a compressed file (with .Z appended to its name) to its original format. It deletes the compressed version and saves the expanded one under the original name.

You can compress files with **compress** and read them with **zcat**.

Examples

To expand the compressed file file.Z, issue

```
uncompress file.Z
```

unexpand

Description:
Replaces spaces with tabs

Compatibility:

OSF/1	Yes
SCO Unix	No
SCO Xenix	No
System V Release 3.2	No
System V Release 4	No
X/Open	No

Syntax:
unexpand [-a] [file]

Options:
-a inserts tabs wherever they would compress the output file by two or more characters

See Also:
expand

Discussion
unexpand replaces spaces with tab characters. By default, it converts only ones at the beginning of lines. Using the -a option converts all sequences of spaces.

Examples

To replace all sequences of spaces with tabs in “MobyDisk”, enter

```
unexpand -a MobyDisk
```

“All that most maddens and torments, all that stirs up the lees of things, all truth with malice in it . . . ”—now on a single white disk with tabs placed appropriately, courtesy of Captain Ahab's Software (New Bedford, MA).

uniq

Description:
Displays all repeated lines in a file

Compatibility:
OSF/1	Yes
SCO Unix	Yes
SCO Xenix	Yes
System V Release 3.2	Yes
System V Release 4	Yes
X/Open	Yes

Syntax:
uniq [-cdu [+n] [-n]] [input [output]]

Options:
-c precedes each line by the number of times it is repeated

-d displays only one copy of repeated lines

-u displays only non-repeated lines

+n ignores the first "n" characters

-n ignores the first "n" fields and blanks

See Also:
comm; sort

Discussion
uniq reads standard input or an input file and compares all adjacent lines. It removes duplicates, leaving only the first occurrence. It is useful for removing duplicates from a list, for example. The -u option displays only unique lines.

To ensure that a file is in the correct order for use with **uniq**, issue **sort** first. If the file is not sorted, duplicates separated by other lines will not be removed. The input and output filenames should not be the same.

units

Description:

Converts units

Compatibility:

OSF/1	No
SCO Unix	Yes
SCO Xenix	Yes
System V Release 3.2	Yes
System V Release 4	Yes
X/Open	No

Syntax:

units

Files:

/usr/lib/unittab

Discussion

units displays conversions between scales interactively. You terminate it with Ctrl-D.

units displays the prompt "You have:" and waits for you to enter the starting units. It next displays "You want:", requesting the units to which you want to convert. It then displays the conversion method.

units can handle only multiplicative scale changes. It recognizes most metric prefixes and:

"au" (astronomical unit).

"c" (speed of light)

"e" (charge on an electron)

"g" or "force" (acceleration due to gravity)

"mole" (Avogadro's number)

"pi"

"water" (pressure head per unit height of water)

A complete list of recognized units is in /usr/lib/unittab.

Notes

units does not recognize "pound", but does recognize "lb".

Examples

To convert inches to centimeters, issue

```
units
You have: inch
You want: cm
* 2.540000e+00
/ 3.937008e-01
```

unpack

Description:

Expands packed files

Compatibility:

OSF/1	Yes
SCO Unix	Yes
SCO Xenix	Yes
System V Release 3.2	Yes
System V Release 4	Yes
X/Open	Yes

Syntax:

unpack file...

See Also:

pack; pcat

Discussion

unpack expands packed files created with **pack**. It deletes the ".z" suffix and saves the file under its original name.

If it cannot expand any files, **unpack** displays a message. Typical problems are that an expanded file with the original name already exists, or the file cannot be created.

Examples

To expand the packed file file.z, issue

```
unpack file.z
```

uptime

Description:

Displays system activity information

Compatibility:

OSF/1	Yes
SCO Unix	Yes
SCO Xenix	Yes
System V Release 3.2	No
System V Release 4	No
X/Open	No

Syntax:

uptime [-m]

Versions:

OSF/1: adds the -m option.

Options:

-m prints the Mach factor instead of the load average (OSF/1 only)

Discussion

uptime displays basic information about the system since its last reset. It displays the current time, how long the system has been up, and the number of users currently logged in.

If your system maintains the information (set by the system administrator), **uptime** also displays load averages. The smaller they are, the higher the current load.

OSF/1 can print the Mach factor instead of the load average. They are similar, but use different algorithms.

users

Description:
Displays a compressed list of users on the system

Compatibility:

OSF/1	Yes
SCO Unix	No
SCO Xenix	No
System V Release 3.2	No
System V Release 4	No
X/Open	No

Syntax:
users

See Also:
w; who; whodo

Discussion
users displays the login names of all users currently on the system. It displays them on a single line if possible in alphabetical order. For more extensive information, use **who** or **whodo**.

Examples

The command

```
users
```

produces a single-line sorted list of all current system users:

```
bill dan geraldo mary mike tim
```

What could Geraldo be doing? Will his next show be, "Obscene News and the Unix Users Who Create It!"? What if he finds out about **fsck** and **fork**ing? How about Ethernet networks operating in promiscuous mode?

uucp

Description:
Copies files between Unix systems

Compatibility:

OSF/1	Yes
SCO Unix	Yes
SCO Xenix	Yes
System V Release 3.2	Yes
System V Release 4	Yes
X/Open	Yes

Syntax:
uucp [-c|-C] [-d|-f] [-ggrade] [-j] [-m] [-nuser] [-r] [-sfile] [-xlevel] source destination

Arguments:

destination	filenames on target machine
source	filenames on source machine

Options:

-c	does not copy to the spool directory for transfer
-C	copies to the spool directory for transfer
-d	creates all necessary directories
-f	does not create necessary directories
-g	sets priority to "grade", a single letter or number. Priority is by ASCII value, with the smallest one having the highest priority.
-j	displays the job identification
-m	sends mail when the copy is complete (does not work with wildcards in filenames)
-n	notifies "user" when the copy is complete

-r does not start the transfer, but queues the job

-s reports the transfer status of "file"

-x sets the debugging level for standard output. Levels are from 0 (lowest) to 9 (highest).

Defaults:

Assumes the -c and -d options unless overridden

Files:

/usr/spool/uucp	spool directories
/usr/spool/uucppublic	public directory

See Also:

uulog; uuname

Discussion

uucp copies files between Unix systems. It allows source pathnames. The destination filename can include machine names separated by exclamation marks. If several system names appear, **uucp** tries to send the files through them in order. It supports wildcards.

uucp owns all files it receives. It retains execute permissions, and sets files to read and write permission.

When you send a file with system names in its name, **uucp** must be able to find them in a file set up by the administrator. You can use **uuname** to verify system names.

Notes

All systems involved must have the same version of **uucp**.

Examples

To send test_file through system1 to system2, issue

```
uucp /usr/tim/test_file system1!system2!/usr/bob/test_file
```

uudecode

Description:

Decodes a binary file after transmission

Compatibility:

OSF/1	Yes
SCO Unix	Yes
SCO Xenix	Yes
System V Release 3.2	Yes
System V Release 4	Yes
X/Open	No

Syntax:

uudecode [file]

See Also:

uucp; uuencode

Discussion

uudecode decodes a binary file after transmission by **uucp** or other mail services. It is usually called automatically by **uucp** upon receipt of an encoded file, but a user can call it.

uudecode strips off all leading and trailing lines added during the encoding and transmission process.

Notes

To use **uudecode**, a user must have write permission for the file.

uuencode

Description:

Encodes a binary file for transmission

Compatibility:

OSF/1	Yes
SCO Unix	Yes
SCO Xenix	Yes
System V Release 3.2	Yes
System V Release 4	Yes
X/Open	No

Syntax:

uuencode [source] destination

Arguments:

destination destination system name

Options:

source source file

Defaults:

Uses standard input if no source file appears

See Also:

uucp; uudecode

Discussion

uuencode encodes binary files for transmission with **uucp** or other mail services. It uses only printing ASCII characters.

uuencode writes to standard output, but it is usually redirected to a transfer program such as **mail**.

Notes

Encoded files are expanded by 35% due to control information.

Examples

To encode and send the binary file "affairs" using **mail** to "gennifer" on system1, issue

```
uuencode affairs system1 | mail system1!gennifer
```

uulog

Description:

Displays **uucp** log files

Compatibility:

OSF/1	Yes
SCO Unix	Yes
SCO Xenix	Yes
System V Release 3.2	Yes
System V Release 4	Yes
X/Open	Yes

Syntax:

uulog [-fsystem] [-num] [-ssys] [-uuser] [-x]

Versions:

SVR3.2: supports only the -s and -u options. It is the only version that supports -u.

Options:

-f	performs a **tail -f** of the log for “system”
-s	displays transfers involving “system”
-u	displays entries for “user” only (SVR3.2 only)
-x	uses the **uuxqt** log instead of the default **uucico** log
-num	performs a **tail** with “num” lines

Files:

/usr/spool/uucp/.Log/uucico/*	**uucp** log file
/usr/spool/uucp/.Log/uuxqt/*	**uuxqt** log file

See Also:

uucp; uuname

Discussion

uulog displays the **uucp** or **uuxqt** log files, printing different information depending on the options.

uuname

Description:

Lists system names known to **uucp**

Compatibility:

OSF/1	Yes
SCO Unix	Yes
SCO Xenix	Yes
System V Release 3.2	Yes
System V Release 4	Yes
X/Open	Yes

Syntax:

uuname [-c] [-l] [-v]

Versions:

OSF/1: supports only the -l option.

SVR3.2: adds the -v option.

Options:

-c displays the names of systems known to **cu**

-l returns the local system name

-v displays information from the /usr/lib/uucp/ADMIN file (SVR3.2 only)

See Also:

cu; uucp; uulog

Discussion

uuname displays the names of systems known to **uucp**. They can be used when transferring files. The -l option displays the name of your local system.

The -c option has no effect unless **cu** and **uucp** use different files.

uupick

Description:

Copies files between public Unix systems

Compatibility:

OSF/1	Yes
SCO Unix	Yes
SCO Xenix	Yes
System V Release 3.2	Yes
System V Release 4	Yes
X/Open	Yes

Syntax:

uupick [-s system]

Options:

-s searches for files sent from "system"

See Also:

rcp; uucp; uustat; uuto

Discussion

uupick finds files sent for you, and stored in the publid directory. They are usually sent by **uuto**. When it finds one, **uupick** displays

```
from system:[file filename][dir dirname]?
```

and waits for you to enter a command. With the -s option, it displays only files sent from "system".

uupick accepts the following commands:

<newline>	next entry
Ctrl-D	quits
a [dir]	copies all files to "dir" (or home directory) that were sent by "system"
d	deletes the file
m [dir]	copies the file to "dir" (or home directory)
p	displays the file's contents
q	quits
!cmd	executes the shell command "cmd"
*	displays a command summary

uustat

Description:

uucp status inquiry and job control

Compatibility:

OSF/1	Yes
SCO Unix	Yes
SCO Xenix	Yes
System V Release 3.2	Yes
System V Release 4	Yes
X/Open	Yes

Syntax:

uustat [-a|-c|-dnumber|-m|-p|-q|-kjobid|-rjobid|-ssystem|-tsystem [-uuser]]

Versions:

SVR4: adds the -c, -d, and -t options.

X/Open: supports only the -k, -q, -r, -s, and -u options.

Options:

- -a displays all jobs in the queue
- -c displays average queue time (SVR4 only)
- -d uses "number" minutes for calculations (default is 60; see -t) (SVR4 only)
- -k kills the **uucp** request "jobid"
- -m displays the accessibility of all machines
- -p performs **ps -flp** for all processes in the lock files
- -q displays the jobs queued for each machine. Also displays machine status information.
- -r **touch**es "jobid" to set its modification time to the current time (prevents cleanup by daemons)

-s displays the status of all requests for "system"

-t displays average transfer rate or queue time for last 60 minutes (see -d) (SVR4 only)

-u displays the status of all requests issued by "user"

See Also:

ps; uucp

Discussion

uustat displays the status of previously scheduled **uucp** requests, or status information on remote machines. It also allows cancellation of requests. Each **uustat** command can perform only one option.

With no arguments, **uustat** displays the status of all **uucp** requests you issued.

The -s and -u options display the job identification, data, and time of the request, S for Send or R for Receive, the user ID who queued the job, the size of the file, and the name of the command.

Notes

SVR4: The new -c, -d, and -t options apply only to remote system performance.

uuto

Description:

Copies files between public Unix systems

Compatibility:

OSF/1	Yes
SCO Unix	Yes
SCO Xenix	Yes
System V Release 3.2	Yes
System V Release 4	Yes
X/Open	Yes

Syntax:

uuto [-m] [-p] source destination

Arguments:

destination	has the form "system!user" where "system" is a system known to **uucp** and "user" is a valid user on the destination system
source	filename on local system including path

Options:

-m sends mail when the copy is complete

-p copies the source file into the spool directory before transmitting it

See Also:

rcp; uucp; uupick; uustat

Discussion

uuto sends files to a remote system using **uucp**. It lets the local system control file access. It sends files to the PUBDIR (public directory, usually /usr/spool/uucppublic) on the remote system. When that system receives a file, it sends mail to the user for whom it is destined.

uuto differs from **uucp** and other transfer programs in that it allows local systems complete control over file access. **uuto** does not override file permissions.

You can move files from the public directory to other locations with the **uupick** command.

Examples

To send /usr/tim/letter.3 to user "bill" on the remote system1, issue

```
uuto -m /usr/tim/letter.3 system1!bill
```

uux

Description:

Executes commands on a remote Unix system

Compatibility:

OSF/1	Yes
SCO Unix	Yes
SCO Xenix	Yes
System V Release 3.2	Yes
System V Release 4	Yes
X/Open	Yes

Syntax:

uux [-] [-aname] [-b] [-c|-C] [-ggrade] [-j] [-n] [-p] [-r] [-sfile] [-xlevel] [-z] command

Options:

- \- uses standard input for "command"
- -a uses "name" as the command initiating user ID
- -b returns standard input if the exit status is nonzero
- -c does not copy a file to the spool directory (default)
- -C copies a file to the spool directory
- -g sets the priority of the transmission. "grade" is a single letter or number. Lower ASCII values have higher priorities.
- -j displays the job ID
- -n does not notify the user if the command fails
- -p uses standard input for "command" (same as "-")
- -r does not start a file transfer, but queues the job
- -s displays the transfer status of "file"

-x sets the debugging output to “level”. “level” is from 0 to 9, with 9 highest.

-z notifies the user when the command executes successfully

Files:

/usr/lib/uucp/Permissions remote execution permissions

See Also:

mail; remote; uucp; uustat

Discussion

uux lets you execute commands on a remote system, or send files. Most installations limit the commands you can execute remotely for security purposes. Usually only **mail** commands are available.

When using **uux**, you can specify files on other systems that it is to gather to execute a command (see Examples). **uux** tries to gather all of them first. Filenames may be a full pathname, or include system names. A filename can be preceded by “~name”, where “name” is your name on the system and is replaced by the login directory when expanded.

Examples

The command

```
uux "!cat sys1!/file.1 sys2!/usr/james/file.2 > !~/new.file
```

collects files from two remote systems and concatenates them on the local machine.

vedit

Description:

Screen editor

Compatibility:

OSF/1	Yes
SCO Unix	Yes
SCO Xenix	Yes
System V Release 3.2	Yes
System V Release 4	Yes
X/Open	Yes

Syntax:

vedit [-c cmd] [-c] [-I] [-L] [-r [file]] [-t tag] [-wsize] [-x] [command ...] [filename ...]

Options:

-c cmd	executes the **vedit** command cmd before allowing editing
-C	enables encryption. Assumes all files are encrypted and need a key. Files are encrypted when saved. (Similar to -x but forces **vedit** to assume files are encrypted.)
-I	sets the *showmatch* and *lisp* options (used only for editing LISP programs)
-L	lists the names of all files saved as a result of an editor or system crash (usually used before the -r option to recover a file)
-r	sets a read-only flag preventing modification
-r file	retrieves the last saved version of *file* (used after editor and system crashes)
-t tag	positions the cursor at the *tag* definition
-wsize	sets the default window to *size* lines

-x enables encryption. Encrypted files need a key to decrypt them. When reading a file, **vedit** tries to determine if it is encrypted.

See Also:

ed; edit; vi

Description

vedit has the same commands as **vi**, but has several default options set differently. See **vi** and the User's Reference Guide included with your Unix documentation for more details.

vi

Description:

Screen editor

Compatibility:

OSF/1	Yes
SCO Unix	Yes
SCO Xenix	Yes
System V Release 3.2	Yes
System V Release 4	Yes
X/Open	Yes

Syntax:

vi [-c cmd] [-c] [-I] [-L] [-r [file]] [-t tag] [-wsize] [-x] [command ...] [filename ...]

Options:

-c cmd	executes the **vi** command cmd before allowing editing
-C	enables encryption. Assumes all files are encrypted and need a key. Files are encrypted when saved. (Similar to -x but forces **vi** to assume files are encrypted.)
-I	sets the *showmatch* and *lisp* options (used only for editing LISP programs)
-L	lists the names of all files saved as a result of an editor or system crash (usually used before the -r option to recover a file)
-r	sets a read-only flag preventing modification (set automatically by the **view** command)
-r file	retrieves the last saved version of *file* (used after editor and system crashes)
-t tag	positions the cursor at the *tag* definition

-wsize sets the default window to *size* lines

-x enables encryption. Encrypted files need a key to decrypt them. When reading a file, **vi** tries to determine if a file is encrypted.

See Also:

ed; edit; vedit; view

Description

vi is a screen editor that uses mnemonic (or somewhat mnemonic!) commands. **view** is the same except that it does not allow files to be modified (the -R option is set). **vedit** has the same commands, but has several default options set differently.

vi uses an editing buffer for all work. If a file exists, **vi** copies it into the buffer, and does not modify the original until the user issues a save command.

The -c option forces the execution of a command before allowing editing. The usual aim is to search for a starting place in the text.

vi has three operating modes. Command mode allows the user to enter commands from the keyboard. Insert mode assumes keyboard entries are text for the editing buffer. Escape mode allows command entry in insert mode. One problem with many versions of **vi** is that they do not indicate the current mode! The result is constant annoying sequences of errors caused by commands being interpreted as text and vice versa.

vi has many commands users can combine to form powerful structures. For more information about it, see the Text Processing Guide and the User's Guide in your Unix manuals. Also see L. Lamb, *Learning the vi Editor*, 5th ed. (Sebastopol, CA: O'Reilly & Associates, 1991).

The following commands are special in insert mode:

BKSP moves the cursor back one character. Removes the last character from the editing buffer, although it stays on the screen.

Ctrl-T indents the same as the preceding line (*autoindent*)

Ctrl-U moves the cursor back to the first character of the current insertion and restarts insert mode

Ctrl-V ignores any special significance of the next character entered. Allows insertion of control characters.

Ctrl-W moves the cursor back to the start of the last inserted word

Ctrl-@ if entered as the first character of an insertion, it is replaced by the last text inserted up to a maximum of 128 characters. If more were inserted, it has no effect.

vi supports the following commands:

Cursor Movement:

+ start of next line

- start of previous line. A number can indicate how many lines to move up.

^ first non-whitespace character on line

$ end of current line. A number can indicate how many lines to move down.

(start of sentence

) end of sentence

" text marked with m command

0 start of current line

b back a word (counting punctuation as words)

B back a blank-delimited word

e end of next word (counting punctuation as words)

E end of next blank-delimited word

G start of line specified by a number (eg., 16G). If no number appears, it moves to the beginning of the last line.

h back a character. A number can indicate how many characters to move. Cannot move past the start of the line.

j down a line

k up a line

l forward a character. A number can indicate how many characters to move. Cannot move past the end of the line.

w start of next word (counting punctuation as words)

W start of next blank-delimited word

Screen Commands:

Ctrl-B moves back one screen. Two lines overlap on each screen.

Ctrl-D scrolls screen down half a window. A number can indicate how many lines to scroll.

Ctrl-F moves forward one screen. Two lines overlap on each screen.

Ctrl-G displays status line showing filename, whether it has been modified, current line number, number of lines in the file, and percentage of the file that precedes the current cursor position

Ctrl-L redraws screen (same as Ctrl-R)

Ctrl-R redraws screen (same as Ctrl-L)

Ctrl-U scrolls screen up half a window. A number can indicate how many lines to scroll.

z redraws screen with current line at top, middle, or bottom. The choice is:

no argument	top
. (i.e., z.)	middle
- (i.e., z-)	bottom

A number can indicate how many lines to display.

Text:

. repeats last insert or delete command

! executes a Unix command

= displays current line number

> shifts text right by default amount (usually eight spaces). A number can indicate how many lines are affected.

< shifts text left by default amount (usually eight spaces). A number can indicate how many lines are affected.

/ searches forward through buffer for a pattern. If none appears, uses the last one. The command /text searches for "text". A number after a second delimiter can indicate how many lines to move the cursor after the match (e.g., /text/2 positions the cursor two lines after the one matching "text").

? searches backward through buffer for a pattern. If none appears, uses the last one. The command ?Unix searches for "Unix". A number after a second delimiter can indicate how many lines to move the cursor after the match (e.g., /Unix/-4 positions the cursor four lines above the one matching "Unix").

; repeats last character search (see f)

, repeats last character search but in opposite direction (see F)

` moves to a mark (see m). The command `a moves to mark *a*.

' moves to the start of the line containing a mark (see m). The command 'a moves to the start of the line containing mark *a*.

: enters escape mode and waits for a command (see Escape Commands below)

a appends text to editing buffer after the cursor position

A appends text to the editing buffer at the end of the current line. Exit with Esc.

c changes text from current cursor position

C changes entire current line

d deletes text using a cursor movement command as an argument to indicate how much (e.g., dw deletes to end of the word)

D deletes from cursor to end of current line

dd deletes entire current line

f finds character on current line searching forward. The command fx searches for *x*.

F finds character on current line searching backward

i inserts text into editing buffer before the character beneath the cursor

I inserts text into editing buffer at the beginning of the current line

J joins current line with following one. A number can indicate how many lines to join.

m marks text with a lowercase letter for rapid movement. To mark a position with the letter *a*, use ma.

n repeats last search in same direction

N repeats last search in opposite direction

o opens new line below current one and inserts text

O opens new line above current one and inserts text

p puts text from an editing buffer after the cursor. Buffers are named *a* through *z*. Uses a double quotation mark to indicate the buffer name (e.g., "dp puts text from buffer *d* after the cursor.)

P puts text from an editing buffer before the cursor. Buffers are named *a* through *z*. Uses a double quotation mark to indicate the buffer name (e.g., "qP puts text from buffer *q* before the cursor.)

Q exits editor

r replaces single character with the argument (e.g., rX replaces the current character with *X*)

R replaces entire current line until terminated with ESC. A number can indicate to replace text several times.

s substitutes text for current character

S substitutes an entire line until terminated with ESC

t moves cursor just ahead of argument. The command tX moves to the character before *X*.

T same as t

u undoes last insert or delete command

U restores current line to original state (before editing)

x deletes character beneath cursor. A number (e.g., 6x) can indicate how many characters to delete to the right.

X deletes character before cursor. A number (e.g., 5X) can indicate how many characters to delete to the left.

y puts text into buffer as indicated by appended movement command. Buffers are named *a* through *z*. Uses a double quotation mark to indicate the buffer name (e.g., "dyy puts the entire line into buffer *d*.) If the name is capitalized, text is appended to its current contents.

yy puts entire line into named buffer. See y. A number indicates how many lines to place. (Same as Y)

Y puts entire line into named buffer. See y. A number indicates how many lines to place. (Same as yy)

ZZ exits editor and writes file

Escape Commands:

e file	begins editing session with a new file. Checks whether the current buffer has been saved, and displays a message if not.
e! file	begins editing session with a new file, suppressing checks on whether the current buffer has been saved
q	exits editor after checking whether buffer has been saved
q!	exits editor without checking whether buffer has been saved
r file	copies *file* into editing buffer
r !cmd	reads output of *cmd* into editing buffer. (A space must appear before the exclamation mark.)
w file	writes buffer's contents to *file*. The filename can be omitted if one has already been specified.
w>> file	appends buffer's contents to the end of the file
wq	same as a w command followed by a q
wq!	same as a w command followed by a q, overriding all checks
x name	if changes have been made and not written, writes them and quits. Otherwise, just quits.

Global Substitution Commands:

The syntax is

```
g/pattern/commands
```

Execution occurs in two stages. First comes pattern matching to mark each match, followed by the commands using the current line set to the marked line. The following formats show variations:

g/str/p	displays all lines containing "str"
g/str1/s//str2/	replaces the first occurrence of "str1" on all lines with "str2"
g/str1/s//str2/g	replaces all occurrences of "str1" with "str2"
g/str1/s//str2/gp	replaces all occurrences of "str1" with "str2," displaying each change on the screen
g/str1/s//str2/gc	similar to the preceding example, but asks user to confirm each change
g/str1/s/str2/str3/g	changes "str2" to "str3" on all lines containing "str1"

vi uses a set of options to control its environment. Most of them are set to default values and can be changed from it or read from a startup file called .exrc. A full discussion of the options is in the User Reference Guide of the Unix manuals.

view

Description:

Screen-oriented file display utility based on **vi**

Compatibility:

OSF/1	Yes
SCO Unix	Yes
SCO Xenix	Yes
System V Release 3.2	Yes
System V Release 4	Yes
X/Open	Yes

Syntax:

view [-c cmd] [-c] [-I] [-L] [-r file] [-t tag] [-wsize] [-x] [command ...] [filename ...]

Options:

-c cmd executes the **view** command cmd before allowing editing

-C enables encryption. Assumes all files are encrypted and need a key. Files are encrypted when saved. (Similar to -x but forces **view** to assume files are encrypted.)

-I sets the *showmatch* and *lisp* options (used only for editing LISP programs)

-L lists the names of all files saved as a result of an editor or system crash (usually used before the -r option to recover a file)

-r file retrieves the last saved version of *file* (used after editor and system crashes)

-t tag positions the cursor at the *tag* definition

-wsize sets the default window to *size* lines

-x enables encryption. Encrypted files need the key to decrypt. When reading a file, **view** tries to determine if it is encrypted.

See Also:

ed; edit; vi

Description

view is the same as **vi** except that it does not allow files to be modified (the -R option is set). See **vi** for more information on commands available to **view**.

w

Description:

Displays a summary of current system activity

Compatibility:

OSF/1	Yes
SCO Unix	No
SCO Xenix	No
System V Release 3.2	No
System V Release 4	No
X/Open	No

Syntax:

w [-f] [-h] [-l] [-m] [-s] [-u] [user]

Alternative:

ps

Options:

-f	suppresses from field
-h	suppresses system summary and header
-l	displays in long format
-m	displays Mach factor instead of load average
-s	displays in short format
-u	displays system summary only
user	displays information about "user" only

See Also:

ps; w; who; whodo

Discussion

w displays a summary of current system activity and information about who is logged in. The summary shows the current time, amount of time since restart, number of users logged in, and the load averages. The load average is calculated from the number of jobs. The smaller it is, the higher the system load. The Mach factor is another algorithm for calculating load factors.

User information includes name, tasks, the device he or she is logged on, location, login time, period of inactivity, current process, CPU time used by the current process, and system time used by all processes.

wait

Description:

Waits for a background process to finish

Compatibility:

OSF/1	Yes
SCO Unix	Yes
SCO Xenix	Yes
System V Release 3.2	Yes
System V Release 4	Yes
X/Open	Yes

Syntax:

wait [n]

Options:

n   background process ID

Discussion

wait forces a wait until specified (or all, if not specified) background processes (ones started with the ampersand character) finish, then reports abnormal terminations.

Many system shells have **wait** built-in.

wall

Description:
Sends a message to all users

Compatibility:

OSF/1	Yes
SCO Unix	Yes
SCO Xenix	Yes
System V Release 3.2	Yes
System V Release 4	Yes
X/Open	Yes

Syntax:
wall [file]

See Also:
mesg

Discussion
wall sends a message to all users who are logged in. You must be superuser to use it. It overrides the **mesg** command. **wall** resembles the broadcast or multicast mode available on some communications systems. An excellent way for the system administrator to remind users of the importance of providing adequate gifts on such important holidays as Flag Day, Grandparents' Day, and the anniversaries of the Battles of Bull Run, Hastings, Lepanto, and Trafalgar.

wc

Description:

Counts lines, words, and characters

Compatibility:

OSF/1	Yes
SCO Unix	Yes
SCO Xenix	Yes
System V Release 3.2	Yes
System V Release 4	Yes
X/Open	Yes

Syntax:

wc [-clw] [file ...]

Options:

-c counts characters

-l counts lines

-w counts words

Defaults:

Counts characters, words, and lines

Discussion

wc examines and counts all characters, words, and lines in files. Options limit the counts performed. Usually, **wc** considers a word as a string of characters with spaces, tabs, or punctuation marks at either end. Be careful about using **wc** in England, where the acronym has a special meaning.

Examples

To count the number of words in newfile, issue

```
wc -w newfile
```

whatis

Description:
Displays information about a command

Compatibility:

OSF/1	Yes
SCO Unix	No
SCO Xenix	No
System V Release 3.2	No
System V Release 4	No
X/Open	No

Syntax:
whatis [-M path] [keyword ...]

Options:

keyword	command to search for
-M	specifies an alternate search path

Files:

/usr/share/man/whatis	keyword database

See Also:
man

Discussion
whatis looks up a keyword in the reference pages and displays basic information about it. It is the same as the **man -f** command.

Examples

To display what the **who** command does, issue

```
whatis who
```

But not in front of an English teacher or anyone familiar with the old Abbott and Costello "Who's on first?" routine!

who

Description:

Lists who is on the system

Compatibility:

OSF/1	Yes
SCO Unix	Yes
SCO Xenix	Yes
System V Release 3.2	Yes
System V Release 4	Yes
X/Open	Yes

Syntax:

who am I

who am i

who [-aAbdHlpqrstTu] [file]

Options:

-a processes /etc/utmp file (or named file) with all options active

-A displays accounting information

-b indicates time and date of last reboot

-d displays processes that have expired and not been respawned

-H displays column headings

-l lists only ports waiting for a login

-p lists only active processes

-q displays only name and number of logged in users

-r indicates current run level

-s lists only name, line, and time (default value)

-t displays the last change to the system clock

-T same as -u but adds the state of the terminal

-u lists only users currently logged in

See Also:

whoami

Discussion

who lists the user's name, terminal, login time, and elasped time since the last activity for each line on the system. It can also list process IDs for all active processes.

The command **who am i** or **who am I** displays the name of the user who typed it. This is particularly helpful for the absent-minded person who must otherwise wear a conference badge with his or her name on it.

whoami

Description:
Displays the user's name

Compatibility:

OSF/1	Yes
SCO Unix	No
SCO Xenix	No
System V Release 3.2	No
System V Release 4	No
X/Open	No

Syntax:
whoami

See Also:
who; whodo

Discussion

whoami is similar to the **who am i** command. It displays the username associated with your current ID. Unlike **who am i**, it displays your effective ID, not the one logged into your tty device. It is useful in shell scripts.

whodo

Description:

Displays who is on the system and what they are doing

Compatibility:

OSF/1	No
SCO Unix	Yes
SCO Xenix	Yes
System V Release 3.2	No
System V Release 4	No
X/Open	No

Discussion

whodo displays the login names of all users on the system, and the program each is running. It uses output from the **who** and **ps** commands.

whodo is particularly helpful for spies, stoolpigeons, efficiency experts, wiretappers, perverts, and other undesirables such as system administrators and evaluators. More fun than listening in on an old-fashioned telephone party line!

xtod

Description:
Changes file formats from Unix to DOS

Compatibility:

OSF/1	No
SCO Unix	Yes
SCO Xenix	No
System V Release 3.2	No
System V Release 4	No
X/Open	No

Syntax:
xtod file1 > file2

Arguments:

file1	Unix source file
file2	DOS destination file

Error Handling:
Reports a syntax error if redirection symbol is omitted

See Also:
dtox

Discussion

xtod converts a file from Unix to DOS format by changing line feeds to carriage return/line feed pairs. It also inserts the terminating Ctrl-Z.

If a filename is omitted, **xtod** uses standard input or output.

Notes

xtod is an extension supplied by the Santa Cruz Operation.

Examples

The command

```
xtod letter.4 > letter.new
```

reads the file letter.4, inserts carriage returns and Ctrl-Zs, and writes the result as letter.new.

zcat

Description:

Displays compressed files

Compatibility:

OSF/1	Yes
SCO Unix	Yes
SCO Xenix	Yes
System V Release 3.2	No
System V Release 4	Yes
X/Open	No

Syntax:

zcat file ...

See Also:

cat; compress; uncompress

Discussion

zcat displays compressed files much as **cat** does ordinary ones. It expands them and sends them to standard output unless redirected. It does not modify the originals.

You can compress files with **compress** and expand them with **uncompress**.

Examples

To display the compressed file file.Z, enter

```
zcat file.Z
```

The ".Z" extension is assumed if not specified. To route the unpacked output to the printer, for example, enter

```
zcat file | lp
```

Acronyms

ACU	Automated Calling Unit
ASCII	American Standard Code for Information Interchange
BSD	Berkeley Software Distribution
CR	Carriage Return
CRC	Cyclic Redundancy Check
CSRG	Computer Systems Research Group (University of California, Berkeley, Computer Science Department)
CTS	Clear to send
CUT	Coordinated Universal Time
DOS	Disk Operating System (Microsoft)
EBCDIC	Extended Binary Coded Decimal Interchange Code
eof	end of file
eol	end of line
FF	Form Feed
FST	Filesystem Type
GMT	Greenwich Mean Time
IEEE	Institute of Electrical and Electronic Engineers
IP	Internet Protocol
KB	Kilobyte
LF	Line Feed
MB	Megabyte
MFS	Memory File System
MS-DOS	Microsoft Disk Operating System
NFS	Network File System
OSF	Open Software Foundation
PID	Process Identification Number
RFS	Remote File System

RPN	Reverse Polish Notation
RTS	Request to send
SCCS	Source Code Control System
SCO	Santa Cruz Operation
SVR	System V Release
SVR3.2	System V Release 3.2
SVR4	System V Release 4
TCP	Transmission Control Protocol
tpi	tracks per inch
TTY	Teletype(writer)
UI	Unix International
UID	User Identification Number
USL	Unix System Laboratories

Glossary

alias
A name assigned to a command sequence (for example, the name **dir** assigned to **ls -l**); also a group name encompassing several user names (e.g., users "bill", "john", and "tim" aliased to the name "programmers" for use by **mail**)

archive
A single file formed from multiple independent files for storage or backup purposes. Often compressed and encrypted.

automated calling unit (ACU)
Obsolete term for a device that dials a remote number. Arose from old hardware that required separate calling units and modems. All recent modems include calling units, so the term nowadays usually just means a modem device name.

binary file
A non-text file, such as executable machine code or raw data. Not directly readable.

block
Physical disk unit, usually consisting of 512, 1024, or 2048 bytes. The smallest unit the inode table manages.

blocking factor
Number of bytes in a block, typically used when describing removable media. Usually given as a multiple of a basic block size (e.g., a blocking factor of 4 may mean 4*512 bytes).

Coordinated Universal Time (CUT)
Replacement for Greenwich Mean Time (GMT) as the standard time reference. CUT is not subject to changes caused by daylight savings time. It is still based on time measured at Greenwich, England.

daemon
Executable program that runs continuously without operator intervention. Usually, the system starts daemons during initialization. **cron** and the print spooler are examples.

filesystem Named structure containing files in subdirectories. Unix can support many filesystems. Each has a unique name, and can be attached (or *mounted*) anywhere in the existing file structure.

inode Data structure that relates a file to actual physical storage; contains user, date, time, size, and permission information. The inode table is used to locate files on the filesystem.

interleave factor The number of physical sectors between consecutive logical sectors on a disk. Used to allow slow systems to read consecutive logical sectors even though they are not fast enough to read consecutive physical ones. A ratio of 1:1 indicates no difference between logical and physical sectors.

interrupt A keystroke or other signal received by a process that causes it to suspend execution or halt.

Julian date An increasing count of the number of days since an arbitrary starting date.

lock Prevent others from using something (such as a file or record).

Micnet Networking protocol used by Xenix systems, rare nowadays.

mount To add a filesystem to the one in use. Unix then understands the filesystem's pathnames.

multiuser Allows more than one user to access the system at a time.

nfs Network File System. Shared filesystem developed by Sun Microsystems. Similar to, but incompatible with, RFS.

pathname Filesystem specification for a file's location (e.g., /usr/tim/book has the pathname /usr/tim).

rfs Network file system developed by AT&T. Similar to, but incompatible with, NFS.

semaphore Indicator that determines which process has current access to a resource.

special file File that is neither executable nor text but is usually associated with the Unix operating system. For example, a special file may hold device access information.

spooling	Using part of the disk as a storage area for files to be printed or transmitted. A daemon manages the operation, queuing the files and sending them when the printer or receiver is available.
sticky bit	Permission bit that prevents anyone except the owner or superuser from deleting a file; applies to directories.
superblock	Block that contains control information for a filesystem such as the number of inodes.
TCP/IP	Transmission Control Protocol/Internet Protocol. A fast, efficient means of transferring data with error checking to ensure data integrity. TCP/IP is currently the most popular networking protocol.

Note:

For more extensive definitions of Unix terms, see K. Christian, *The C and Unix Dictionary* (New York: Wiley, 1990). For telecommunications terms, see H. Newton, *Newton's Telecom Dictionary* (New York: Telecom Library, 1992).

Resources

Magazines

Open Systems Today
CMP Publications Inc.
600 Community Dr.
Manhasset, NY 11030

SCO Magazine
CMP Publications Inc.
600 Community Dr.
Manhasset, NY 11030

UniForum Monthly
2901 Tasman Dr., Suite 201
Santa Clara, CA 95054

Unix Review
Miller Freeman Publications
600 Harrison St.
San Francisco, CA 94107

Unix World
1900 O'Farrell St., 2nd Floor
San Mateo, CA 94403

Organizations

UniForum
2901 Tasman Dr., Suite 201
Santa Clara, CA 95054
(800) 255-5620 (408) 986-8840
986-1645 (fax)

Usenix Association
P.O. Box 2299
Berkeley, CA 94710
(415) 528-8649

Vendors/Suppliers

Computer Systems Research Group
457 Evans Hall
University of California
Berkeley, CA 94720
(510) 642-7780

Open Software Foundation
11 Cambridge Center
Cambridge, MA 02142
(617) 621-8700 621-0631 (fax)

The Santa Cruz Operation
425 Encinal St.
Santa Cruz, CA 95060
or
P.O. Box 1900
Santa Cruz, CA 95061
(800) 726-8649 (408) 725-2222
458-4227 (fax)

UNIX International
Waterview Corporate Center
20 Waterview Rd.
Parsippany, NJ 07054
(800) 848-6495

UNIX System Laboratories
190 River Rd.
Summit, NJ 07901
(800) 828-UNIX (908) 522-6000
522-5466 (fax)

Reader Comments
Unix User's Handbook

This book has been edited, the material reviewed, and the programs tested and checked for accuracy, but bugs find their way into books as well as software. Please take a few minutes to tell us if you have found any errors, and give us your general comments regarding the quality of this book. Your time and attention will help us improve this and future products.

Did you find any mistakes? ______________________________

____

____

Is this book complete? (If not, what should be added?) ______________

____

____

What do you like about this book? ______________________

____

____

What do you not like about this book? ____________________

____

____

What other books would you like to see developed? ____________

____

____

Other comments: ______________________________

____

____

To be notified about new editions of this and other books of interest, please include your name and address, and mail to:

Name ______________________

Address ____________________

City/State/Zip ______________

Microtrend® Books
Slawson Communications
165 Vallecitos de Oro
San Marcos, CA 92069-1436

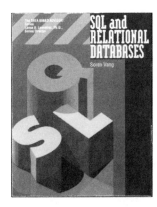

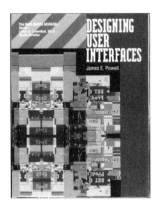

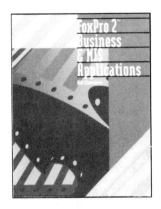